CENTRES OF CATACLYSM

DAVID CONSTANTINE has published several volumes of poetry (*Elder* – 2014 – being the most recent); also two novels (the second, *The Life-Writer*, in 2015) and four volumes of short stories. He is an editor and translator of Hölderlin, Goethe, Kleist and Brecht. For his stories he won the BBC National and the Frank O'Connor International Awards (2010, 2013). With Helen Constantine he edited *Modern Poetry in Translation*, 2003-12.

HELEN CONSTANTINE taught languages in schools until 2000, when she became a full-time translator. Her volumes of translated stories, *Paris Tales*, *Paris Metro Tales* and *French Tales* are published by OUP, and a fourth volume, *Paris Street Tales* will be published in September. She is general editor of a series of 'City Tales' for Oxford University Press. Her translations include *Mademoiselle de Maupin* by Théophile Gautier, *Dangerous Liaisons* by Choderlos de Laclos, *The Wild Ass's Skin* by Balzac, *The Conquest of Plassans* by Zola and Flaubert's *Sentimental Education* for OUP. She is married to the writer David Constantine, and formerly co-edited *Modern Poetry in Translation*.

SASHA DUGDALE is editor of *Modern Poetry in Translation*. She has translated a number of contemporary Russian poets, including Tatiana Shcherbina, Elena Shvarts and Maria Stepanova. Her translations of Elena Shvarts' *Birdsong on the Seabed* (Bloodaxe Books, 2008) were shortlisted for the Popescu and Academica Rossica Awards. She has published three collections of poetry with Carcanet, the most recent being *Red House* (2011), and she co-edited *The Best British Poetry 2012* (Salt). She is co-director of the Winchester Poetry Festival.

CENTRES
OF CATACLYSM

CELEBRATING FIFTY YEARS OF
MODERN POETRY IN TRANSLATION

EDITED BY SASHA DUGDALE
AND DAVID & HELEN CONSTANTINE

BLODAXE BOOKS

ISBN: 978 1 78037 264 8

First published 2016 by
Modern Poetry in Translation
The Queen's College
Oxford OX1 4AW,
in association with
Bloodaxe Books Ltd,
Eastburn,
South Park,
Hexham,
Northumberland NE46 1BS.

www.mptmagazine.com   *www.bloodaxebooks.com*
For further information about Bloodaxe titles please visit
our website or write to the above address for a catalogue.

 Supported by
**ARTS COUNCIL
ENGLAND**

Modern Poetry in Translation gratefully acknowledges
the support of the Unwin Trust.

 SUPPORTING AND
EMPOWERING
REFUGEES

Royalties from the sale of this book are paid to Refugee Council.

Printed in Great Britain by Bell & Bain Limited, Glasgow, Scotland, on
acid-free paper sourced from mills with FSC chain of custody certification.

CONTENTS

(Dates in brackets refer to the publication date
in *Modern Poetry in Translation*)

Preface

More than fifty years ago Ted Hughes began thinking about founding a poetry magazine which would publish only translations. The timing was propitious: after what Hughes characterised as a 'solid wall of dismissal (and derision)' in the 50s, a 'passionate affair' with translated poetry was beginning. Hughes began gathering and considering work, and by the time he came to discuss the magazine with his friend and fellow poet Daniel Weissbort he had already amassed material and ideas. Weissbort's immediate enthusiasm was a catalyst and the two men set about the practical job of founding the magazine: finding a designer, Richard Hollis; publisher; advertisers; money and subscribers. They chose the austere and functional title *Modern Poetry in Translation*. There was no need to search out contributors because they came flooding in of their own accord – as Hughes later wrote 'it seemed easier to let the magazine take off than to keep it grounded. The sheer pressure of material forced the issue.'

The first issue was published in 1965. Hughes favoured a 'scrappy-looking' aesthetic and in his letters he suggests that the magazine should be published on thin airmail paper and, in a utopian gesture, sent out free to all poets. Hollis's broadsheet design, with its columns of poetry set out like broadside ballads, encapsulated the handout spirit of the venture. It was never sent out free to all poets, but it sold for 2s 6d (the same price as Ladybird's *How it Works: the Motor Car*), had a print run of over a thousand and quickly went into a reprint. Although function was the watchword, the paper is delicate and white and the butterfly-fragility of its pages made this first *MPT* a thing of great beauty.

The issue published generous selections of the poetry of Yehuda Amichai, Zbigniew Herbert, Miroslav Holub, Ivan V. Lalić, Vasko Popa, Czesław Miłosz and Andrei Voznesensky. Some of these poets were already known but most were not, and the magazine stimulated interest and attention in their work. Hughes and Weissbort saw the magazine as an 'airport for incoming translations' and they were determined that the work they published should find a home in the English-speaking landscape, as it mostly did. George Theiner's translation of Holub's poem 'The fly', first published in that issue was later published in an anthology of *British* poems, Amichai was published in book form soon after, in a venture inspired by *MPT,* and all the other poets had great recognition in the English-speaking world in the following decades.

All the poets published in the first issue, with the exception of Israeli poet Amichai, were from Eastern Europe, the region 'at the centre of cataclysm', as the editors described it. By the mid-60s the Cold War was an established fact of European life. The brutal Soviet repression of the Hungarian Uprising in 1956 had shocked the West and made it apparent that Soviet rule cared little for human rights and freedom of speech in the countries of Eastern Europe. It was a troubling time to be a European. The ugly concrete symbolism of the Berlin Wall, built in 1961, was a constant reminder of the un-peace between West and Eastern Europe.

But the poets of the Eastern Bloc were already being translated and read and Hughes and Weissbort felt this poetry to be the 'most insistent' of all the material they had received. They wrote unequivocally: 'This poetry is more universal than ours.' It seemed to them as if the political repression of the East and the urgency of the situation produced poetry that was of a higher order, full of confidence, philosophy and universality; poetry that was psychologically subtle and yet spoke to millions. Seamus Heaney, a few decades later, said much the same thing in his essay 'The Impact of Translation'. He considered that the locus of greatness had shifted to the East and to those poets like Miłosz who testified to the 'efficacy of poetry itself as a necessary and fundamental human act'.

With hindsight we may choose to disagree, or perhaps to soften the picture: this poetry was important, but the snapshot was partial and it favoured a few European male voices, a new canon in place of the old. Some of the poets, stripped of context, have fared less critically well in recent times. Even within Poland and Czechoslovakia there was a multitude of different poetic responses, many of which we are still discovering. But Hughes and Weissbort were stating a case in the most urgent terms they had, and it is undoubtedly true that poetry in translation has a beneficial effect on English-language poetry: it is by its very existence more universal than ours because it adds to our partial understanding of what poetry is able to do. Reading translated poetry and translating poetry encourages a poet to extend the elastic potential of language, to inhabit other voices, and the proof of this is immediately manifest in the effect that translation had on Hughes's own poetry. Poet and scholar Tara Bergin has written extensively on how Hughes's work, particularly the songs of *Crow* – 'songs with no music whatsoever', as Hughes phrased it – owed a great deal to his proximity with the deliberately unadorned poetry of János Pilinszky.

Hughes began the magazine with a particular view of translation. He wrote in a 1967 editorial:

> Nevertheless, after our experience as editors of this paper, we feel more strongly than ever that the first ideal is literalness, insofar as the original is what we are curious about. The very oddity and struggling dumbness of a word for word version is what makes our own imagination jump.

We know that this view was Hughes's own, as Weissbort (amongst others) recorded Hughes's instinct to cleave to literalness in a piece about his translations published in *MPT* in 2003. Whilst it is important to see this as a stand against the practice of adapting and making versions in the way Lowell did in his *Imitations*, we can also see this as Hughes's desire to seek out something authentic and strange for his own purposes as a poet. Hughes spoke no other languages and all his translations were done with the help of a co-translator, usually a native speaker. We might take issue with Hughes's belief that this method of working, the capturing of 'fumbled and broken' language, is more authentic than the work of an experienced translator of poetry with knowledge of both cultures, but the urgent hunger for something quite other is what gives Hughes the energy to found a magazine, and the Poetry International Festival, in 1967.

Over the fifty years of *MPT*, the practice of poetry translation has become increasingly diverse in approach and concern and the magazine never again made a claim for a particular style of translation – perhaps because all the other editors of *MPT* have been practising translators themselves and aware of the many ways a translator can make a poem sing in another language. The number of translators who work particularly with poetry seems to rise exponentially, thanks in part to the important advocacy work done by centres of translation such as the British Centre for Literary Translation. The internet has allowed us access to translators all over the world and to poetry from many regions.

But *MPT* is also filled with examples of English-speaking poets, whose poetry was enlivened by the practice of translation from literals. In 1996 Elaine Feinstein wrote in *MPT* of her earlier engagement with the poetry of Marina Tsvetaeva:

I recognised something in Tsvetaeva's work I could not find expressed elsewhere: an unguarded passion, and a desperation that arose from it, which was willing to expose the most undignified emotions. Even as I struggled to find ways of channelling such intensity into a workable English idiom, I was beginning to be seduced by her example. I wanted to take the same risks in my own writing.

There are many more examples of such creative symbiosis between poets and their translators in this anthology. The editors of the first issue hoped that the work published would 'stimulate poetry-making in this country' and MPT did this, and does it still, by offering persuasive and different work to its readers, but also by providing a space for poets to experiment with translation.

Modern Poetry in Translation continued to publish a great deal of work from Eastern Europe over the following decade. In 1969, just months after the Prague Spring and Soviet invasion of Prague one of MPT's most important collaborators, George (Jiří) Theiner, published his translations of a number of Czech poets in a Czech issue of MPT. Theiner was born in Czechoslovakia, but left his country as a child to escape the Nazis in 1939 and came to Britain. He returned to his native country after the war, but was subject to internment and forced labour under the Communists. In 1968 he left again, writing to Weissbort in a letter dated September 1968, a few weeks after the Soviet invasion:

Just a few lines to let you know that we've left Prague and are on our way to London. We have been through a ghastly time and I feel that I've had enough of Central Europe, however much I had hoped that life might soon become quite tolerable in Prague. August 21 has effectively dashed all such hopes...

With this letter Theiner sent new translations of Holub and Jiří Kolář which went into the hastily-assembled Czech issue. Later Czech work, gathered and sent by other collaborators was subject to increasing censorship. As one contributor wrote in a letter to Weissbort in 1969: 'Please let me know when you get it and refer to it as the "folk poetry".'

MPT exists because of excellent translation and translators, and the stories of the translators and collaborators occupied us in our selection for this anthology almost as much as the poems themselves. A number of translators, like Theiner, lived between two worlds and attempted to foster contact between the cultures through the medium of poetry. Many of these, like Theiner, Michael Hamburger and Ewald Osers, had fled Nazi Europe: their particular cataclysm was fascism and war in Europe.

Weissbort himself was from a migrant family. His parents were Polish Jews and they had moved to Britain in the 1930s. In the house they spoke French although Weissbort as a child would answer in English. Unlike Hughes, who was confidently 'local', a poet of place, Weissbort shared with many of the translators a more complicated sense of national identity and language. He had begun his career as a historian of Soviet Russia, and learnt Russian and he too began to translate for the magazine, eventually dedicating himself to the teaching and practice of translating poetry. In 1973 he became Professor of English and Comparative Literature at the University of Iowa and directed the International Writing Program there. Over his lifetime he contributed many translations to *MPT*, among them moving poems by the young poet and human rights protester Natalya Gorbanevskaya, who was incarcerated in a Soviet psychiatric ward in the 1970s for her protests on Red Square against the Soviet invasion of Czechoslovakia.

But Weissbort's greatest legacy was the magazine itself. We can see from the letters that Ted Hughes began with enormous and engaging enthusiasm, but was quickly overwhelmed with the business of the magazine: 'I don't want to be a poetry telephone exchange operator' as he wrote to his co-translator of Pilinszky, János Csokits. By 1967 his interest was waning, and he left Weissbort increasingly to make the business and practical decisions, and even the selections of poetry. By 1970 he had detached himself entirely. Weissbort went on loyally editing the magazine for three more decades, publishing much extraordinary work, and increasing the global reach of the magazine. By the 90s the 'scrappy-looking' magazine was a large annual anthology of poems and prose.

Weissbort was not, however, alone in this venture. He often worked with guest editors on country-specific or author-led issues – Anthony Rudolf, Stephen Watts, Saadi Simawe, David Ricks and Norma Rinsler all guest-edited later issues of the magazine. Norma Rinsler worked with Weissbort for over twelve years towards the end of his editorship, effectively co-editing the magazine. She remembered: 'Working with Danny was never a matter of routine. [...] We would take a bus along the Finchley Road, he from the north and I from the south, and meet at Swiss Cottage for coffee, where the café tables were always too small for the jumble of papers that Danny brought with him.'

Many collaborators of *MPT* offered their time and effort generously. Throughout its long history *MPT* has inspired acts of kindness and self-sacrifice: contributors who quietly refuse payment for their contributions, poets who waive permissions fees, colleagues who work long hours for no pay. The magazine, founded in wayward generosity (free issues to all the world's poets!), expresses itself with the same utopian gestus even now: it is not for nothing that John Berger wrote 'MPT is the Fifth International. Anyone who wants to change the world and see it changed should join.' David and Helen Constantine's nine-year editorship was entirely true to this spirit. The magazine flourished like a tended garden, much of the excellent work published in this anthology was sought out and published by the Constantines, and they worked hard to establish the magazine as an independent and self-sustaining organisation.

This anthology, *Centres of Cataclysm*, is not a summing up of MPT's large publishing output or even a scientifically representative selection. Between 1965 and 2016 MPT published ninety-four issues and many thousands of poems. We (the editors) were caught in a double bind: reading everything was necessary, but also induced terrible poem-blindness.

After many days reading through the issues and alternating between despair at the quantity and delight at every new find, we decided to make a shape for the anthology which would allow us to present a tiny fraction of the work in the spirit of the magazine's history. Hughes and Weissbort had described a 'Centre of Cataclysm' in the first editorial and this struck us vividly as a visual form: the centre of a circle around which ran concentric rings, like ripples or tremors (the cover is MPT designer Katy Mawhood's imagining of this idea).

Applied to an anthology of poetry this form can only be the loosest sort of organisation: poems shoot like sparks away from a central fire and where we have chosen to present them is conditional, a matter of personal imagination. Nonetheless, the zoning of poems and prose around a core was a satisfying concept: dynamic in intent, the outwards movement seemed to represent the trajectory of a translated poem out into a new world.

The central core, and first section of the anthology was the zone of lived 'Cataclysm' where the magazine began: poems about war, revolution, upheaval, genocide, dissidence and resistance, and also ways and images of hope and survival. This core spread into a surrounding ring which we called 'The Gate of Secrets' in reference to the Hungarian poet Ferenc Juhász's poem 'The Boy Changed into a Stag Cries Out at the Gate of Secrets'. Ted Hughes made a version of this poem in the 60s after reading Kenneth McRobbie's version and we publish it here alongside Pascale Petit's version of Ted Hughes's version, and Tara

Bergin's poem 'The Stag Boy'. The chain of translation and inspiration which stretched from the original Hungarian poem (described by W.H. Auden as 'one of the greatest written in my time') deep into our own poetry expressed something very important about the magazine's role in English-language culture.

The gate of secrets opened into a wider garden of translation, with poems that examine the nature of language and translation, a prose piece on Michael Hamburger and a study (in poetry) of the practical, metaphorical and humane sense of translation.

The next zone relates to the human experience of migration and exile and it takes in survival in a new language and territory, the looking back and longing for home and the transplanting of experience into new contexts. It is hardly a matter of surprise that many of the poems we looked at, over the fifty years of *MPT*, dealt with the migration of peoples and communities, for it has been a defining feature of human life over the last century, and perhaps always. It is also noticeable that *MPT* has been a point of entry for writers who have migrated to an English-speaking country, a metaphorical 'airport', as Hughes described it, where poets are first published.

The final outer ripples are concerned with protecting and saving: the ecology and survival of languages and cultures and finally protecting and saying the human. So the burning heart of cataclysm at the centre of the anthology is drawn out; through translation, migration and exile, it is transplanted into another soil. The word spoken under duress becomes a word of affirmation: a protection and a stating of our own humanity.

Introduction

When Daniel Weissbort asked us to take over *MPT* in the autumn of 2003, and as we began to learn more about the spirit and the social and political context of the magazine's foundation in the mid-1960s, we felt the forces of change and of continuity in equal measure. We felt the urgency of the project, the same spirit, in very differerent times. Not that the old 'centres of cataclysm' – 1968 in Czechoslovakia, for example, or 1989 in Berlin – had worked themselves out and were done with. On the contrary: the Wall coming down, the removal of that barrier, far from signalling 'the end of history', caused a mêlée of possibilities, some good, some bad, in a colossal unrest. It seemed to us then that our editorial context was not the longing and the bid for the end of fixity, but rather the consequences of a continuing revolution: the break-up of blocs, the opening of borders, the march of capital, the voluntary or forced movement of many thousands of people, their going abroad for work or into exile, seeking asylum, everywhere people and their languages on the move, those languages themselves, spoken abroad, adding to a new mix or falling silent and being extinguished among the more powerful dialects of the human tribe.

In that situation *MPT*, open to the poetry of all the world, again came truly into its own. For the spirit was the same. We believed as passionately as Hughes and Weissbort did that poetry matters: because it tells the truth in mendacious times and because that truth, through the forms and rhythms of poetry, excites in people under whatever repressive and demeaning structures the demand for greater freedom. That was our first premise, as it had been theirs. Our second was that translation matters: because it brings valuable things from abroad into our home country. English is a major world-language and, precisely for that reason, its native speakers need to be continually confronted with what is foreign to them, or they risk sticking fast in complacency and insularity. And like Weissbort, only more so, we understood the 'modern' in the magazine's title to mean any new and lively version of any poetry of any age. So translation crosses frontiers of both space and time. The past is a foreign country just as much as anywhere else beyond our frontiers now. We need the imports from both foreign time and space.

Exile and diaspora, the movement of peoples, already the hallmark of our time when we began to edit *MPT* in 2003, appears now, in 2015, day by day like a mark of Cain or an obscene disfigurement on the front page of every newspaper and on every television screen. A man can't hold his wife and their two little boys: they slip from his grasp and wash up drowned on a shore that does not want them. Thousands upon thousands, day after terrible day. And in Turkey, Jordan, the Lebanon, millions more backed up in wretched conditions, always liable to be evicted into the next stage of exile in another place where they will not be welcome. We always believed – and, since Sasha Dugdale succeeded us, with accumulating evidence we continue to believe – that *MPT* is a benign version of the crossing of frontiers, a world-wide generous, mutually enlivening exchange. And that utopian gesture is not cancelled out but is made more necessary by the real present context of our celebratory anthology, namely the biggest wandering of peoples since the Second World War and the ceaseless annexation of life by the markets.

MPT seeks a real diversity of voices: women and men equally, different centuries, countries, races, creeds, languages, cultures, ideas. The very essence of the founding principle was: Your view is not the only one. Set that against the maniacal, life-hating, life-destroying monotheism now advancing bloodily across the Middle East.

In a context of hateful fundamentalisms and the movement of millions of people from their homes, we, former editors, and Sasha, the editor now, have made an anthology of fifty years of good writing first published in *MPT*. This volume and every new issue of the magazine are a profession of faith in the virtue of poetry and translation. Through the act and the metaphor of the translation of poetry *MPT* will continue to show what pluralism and free exchange are like. It will be those things *in practice*, we might say. And so it will do what poetry always does: it will prove that human beings can still imagine a world more in accordance with them at their best. Poetry can't bring that better condition about; but by its most characteristic workings, by its liveliness, its freedom, its natural sympathy for plurality of being, poetry, and the act of translating it, can and must keep on insisting that we are capable of living together better than we do at present.

✧

This poetry is more

universal than ours.

TED HUGHES & DANIEL WEISSBORT

From the Editorial to the First Issue

Our policy is to concentrate on a limited number of poets in each issue and to represent each one by a larger sampling of his work than is usually possible in less specialised magazines, rather than to include many poets each with one or two pieces. The type of translations we are seeking can be described as literal, though not literal in a strict or pedantic sense. Though this may seem at first suspect, it is more apposite to define our criteria negatively, as literalness can only be a deliberate tendency, not a dogma. We feel that as soon as devices extraneous to the original are employed for the purposes of recreating its 'spirit', the value of the whole enterprise is called into question. Also 'Imitations' like Robert Lowell's, while undeniably beautiful, are the record of the effect of one poet's imagination on another's. They may help in the appreciation of the original, they may simply obscure it. In any case, the original becomes strangely irrelevant. Poetry inevitably loses hugely in translation, but those purists who claim that it is precisely 'the poetry' which is lost are speaking as though 'the poetry' were some separable ingredient, some additive like the whitening agent in a detergent. We feel that enough of the whole is preservable in some, though by no means in all, poetry.

It will be noted that in our first issue there is a minimum of comment. Indeed there is virtually no comment, simply bare biographical and bibliographical data. This is to some extent the result of our embarrassment at the amount of material we had. As it is we have had to leave out much we should like to have included. We were reluctant to have to leave out still more to make room for critical surveys. Furthermore we are convinced that experience should, in any case, come before judgement, that it is more important to be somewhere than simply to have the illusion that one knows where one is. There has been little attempt to impose any unity on this first issue, but the unity, such as it is, has imposed itself on us. While we had material coming from many other areas of the world, it was that which came from Eastern Europe, which was somehow the most insistent. It is this region which has been at the centre of cataclysm. One of the most remarkable features of the poetry printed in this first issue is its sense of purpose, its confidence in the social as well as private value of poetry, its confidence that it is being heard. This poetry is more universal than ours. It deals in issues, universally comprehensible. It does not fight shy of philosophy. It does not hide behind perverse imagery. As compared with our poetry it comes out into the open. We feel then that this magazine, could it but reach a wider audience than poetry magazines generally do, could not fail to engage that audience. But it is not our aim to disparage English poetry by invidious comparison. We feel, on the contrary, that closer acquaintance with what is being written elsewhere can only stimulate poetry-making in this country.

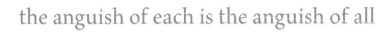

the anguish of each is the anguish of all

MIROSLAV HOLUB

The fly

She sat on a willow-trunk
watching
part of the battle of Crécy,
the shouts,
the gasps,
the groans,
the trampling and the tumbling.

During the fourteenth charge
of the French cavalry
she mated
with a brown-eyed male fly
from Vadincourt.

She rubbed her legs together
as she sat on a disembowelled horse
meditating
on the immortality of flies.

With relief she alighted
on the blue tongue
of the Duke of Clervaux.

When silence settled
and only the whisper of decay
softly circled the bodies

and only
a few arms and legs
still twitched jerkily under the trees,

she began to lay her eggs
on the single eye
of Johann Uhr,
the Royal Armourer.

And thus it was
that she was eaten by a swift
fleeing
from the fires of Estrées.

Translated from the Czech by George Theiner

Miroslav Holub (1923–1998) was a Czech immunologist and poet. His work is remarkable for its precision of tone and voice and its preoccupation with the material and everyday. George Theiner's translation of 'The fly' was first published in the first issue of MPT, and subsequently became so popular with English-speaking readers it was actually included in the *New Penguin Book of English Verse* in 2000.

JAN BOLESŁAW OŻÓG

Ash

Storms have rumbled by like German tanks
and the black oxen of clouds have flattened out the weather with their bellies;
only the horse of the wind galloping over fences and fields
moves lightly in the company of peasant carts back of beyond.

A church on the hill
sings the praises of him, who didn't run away to the city,
but stayed behind.

Lady's smock, ah, like belated snow on a greened meadow –
and birches in white stockings and short skirts
the colour of celadon and air –
the only women of this landscape.

The men, who have stayed in the villages, are the young oaks bent over the dell,
elms and hawthorn, with a bird-nest in its briars,
not yet covered by a curtain of green.

And those of the peasants who have remained in the villages
are such solemn priests of their own and others' acres
that the field-crosses like spiders bow to them from afar,
when, taking huge and slow strides, as at sowing time,
they gaze from balks to see if the corn is growing as it used to grow.

One solitary old man, like an insubordinate vicar,
is sowing in the valley, scattering white, fine ash, his last, over a late field.

Translated from the Polish by Andrzej Busza and Bogdan Czaykowski

Jan Bolesław Ożóg (1913–1991) was a Polish poet and schoolteacher. His early
work was characterised by imagery drawn from rural life, but the destruction
of rural culture in postwar Poland turned Ożóg from a poetic witness of a way
of life to its angry priest and mourner.

The Girl at Pompeii

Since the anguish of each is the anguish of all
Let us relive your own once more, skinny girl
Who clung convulsively to your mother
As if you wanted to vanish back inside her
That midday when the heavens turned black.
In vain, since the air had turned to poison,
Seeking you out, slipped through the barred-up windows
Of your house calm behind the solid walls
Which once echoed your singing and timid laughter.
Centuries went by, the ash became stone
Imprisoning forever those graceful young limbs.
And so you are with us still, a twisted cast,
Agony without end, dreadful testimony
To how the gods rate our proud seed.
But of your distant sister nothing remains,
The girl from Holland closed within four walls
Yet who wrote her story without tomorrows:
Mute her dust is scattered upon the wind,
Her brief life shut in a crumpled notebook.
Victim sacrificed upon fear's altar,
Nothing remains of the Hiroshima schoolgirl
But a shadow fixed to the wall by the glare
Of a thousand suns. Potentates of the earth,
Sad secret custodians of the definitive thunder,
Procurers of new poisons, we have had our fill
Of afflictions rained down from heaven.
Before pressing the button, stop and consider.

Translated from the Italian by Martin Bennett

Primo Levi (1919–1987) lived most of his life in Turin. During the Nazi occupation of Italy, he joined a partisan group in the Alps, but was soon arrested and sent to an internment camp at Fossoli and then to Auschwitz. After the war he worked as a chemist in a paint factory and wrote many books, including *Survival in Auschwitz* and *The Periodic Table*, which London's Royal Institute voted in 2006 'the best science book ever'. The measured intensity of Levi's prose also infuses his poetry – each poem poignant testimony of a suffered and enduring integrity.

Choman Hardi (1974–) was born in Iraq but her family fled to Iran when she was a baby. She returned to her birthplace as a child but was once again forced to leave when Saddam's army attacked Kurds with chemical weapons in 1988. In 1993 she was granted refugee status in the UK. The poem here refers to the Iraqi attack on the Kurdish city of Halabja and to the Anfal campaign, when many thousands of people were killed by poisonous gas. Hardi wrote that the poem rose out of a sense of dissatisfaction with the official Kurdish commemoration of the genocide: 'I found the repeated displays of gassed bodies disrespectful and unfair. People were reduced to broken victims and their humanity was lost. I wanted to remember the victims as people who were once full of life and hope.'

CHOMAN HARDI

One Moment for Halabja

To honour the victims

One moment of no silence, no sorrow.
One moment of thinking not of your entangled,
twisted bodies, your blistered eyes,
your poisoned blue lips.

This time, one moment of applause for your
remembrance, dear ones. One moment
of smiling. One moment of thinking
of your dreams, colourful as finches.

One moment of standing, not in front of
the pictures which turned to stone
your shattering. This time one moment of
standing to pay respect

to the people who wanted to live longer,
to those who were scared and those who weren't,
those whose hearts were full of kindness
and those who were cold-hearted,

to you, all of you, from the old to the young,
to you who used to walk the streets,
remembering yesterday,
and thinking of tomorrow.

Translated from the Kurdish by the author

Punjabi Folksongs from World War One

The Punjab as a sovereign state was occupied by the British East India Company Army in 1849. Sikh soldiers were first taken in the army in 1846. In 1860 the Loodhiaah (Ludhiana) Regiment conquered Hong Kong and Peking. For half a century Sikh 'soldiers of the Queen' were instrumental in suppressing revolts by Pathans in the North West Frontier Province. The best Indian material for the British army, to quote Sir Michael O'Dwyer, the Governor of the Punjab, was found mainly in the province. His remarks were consonant with the period's socio-biological ideology of martial races.

At the outbreak of the First World War half of the Indian Army was drawn from the Punjab, 'the sword arm of the Empire'. The total number of Indians serving in all areas of the war in France, East Africa, Meso-potamia, Egypt, Gallipoli, Salonika, Aden and Persian Gulf was 943,344. The price paid by these soldiers was high: 61,041 died and 67,771 were wounded in battle.

The Dhan-Pothohār region of the division of Rawalpindi produced most of the folk songs on world wars. In the folk songs the womenfolk – mothers, sisters and wives – are the protagonists. They curse the *firangees* (white foreigners) for the suffering. They hate war and the warmongers, whether British or Germans. The women know their men are mercenaries and have no allegiances.

Here are some Punjabi folksongs of the time in English translation. The songs mostly refer to the battle of Basra although there are a few references to Germany. The French word *l'arme* (laam) is used to mean 'war' in Punjabi common parlance.

ਗਲ ਕੁੜਤਾ ਟਸਰੇ ਦਾ
ਹੌਲੀ-ਹੌਲੀ ਚਲ ਗੱਡੀਏ
ਵਿਚ ਮੁਸਾਫ਼ਰ ਬਸਰੇ ਦਾ।

He wears a tussar shirt
O train, move slowly
You carry a passenger bound for Basra

ਮੇਰਾ ਲਿਖ ਰੰਡੀਆਂ ਵਿਚ ਨਾਮਾ
ਬਸਰੇ ਨੂੰ ਜਾਣ ਵਾਲ਼ਿਆ

Better you enter my name amongst the widows
You who are off to Basra

ਮੈਂ ਰੰਡੀਓਂ ਸੁਹਾਗਣ ਹੋਵਾਂ
ਬਸਰੇ ਦੀ ਲਾਮ ਟੁੱਟ ਜਾਏ

May the battle in Basra come to an end
The one who is destined to be a widow
May yet be wed

ਪੱਤ ਬਿਰਛਾਂ ਦੇ ਲੂਸ ਗੇ' ਸਾਰੇ
ਜੰਗ ਦੀ ਸੋਅ ਸੁਣ ਕੇ

Hearing the news of the war
The trees caught fire

ਐਸ ਦੇਸ ਮੇਰਾ ਜੀਅ ਨਈਂ ਲਗਦਾ
ਬਸਰੇ ਲੈ ਜਾ ਤੂੰ
ਮੈਂ ਸਾਰੀ ਰਾਤ ਕੱਤਿਆ ਕਰੂੰ

Without you I feel lonely here
Come and take me along to Basra
I will spin the wheel for you the whole night

ਦਿਨ ਚੜ੍ਹਦੇ ਨੂੰ ਘੋੜਾ ਬੀੜਿਆ
ਬਸਰੈ ਦੀ ਆ ਪਈ ਮੁਹਿੰਮ
ਦਿਲੈ ਦੀਆਂ ਦਿਲ ਚ ਰਹੀਆਂ

In the morning he saddled the horse
For the Basra expedition
Alas, I couldn't talk to him to my heart's content

ਉਡ ਗਈ ਪਤੰਗ ਪਿੱਛੇ ਡੋਰ
ਬਈ ਮਹਿੰਡੀ ਤੋਬਾ ਤੋਬਾ
ਜਰਮਨ ਨੇ ਪਾਇਆ ਡਾਢਾ ਜੋਰ
ਬਈ ਮਹਿੰਡੀ ਤੋਬਾ ਤੋਬਾ
' ਗਰੇਜਾਂ ਦਾ ਚਲਨਾ ਨਹਿੰ ਜੋਰ
ਬਈ ਮਹਿੰਡੀ ਤੋਬਾ ਤੋਬਾ

The kite has lost its string
God forbid
Germany is on the offensive
God forbid
The English are on the defensive
God forbid

ਮਾਵਾਂ ਦੇ ਸਭ ਬੱਚੜੇ ਪਰਦੇਸ
ਮੋਡੇ ਬੱਚੜਿਓ ਵੇ, ਮੋਲਾ ਲਾਮ ਤੁੋੜੈ ਨੇ
ਪੰਜ ਤਨ ਰਾਖਾ ਨੇ, ਅੱਲ੍ਹਾ ਖੈਰੀਂ ਮੋੜੈ ਨੇ।

Each and every son has gone to the *laam* in the foreign lands
May Allah end the *laam*
May the Five Souls of the Prophet's family guard you my children
May Allah bring you back home safe

ਛੱਲਾ ਰੂੰ ਨੇ ਗੋਹਤੇ

Chhalla my darling I spin the cotton wool

ਮੋਲਾ ਲਾਮ ਤਰੋੜੇ

May God stop the war

ਸੱਜਣਾਂ ਕੂੰ ਮੋੜੇ

And bring back my loved ones

ਸੁਣ ਢੋਲ ਜਾਨੀ

Listen my darling

ਅੱਲ੍ਹਾ ਖੈਰੀਂ ਆਨੀ

Return home safe

ਛੱਲਾ ਸਾਂਝੀ ਝੰਗੀ ਏ

Chhalla...

ਹਾਕਮ ਅੱਜ ਫ਼ਰੰਗੀ ਏ

Firangee is the ruler

ਡਾਢੀ ਹੱਥ ਨੀ ਤੰਗੀ ਏ

We are in much hardship

ਕਿਹੜੇ ਪਾਸੇ ਜਾਵਾਂ

Where shall I go

ਪੋਹਲੀ ਪਈ ਖਾਵਾਂ

I have to eat weeds

ਛੱਲਾ ਰੂੰ ਨਾ ਗੋਹਤਾ

Chhalla here is the cotton ball

ਡਾਢਾ ਪਿਆ ਵਛੋੜਾ

Terrible separation I suffer

ਦੇਸ ਯਾਰਾਂ ਛੋੜਾ

My darling has left home

ਅੱਲ੍ਹਾ ਮੀਂਹ ਵਸਾਈਂ

Oh God make it rain

ਸੱਜਣਾਂ ਨੂੰ ਮਿਲਾਈਂ

And let me meet my beloved

ਛੱਲਾ ਆਈ ਲਾਰੀ

Chhalla here comes the lorry

ਸਿਰੇ ਉੱਤੇ ਖਾਰੀ

I carry a heavy basket on my head

ਐ ਵੀ ਡਾਢੀ ਭਾਰੀ

I stand and wait for him on the road

ਖਲੀ ਪਈ ਤਕੇਨੀ ਆਂ

With tears in my eyes

ਹੰਝੂ ਪਈ ਵਹੇਨੀ ਆਂ

Late One Melancholy February Night

(for Galina)

Late one melancholy February night
a friend knocked at my door:
'Olga, I've just buried my son!
I cannot cry out, cannot even sigh.
Tell me, don't hide anything –
you yourself have lost children –
will the tears come soon,
will this terrible darkness lighten?'
All night I spoke with my friend,
Soothing her, comforting her.
So my grief was turned to good use,
my inconsolable grief.

Translated from the Russian by Daniel Weissbort

Olga Berggolts (1910–1975) was born in St Petersburg and was a much-loved radio announcer during the Siege of Leningrad. Her first husband was a victim of Stalinist repression, and she too was imprisoned in 1938. She gave birth to a stillborn child as a result of the beatings she received in prison.

Dear Fahimeh

That day,
that hot day in July,
when the Evin loudspeakers
called out your beautiful name and your lips
smiled, your eyes said to your friends,
'So today is the day.'

You went and your walk
was a perfume filling the corridor.
Everyone gasped, everyone asked with their eyes,
'Is today then the day?' The Pasdar
flung back an answer: 'Where is her bag?
Where are her veil, her socks, her money?'

A rumour went round that you'd given a sign
that yes, today was the day:
'I don't need my food,' you had said.

So tonight is the night.
A silence hangs in the heart of it.
Friends look at friends and tell themselves
that perhaps you'll come back.

Fahimeh dear, tell us, spare
a word for your friends. Is
the sky sad where you are, does it weep?
And the wind, does it ruffle your veil?
Back here, the ward sweats for your news.

And a message gets through:
wind-blown breathless dandelion
comes from the mountains to say that clouds
are massing up there and they're big with child.

Head held high, you are standing and waiting for this,
for the clouds to open, for you
to be mother of change.

Rifles crack.
The moorland holds its breath
at a star shooting across it.

It would be good to sing and go with friends
to face the firing squad, to dance,
to float in the rain.

In the long sea-silence,
a wave lifts, oars clip at the water.

A young fisherman bringing his boat to land,
rice-growers trudging home,
they shape their lips to your name.

Your name is beautiful for young girls born in July.

Translated from the Farsi by Hubert Moore and Nasrin Parvaz

This poem is for Fahimeh Taghadosi, executed in Iran in 1982. The writer is
unknown. Farkhondeh Ashena, who escaped from Iran, heard it when she
was in solitary confinement in the notorious Evin Prison, and memorised it.

NATALYA GORBANEVSKAYA

That time I did not save Warsaw, nor Prague later...

That time I did not save Warsaw, nor Prague later,
not I, not I, and there's no atoning for this guilt.
Let my house be tightly shut and let it be cursed,
house of evil, of sin, of treachery and of crime.

And chained by an eternal, invisible chain to this terrible house,
I shall find pleasure in it and I shall find comfort where lives
in a dark, dirty corner, drunkenly, wretchedly,
my people, guiltless and godless.

Translated from the Russian by Daniel Weissbort

Natalya Gorbanevskaya (1936–2013) was a poet, translator and human rights
activist. In August 1968 she was one of a very few dissidents who protested on
Red Square against the Soviet invasion of Czechoslovakia. She took along her
three-month-old son in a borrowed pram. As a direct result of her protest she
was arrested and imprisoned for over a year in a Soviet psychiatric ward.

NATALYA GORBANEVSKAYA

This, from the Diagnosis...

'The children's fate doesn't bother her.'

This, from the diagnosis,
rings out like a silvery clarinet,
has lost the colour of danger,
but my memory's not been wiped clean of it.

It's good when the breathing in the next room
is my sons' and not a cell-mate's;
it's good to wake up, not groaning
at an envenomed reality.

It's good not to feel the brain's convolutions –
has there been a change? – is it you or isn't it? –
not settling down to breathe in, from underneath the rubble
the dust of what, please God, is irrecoverable.

Translated from the Russian by Daniel Weissbort

The Hedgehog

The hedgehog that you pointed out with your fierce
glowing eyes, 'Look how all rolled-up he
waits.' That I never saw,

like the dead in their deserted world he lives
outside of me. How else do you explain
now that it's colder and he
asleep as far as I know, that I hear him
rasping over tiles, chirping and growling
behind the back door, every
restless night.

Translated from the Dutch by Virginie Kortekaas

Eva Gerlach (1948–) is a *nom de plume*, chosen by a poet who values anonymity and feels her work should speak for itself.

WISŁAWA SZYMBORSKA

Innocence

Conceived on a mattress of human hair,
Gerda, Erica, perhaps Margarette.
She doesn't, really doesn't know anything about it.
That kind of knowledge is impossible
to accept or transmit.
The Greek Furies were simply too just.
We'd be put off today by their winged savagery.

Irma, Brigide, perhaps Frederike.
Twenty years old, scarcely more.
Fluent in the three languages useful for travel.
Her firm offers for export
only the best mattresses of synthetic fibre.
Export draws nations together.

Bertha, Ulrika, perhaps Hildegaard.
No beauty, but tall and slim.
Her cheeks, neck, breasts, thighs, belly
in full bloom just now and glorious sheen of novelty,
treads in barefooted joy on Europe's beaches,
shaking loose her blond knee-length hair.

Don't have it cut – said her hairdresser –
once cut, it never grows again so rich.
Please believe me – it's been tested
tausend – und tausendmal.

Translated from the Polish by Jan Darowski

Wisława Szymborska (1923–2012) wrote of herself that she 'borrows words weighed down with pathos, and then tries to make them appear light'. She received the Nobel Prize in 1996 and is widely considered to be one of Poland's greatest 20th-century poets.

A Room by the Sea

Will, like the fingers of an empty glove.
A table weighed with silence like a parting.
The sea outside. And a shoe filled with nothing,
Looking for a foot that took its leave.

A fortress of restraint moved by two feet.
Almost books. And a glass without a use.
A bit of old air: two years, perhaps, since it
Refused to go out, and stayed here for always.

And suddenly a seawind feels me
As women feel the cloth in a store;
Is he good, will he wash well in the laundry?

Later I wove a flag of doubt once more.
I hung it up, and looked outside to find
How it clatters, moving in the wind.

Translated from the Hebrew by Dom Moraes

Israeli poet Yehuda Amichai (1924–2000) was born in Germany and went to
Israel as a boy with his family, where he fought in the 1948 Arab-Israeli war.
He is considered to be one of the finest poets in the Hebrew language and he
has been translated into many languages. This poem appears in the very first
issue of *MPT* as part of the earliest published selection of Amichai's poetry in
English translation. It is the first poem in the selection and therefore the first
poem *MPT* ever published.

The selection opens with this statement by the poet: 'Yosef ben Matityahu
(Josephus Flavius) was a field-commander of the Judaean Army in Galilee
that fought Vespasian and Titus. He went over to the Romans, and wrote the
history of the campaign he had fought. He chose to write about what he had
been involved in. I agree with Josephus. I want to be involved and avoid
writing, and then to be detached and write. The debate continues as to
whether Josephus was, or was not, a traitor.'

GEORGE GÖMÖRI

Polishing October

Like cleaning a silver bowl years locked away,
the shine of it all tarnished now and spotted:
that's how, Revolution, I clean you.
I won't tell facts about you any longer:
in the October wind the holed-through banners fluttering,
the words fleeing freely, that wild ecstasy,
tanks charging along in terror, their guns firing,
graves for teenagers dug in public squares...
No, what I'll say can be grasped by anyone,
by those not there to see it or born later:
I could never before say the word 'Hungarian'
with my head raised so high and with such certainty,
so conscious of my integrity as a human.
I never before had the right to be proud of my nation.
And I'm sure that when at the bar of posterity
are judged the glorious deeds and the pitiful deeds of nations,
I need say no more than '56' and 'Hungary' –
and then our countless sins will be forgiven
and if anything survives of us, this will, and will forever.

Translated from the Hungarian by Clive Wilmer and the author

George Gömöri (1934–) was born in Hungary but fled to the UK in 1956 after
the Hungarian Uprising. He was involved in the Uprising, which began as
spontaneous protests against Soviet-influenced rule in Hungary and was
suppressed with great loss of life in November 1956 by Soviet tanks. He is a
prolific poet and translator of Hungarian poetry.

Roll Call in the Concentration Camp

He stands, cold in the morning wind,
stamping his feet, rubbing his hands,
death's diligent angel
who worked hard and rose in rank.
Suddenly he feels he has made a mistake. All eyes,
he checks again in his open book
the bodies waiting for him in formation,
a square within a square. Only I
am missing. I am a mistake.
I extinguish my eyes quickly; I erase my shadow.
Please God, let me not be missed, let the sum
add up without me.

Here, forever.

Translated from the Hebrew by Robert Friend

Dan Pagis (1930–1986) was born in Bukowina and spent several years in a concentration camp as a child. In 1946 he went to Israel and began writing in Hebrew. He taught medieval Hebrew literature at the Hebrew University of Jerusalem. Many of his poems are concerned with his experiences as a Holocaust survivor.

DAN PAGIS

Scrawled in Pencil in a Sealed Car

Here in this transport
I Eve
and Abel my son
if you should see my older son
Cain Adam's son
tell him that I

Translated from the Hebrew by Robert Friend

BARTOLO CATTAFI

Winter Figs

Winter figs
arrive on branches convulsed by cold.
Tight-shut hard stubborn
unlike their easy-going
summer companions
they're red inside like
an icy sunset with no yellow
wild suspicious
at every rustle of a bough
between sour lips they lock
a streak of sugar.
Arriving unexpected
they leave
the way they came
fragments roaming
in the void in the dark
struck for an instant by the light.

Translated from the Italian by Ruth Feldman and Brian Swann

Bartolo Cattafi (1922–1979) was born in Sicily and came to prominence in the postwar period in Italy. This poem comes from a 1975 issue of *MPT* dedicated to introducing lesser-known Italian poets to an English readership.

MIKLÓS RADNÓTI

Letter to My Wife

Soundless worlds are listening somewhere deep
In the earth; the silence roars in my ears and I keep
On crying for help but from Serbia stunned by war
No one can give me an answer and you are far
Away. The sound of your voice becomes entwined
With my dreams and, when I awake next day, I find
Your words in my heart; I listen and meanwhile the sound
Of tall, proud ferns, cool to the touch, murmurs all round.

When I'll see you again, I can no longer promise – you
Who once were as grave as the psalms, and as palpably true,
As lovely as light and shade and to whom I could find
My way back without eyes or ears – but now in my mind
You stray through a troubled land and from somewhere deep
Within it your flickering image is all I can keep
A hold of. Once you were real, but now you're a dream,
I tumble back into memory's depths till it seems

I'm a boy once more, wondering jealously whether
You love me and if, at the height of youth, you'll ever
Become my wife – I begin to hope once more
And, tumbling back, my wakeful state is restored
And I know you are – my wife, my friend, yet how
Far off. Beyond three savage frontiers. Now
Autumn's coming. Will it forget me here?
The vivid memory of our kisses still endures.

I believed in miracles once, but now they've fled
And squadrons of bombers slowly drone by overhead;
In the sky I saw with amazement the blue of your eyes;
But then it grew dark and the bombs in the aeroplane high
Above were longing to fall. All the same, I came through
And now I'm a prisoner. And though I've measured the true
Scale of my hopes, I'm certain I'll reach my goal;
For you I've already travelled the length of the soul,

The roads that seek distant lands; if I must, I'll contrive
To conjure myself over red-hot coals and survive
Among showers of flames – yet still I will return
To be with you one day; if I have to, I'll learn
To be tough like the bark on a tree – and now I'm soothed
By the calm of men who, achieving power, move
Through endless trials – and the knowledge that I'll pull through
Descends, like a wave, with the coolness of 2 x 2.

[Camp Heidenau, in the hills above Zagubica, 1944. August–September.]

Translated from the Hungarian by Stephen Capus

Miklós Radnóti (1909–1944) was a Hungarian poet born into an assimilated
Jewish family. His real stature as poet became apparent only during the
Second World War when he managed to articulate the anguish of the
threatened and persecuted individual in classical form and created work of
great compassion and beauty. In 1944 he was called up to a labour battalion
and sent to a labour camp in Bor, Serbia, from where he was evacuated and
forced to march towards Germany. When he grew too weak to continue his
march, he was shot dead on 10 November 1944 by militiamen accompanying
the forced labourers near the village of Abda in north-western Hungary. A
notebook of poems telling the story of his last six months was found on his
body when it was exhumed from a mass grave for reburial after the war, 18
months after his death.

SHASH TREVETT

In Memory

Her father scooped her up,
a senseless bundle in a senseless world,

stroked a grit-lined eye
and slackened lips,

and screamed a lonely 'aiyo'.

As she had done
a few days before.

Until silenced by a gun-shot-groin,
until held hurriedly under water,

until gathered by the sea
she flowed to the seashore,

where she now lies,
wearing her corals and pearls.

'When I left northern Sri Lanka at 13, scarred by the civil war, I stopped
speaking and thinking in Tamil. I shut my ears to its music and my tongue
was refused its songs. I was encouraged by the poet Jack Mapanje to re-engage
with my mother tongue. I began to write in English while using the rhythms
and cadences of Tamil; I then translated the resulting poems into Tamil
itself. However, to my surprise I found that as the Tamil translations took
shape, they forced changes onto the English originals. What had seemed
complete and satisfactory before now seemed guttural and stilted when set
against the lyrical fluidity of their Tamil counterparts. Thus the English
versions had to be re-written, and in doing so, it seemed as if I was translating
original Tamil poems into English. Repeatedly the line between source and
target was blurred and what emerged, I hoped, were poems that seemed
richer for being imagined within the linguistic traditions of two language
systems.' ST

Bitter Waters

See these lines on my upturned palm.

They are the rivers of tears
that have washed my face.

They are the rivers of blood
that have washed my land.

Flowing first in trickles, then streams,
then in torrents:

they are the swell of voices
that have cried out our shame.

They lie etched on my skin,
coursing through the creases and ridges

to pool into stories and tales,

I shall tell of these
for the generations to come.

See these hands all twisted and bent.

These are the scars I bear
instead of children.

O Motherland, look not to me
for your warrior.

What should a man do if he is not a fighter

ATTILA JÓZSEF

What Should a Man Do

What should a man do if he is not a fighter, if he
can't throw stones through windows or build barricades?
What should he do if he is not a fighter,
and doesn't know if he's happy or not?

What should I do? he asks, his face unshaven
his fish eyes gazing at me, seeing nothing.
He is so frail and sad, with a strong and sturdy sadness!
He cannot give his life, but if a train ran over him, he'd face death bravely.

He knows the same things I know, but from a different source.
A single word must find separate flights to his brain and to his heart.
He sees a bird as a puff of feathers, a distant skeleton on the tip of a bare branch –
for him, concepts are made of cold steel, to be contemplated from far off.

Look, I'd speak to him, but what can I say? Although he
hears me, deep inside he's listening to an old man,
an old man who wanders through the autumn rain,
with wild hair and a melancholy smile – even I can feel
that cool wind and it moves me.

O get him out of here, away –
he is our enemy, he and his misty eyes –
our problems squat right in front of us, with iron claws on the cold stove.

Translated from the Hungarian by John Bátki

Attila József (1905–1937) was born into a proletarian family in the slums of
Budapest. His life, as well as his poetry, was marked by active dissent and
revolt against the social injustices of inter-war Hungary. His suicide at the age
of 32 has been interpreted by some as the ultimate protest in the name of a
generation that was forced to witness the destruction of its humanistic hopes
at the hands of Fascism.

ANNA AKHMATOVA

Wild Honey

Wild honey smells like freedom,
dust – like a ray of sun.
Violets – like a girl's mouth,
and gold smells like nothing.
Honeysuckle smells like water,
and an apple – like love.
But finally we've understood
that blood just smells like blood.

And in vain the president from Texas
washed his hands in front of the people,
while cameras flashed and correspondents shouted;
and the British minister tried to scrub
the red splashes from his narrow palms
in the basement bathroom, outside
the strangers bar, in the Palace of Westminster.

In a version by Jo Shapcott

This translation was commissioned by the Southbank Centre in London for a
celebration of Russian poet Anna Akhmatova (1889–1966) in 2004. Poet Jo
Shapcott writes of the commission: 'I was given one of Akhmatova's most
famous poems, "Wild Honey", to work on. I stayed as close as possible to the
tight beautiful images she creates for the first section of the poem. In the
second half, she uses the figure of Pontius Pilate, washing his hands in front
of the people. I changed him to George Bush, reasoning (rightly or wrongly, I
don't know) that she might have spoken more frankly if she could; and since I
live in a more open time and place, then I should.'

FRANCES LEVISTON

Reconstruction

The future creates these fabulous blueprints
from cities it pulls to the ground. What seems the work of giants
lies diminished: domes cave, towers like telescopes
collapse upon themselves, the icy gate
like a berg breaks up, and hoar-frost serves as poor man's grout.
All promises of sanctuary disband into dust
as the centuries pass. The earth's fist closes
on the architects, cold and catacombed, its bloodless grip,
while a hundred generations live above their heads.

Here, for example: here stood a wall,
bearded with lichen and swabbed with blood, not swayed by storms
or the rise and fall of kingdom after kingdom.
Tall or deep, it tumbled at last;
only thrown stones remain, moulded by the wind,
going on milling against themselves
down in the grass. Where once the light of knowledge lay
across these fiddly crafts, mud-crusts offer up
proof of a mind that quickly wove
its ringed design, and that someone sharp
bound the wall-braces together with wire.

Think how intricate the city must have been: archipelagos
of bathing-pools, bristling gables, the bored glint of swords on patrol,
and open casks at every corner
round which camaraderie spiralled like confetti
orbiting a plug-hole –
until the future finished all that.

Bodies piled three men deep for miles. A city of bones
it must have been, and what disease bred
in that grand decomposition claimed the remaining artisans.
Time turned their temples into desecrated tombs.
The whole endeavour came undone. Idols of clay and the talented hands
that shaped them lay in bare scratched graves. Fences flattened.

This red curved ceremonial roof
drops its tiles from the ceiling-vault: civilisation
falls to the floor in dribbling heaps

like everything else, here, where many a man of the past,
blazing with wine, blinding in the spoils of war,
bounced his gaze from treasure to treasure, gold to silver, coins to trinkets,
rings to cups, pinballing angles round the faceted rock
of the mirrored enclosure's endless reign,
here, where stone buildings stood, flowing water threw out heat
in massive clouds, and the mortar circled
the known world within its embrace, where the baths lay, hot as hearts
that prize their own convenience.

'The late 10th-century Exeter Book codex, in which the anonymously
composed Old English poem "The Ruin" appears, famously bears a diagonal
burn-mark that obscures several lines at the centre and end of the poem.
Scholars often note how appropriate this is for a text concerned with damage
and decay. I experimented with keeping these holes in the text, to preserve a
sense of ruination, but in the end found it more interesting to bridge the gaps
instead. The title, "Reconstruction", acknowledges both this and the sense in
which the speaker glimpses another time and place through the act of
dustsceawung – contemplation of the dust – a vision that "The Ruin" itself
might induce for contemporary readers.' FL

✦

Then

she locked up carefully

lest someone steal

Sirius

or Aldebaran

from her kitchen

MIROSLAV HOLUB

Five minutes after the air raid

In Pilsen,
at twenty-six Station Road,
she climbed to the third floor
up stairs which were all that was left
of the whole house,
she opened her door
full on to the sky,
stood gaping over the edge.

For this was the place
the world ended.

Then
she locked up carefully
lest someone steal
Sirius
or Aldebaran
from her kitchen,
went back downstairs
and settled herself
to wait
for the house to rise again
and her husband to rise from the ashes
and for her children's hands and feet to be stuck back in place.

In the morning they found her
still as stone,
sparrows pecking her hands.

Translated from the Czech by George Theiner

A Teardrop

He picks up a teardrop with a pair of tweezers. My room is lifted up. My face, too, of course. When I calmly sit with my knees raised, it feels as if he is holding in his hands a room where the water flows in through the ears. He places the room under a microscope. An eye bigger than my room looks down at me. I wonder if looking through the lens is like looking into a kaleidoscope. He rolls the room around this way and that. He even blows it about huff huff. Every time his breath touches the room that can so easily burst, it shakes wildly. An eye larger than the house encloses the room. It's as if the blinking sky has drawn near. He uses a stronger lens. A single ray of light enters like a freezing cold sun rising inside the room, the room that is like a wrecked ship. A clutch of eggs is found hidden beneath a wardrobe. Seaweed uncoils. Plankton from the inside of the body that fills up the teardrop is also found. Like a diver, he makes his way through the teardrop. As if a plug has been removed, things swirl inside my head. He whom I called out for in the middle of the night, stirs me about. Unable to endure any longer, the room built with water finally bursts. A teardrop courses down my face and spreads. The wave that shakes my shoulders gnaws away at this entire dark room. At dawn, far away, outside the window, someone as small as a dot walks by, dragging a dog.

Translated from the Korean by Don Mee Choi

'Kim wrote these poems just after the end of decades of military dictatorship in South Korea, when freedom of expression was guaranteed for the first time. It was only at this point that critics and poets started to pay attention to Kim's poetry. Kim has always experimented with form and always written about being in the world as a woman poet. Her work did not fit the conventions of Korean poetry, nor did it fit the camp of poetry that expected a direct display of resistance to political oppression. As a result her poetry was often dismissed or neglected before the 1990s. When South Korea attained its first civilian government, Kim suddenly fell ill with post-traumatic stress disorder: for the first time she was able to see the self, the "I". She turned her outward gaze onto herself and was able to shift her focus away from the dark periods of South Korean history and on to her daily existence, her freedom, her time. Kim says what made her write these poems was anxiety, anxiety about form.' DMC

JÁNOS PILINSZKY

The Passion of Ravensbrück

He steps out from the others.
He stands in the square silence.
The prisoner's uniform, the convict's skull
Blink with a projection.

He is horribly alone.
His pores are visible.
Everything about him is so huge –
Everything is so tiny.

And that's it.

     The rest
The rest was simply
That he forgot to cry out
Before he dropped to the ground.

Translated from the Hungarian by Peter Siklós and Ted Hughes

Hughes and Siklós made one mistake in their translation: Ravensbrück was a concentration camp for women and the poem refers to a female prisoner, but in Hungarian 'he' and 'she' are the same word, and the translators assumed the poem referred to a man.

The Catholic Hungarian poet János Pilinszky (1921–1981) is described in the Poetry International 1970 Special Issue as 'preoccupied with the calamities of the Nazi Holocaust, in particular the massacre of European Jewry'. Poet and scholar Tara Bergin notes how Hughes's desire to maintain in his versions of Pilinszky the 'rawness' of a collaborator's literal translation has strong parallels with his own poetic aims for *Crow* which he was composing when he first began translating Pilinszky's work.

From the Editorial to Issue Three

In the present unusually fertile period of translations, it is right that there should be plenty of theories in the air – the more opposed the better, in our opinion. Nevertheless, after our experience as editors of this paper, we feel more strongly than ever that the first ideal is literalness, insofar as the original is what we are curious about. The very oddity and struggling dumbness of a word for word version is what makes our own imagination jump. A man who has something really serious to say in a language of which he knows only a few words, manages to say it far more convincingly and effectively than any interpreter and in translated poetry it is the first hand contact – however fumbled and broken – with that man and his seriousness which we want. The minute we gloss his words, we have more or less what he said but we have lost him. We are ringing changes – amusing though they may be – on our own familiar abstractions, and are no longer reaching through to what we have not experienced before, which is alive and real.

DU FU

Ballad of the Military Waggons

The waggons rumble and creak, horses snort and whinny.
The marching men all carry a bow and arrows at their waist.
Fathers, mothers, wives, children run by their sides, seeing them depart,
While swirls of dust blot out the view of Xianyang bridge.
Tugging at the clothes of their loved ones, stamping their feet in protest, they cry out
      and weep.
The sound of weeping rises to the very heavens.
To the question from a passer-by on the roadside,
All the men can say is: They are levying soldiers, Sir.
Some of us were sent north at fifteen to defend the Yellow River region.
And even at forty we have to go west to man the farms and grow the food.
When we left, we were so young the old people had to fasten our headwear for us.
When we came back, our hair was white, and we still have to go and defend the frontier.
On the frontier it's like a sea of blood.
But the Emperor still means to extend his lands.
Haven't you heard, Sir, how all the villages round about are overgrown with thorns and
      brambles?
Though the women are strong and know how to handle a hoe and drive a plough,
The grain grows all over the place.
Because they know the soldiers of Qin will put up with anything,
We're herded around no better than dogs or poultry.
'Why do we let them?' you ask. We don't dare complain.
Take this winter, you see, they need even more of us,
While the county officials press for more taxes.
I ask you, where is it all to come from?
People say now it's better to give birth to daughters. Having sons is nothing but trouble.
At least you can marry a daughter to a neighbour.
But a son will only end up six feet under.
Do you know, far away by the Kokonor,
Where for ages and ages soldiers' bleached bones have lain uncollected,
New ghosts now come to haunt those who have gone before,
While the wet wind wails against a surly sky.

Translated from the Chinese by Paul Harris

GABRIEL LEVIN

Self-portrait in Khaki

battle-fatigues: booted and stamped
with fierceness, leaning against
the cracked lid of a sarcophagus, half
buried in debris by the hippodrome.
Tyre, '84. Reading Bashō in snatches,
when not in the pillbox
facing the rutted, coastal road.
Mitrailleuse. Rolling the moist syllables,
like pin tumblers, in your mouth.
Rounds of fire beyond the filling
station with the rebus ECOREVE

hanging by a nail above the pump.

'Vanity boxes abandoned in the sedge.
Rare musical instruments, swaddled
in quilt, splash overboard in the mad
scramble to man the small vessels.
This is why even after a thousand
years, the surf riddles the shoreline
with such a melancholic sound.'

Gabriel Levin (1948–) was born in France and lives in Israel. This is one of a
few poems written in English and published in *Modern Poetry in Translation*.
This poem was published in an issue in 1993 on the occasion of the Second
International Poets Festival in Jerusalem in March 1993. The last stanza
adapts lines from the English version (translated by Nobuyuki Yuasa) of
Bashō's 'Records of a Travel-Worn Satchel'.

Du Fu (712–770, also known as Tu Fu) wrote during what is usually regarded
as the Golden Age of Chinese poetry, the Tang Dynasty, more specifically the
reign of the Emperor Ming Huang ('Brilliant Emperor'). Whilst ostensibly
about the hardships caused by the expansionary territorial policies of an
earlier dynasty, this poem is probably meant as a criticism of Ming Huang
himself.

✵

& news of it as tongue-torn as ever

ZIBA KARBASSI

Writing Cells

What thread of rain can we hold onto   not to let it fall
there is no tear here for your teargas   brother
and nothing of blood to pour down the gutter-runnels a little bit
                              south of the east of us here
cult of the body-gobblers in the formality of gorged cities
the swollen corpses of the dead under Shogholle are witness
our dead ones are being shoved under the table
& news of it as tongue-torn as ever   between the teeth of white lines
& every which media hung in dumb formation & with each belch
                        you can smell the blood
like a cloudburst on a napping street handcuffs of the disappeared,
                        blocked bridges, blocked roads
my keenings have more edge than all those words
more blood-dark than their bomb-nights the morning call to prayer
words that try to avoid walking start to dodge bullets & zigzag
breaking of voice-sounds shrieking & at the end ooohf it can kill
I   us
us   Iran
with all its borderlands, its little corner-lands
we with our wounds
wounds that go in deepest at home
I   us
all of us people & breathing   & drrmm drrmm drrmm
drum-filled & bomb-full   (& bom bom bom)
our hands are emptied of guns   our throats are stuffed with bullets
I   us
us   Iran
we with our wounds
wounds that go in deepest at home
& corruption as ever comes from commerce & scamming & scabbing,
                        from market-bazaar & hanging tree
hubble-bubble toil & rubble   not to work works better than
                        all their babble

what can we hang onto not to let it fall
there's no tear here left for your teargas brother
they have threaded our blood vessels   to gas pipelines
boiling boiling blood-bubbles   break the fasts of morning
so, we give you Iran
voice of revolution

Revolution   revelation   revelation

revolution   revolution

revelation   revolution   revolution

Revolution!

Translated from the Persian by Stephen Watts and the author

Shogholle or Shahgoli is a park with a lake in Ziba Karbassi's native Tabriz.
At the time of the Green Movement the bodies of murder victims were
thought to have been dumped in the lake.

Ziba Karbassi (1974–) was born in Tabriz in northwestern Iran in 1974 and fled
Iran with her mother and sisters when she was in her teens. She has lived in
London for much of the last 25 years. She gained attention with her
astonishing poem 'Sangsar' ('Death by Stoning'), written in her early 20s, and
concerning the stoning to death of a relative of her mother. Translator
Stephen Watts writes: 'The dense and open-meshed lyric of her poetry is
mapped onto her senses of reality and justice and achieves a balance rarely
managed in contemporary poetry.'

Hope Climbed

Once upon a time I saw:
hope climbing jagged crags,
while our eyes were lowered to its reality.
Our life was a garden
longing for footsteps,
a short journey
in unhitched sleeping-cars.
Once upon a time I saw:
the doorstep moving to meet
the weary body of the traveller,
a hand lowered to the clothes on the chair,
a bird landing on the dust on the lampshade
seeking attention.
A hope
was climbing towards the roof of the house
and no one woke to throw a stone at it.

Translated from the Macedonian by Peggy and Graham Reid

Nikola Madzirov's (1973–) life and poetry are bound up with the history of the Balkans. He was born into a family of historically displaced people (his very surname 'Madzirov' means 'homeless') and by the time he came of age in Macedonia, his region was once again plunged into dislocation and conflict. Madzirov's poetry reflects this only obliquely. He writes spare poems of remembrance, striking poems of images which constitute a personal metaphysics.

VASKO POPA

The Poplar and the Passer-by

They're widening the street
Clogged with traffic
They're felling the poplars

The bulldozers take a run-up
And with a single blow
Knock down the trees

One poplar just trembled
Withstood the iron

The bulldozer pulls back
From her noisily
Prepares for the final charge

In the huddle of passers-by
There's an elderly man

He takes his hat off to the poplar
Waves his umbrella at her
And shouts at the top of his voice

Don't give in love

Translated from the Serbian by Anne Pennington

Vasko Popa (1922–1991) was a Serbian poet and one of Eastern Europe's foremost 20th-century poets. He was frequently published in *Modern Poetry in Translation* from the very first issue. Ted Hughes was an enthusiastic supporter of Popa's poetry, writing in his introduction to Popa's *Collected Poems 1943-1976*, that 'Popa's imaginative journey resembles a Universe passing through a Universe. It has been one of the most exciting things in modern poetry, to watch this journey being made.'

Usual Story

And my friend
Was immersed in Sufi texts
And he liked to maintain that the world
Meant less to him than a goat's fart.

And my friend was intrigued by the bar
    and his bar-room mates,
Weren't they the key to some expansive vision?

But the world sharpens more than one sword:
The Other is a sword,
    and the Word is a sword,
And the Homeland held a sword above each head,
And the Leader held up the swordsmen.

And so my friend withdrew
    into aloneness.
Didn't trust anyone but his own shadow,
And one day, which was filled with Iraqi night,
His shadow wife hid a wire beneath the bed,
Took off all her clothes, and flirtatiously
Begged him to vilify the state.

And my friend
Is now a prisoner
Wrapped in the national flag,
Learning how to love the Leader's photo.

Translated from the Arabic by Anthony Howell and the author

Fawzi Karim (1945–) was born in Baghdad and lives in London. He is a major contemporary writer: a deeply influential and much-loved poet of the Iraqi exiled generation. His translator Anthony Howell writes of this poem: 'It's the subtext of "Usual Story" that intrigues me, the ghost of another story which we are left to imagine.'

ADRIAAN MORRIËN

National Anthem (to be sung standing)

I do not lie
although I do violence to the truth

I am no thief
though I daily appropriate others' property

I have never committed a murder
yet there is blood on my hand

Translated from the Dutch by James S. Holmes

Adriaan Morriën (1912–2002) was a poet and translator. His poetry was
published as part of a selection of Dutch poetry put together by James S.
Holmes, who writes in Modern Poetry in Translation of 'The Generation of '50'
that 'Dutch literary life has seldom been so thoroughly shaken as it was in
1950 with the explosive eruption of a generation of writers whose avowed
intent was to overturn all established values.'

✲

As powerful as a regime seems, if it needs

to silence poetry then it is built on sand

Editorial to 'Scorched Glass'

In 1969, a year after the Soviet invasion of Czechoslovakia, a Czech translator who was working with *MPT* wrote to Daniel Weissbort about some poetry he was attempting to get out of Czechoslovakia: 'as you can see there are still ways how to deliver the right things to the right hands'. 'Please let me know when you get it and refer to it as to the "folk poetry",' he notes. At the end of another long and amusingly veiled letter he explodes in exasperation: '/Go fuck yourself, Mr Letter-censor!/'

All these letters (and the poems they speak of) arrived and were published, despite the increasing Soviet censorship. They illustrate what a dance censors and poets have led each other, and how even in retrospect it is not always possible to say who had (or who removed) the last word. For every word wiped from a poem in the name of 'public morality', for every poem torn from a printing press, there has been another poem, learnt by heart, or typed out and passed on, sent abroad or put online. Underneath the potted aspidistra that is official literature at any time and in any country, there is a thriving community of dissidents and nonconformists who will be heard and will express themselves whatever the cost.

I do not make light of censorship: the cost is the closing down of magazines and presses, the destruction of the link between poets and their wider audiences and the hardship, imprisonment, murder and suicide of poets. But we should take consolation from poets' refusal to be silent victims. The Russian poet Larisa Miller noted in an interview for *MPT* that every collection of poems she published in the USSR needed a couple of 'locomotives' – model Soviet poems – for the rest to be left alone. There were, it was well known, parts of the country where the censor didn't operate with such zeal, or political situations when the censor was minded to care less. And there was *samizdat*, that beautiful and physical practice of typing up poems to pass on to others. Poetry survives, writers and readers carry on communicating, because it is a human need.

But how does it feel to be censored or to read a censored line? The censor's ███████ has historically including blanking out a ███, or a

██. Or perhaps the whole ██████████████████████████
██████: so the reader was aware of the might of censorship.

Sometimes a line might be rewritten in a crude, but politically aligned way AS THE DELETERIOUS EFFECT OF POETRY ESPOUSING SO-CALLED FREEDOMS CAN BE CLEARLY SEEN. The censor may strike in a seemingly random way, erasing inexplicably so the poet and reader are no longer sure what ██████████████████████. Sometimes the censored material is removed subtly so its absence cannot be felt. [...] At other times all that can be seen is the absence

    404 not found

But poetry thrives in such constrained circumstances – until the mouth is absolutely stopped, that is. 20th-century Eastern European poets particularly noted how one effect of censorship is to deepen the poetic well, the poet forced to use his or her poetic gift to evade the censor and yet say something of importance. Censorship thickens the fibres of metaphor and develops the reader's close reading skills.

The Polish satirist Stanisław Jerzy Lec wrote, 'I had lost faith in the word, censorship restored it to me'. Censorship restored faith in the poem – for how marginal is a genre if the censor needs to clap a hand over it to protect people's morals? As powerful as a regime seems, if it needs to silence poetry then it is built on sand.

WISŁAWA SZYMBORSKA

Hunger Camp near Jasło

Write it. Write. In everyday ink
on everyday paper; they were given no food,
they all died of hunger. *All of them? How many?*
The field is big. How many blades of grass
fell for each one? Write: I do not know.
History counts her skeletons in round numbers.
A thousand and one is still a thousand.
As though that one had never existed:
an imagined embryo, an empty cradle,
an ABC opened for nobody,
air that laughs, cries and grows,
steps to the garden for emptiness to run down,
a place in the queue for no one.

We are in the field where it became flesh.
And it keeps silence like a false witness.
In the sun. Green. There nearby is a forest,
wood to chew for a drink from under the bark,
a day's ration of a view
while we are still not yet blinded. A bird in the mountains,
that moved its shadow of life-giving wings
across their mouths. Their jaws opened,
tooth struck tooth.

At night a sickle shone in the sky
and reaped the loaves of a dream.
Hands came flying from blackened icons
with empty cups in their fingers.
On a spit of barbed wire
a man turned.
They sang with earth in their mouths. *A pretty song,*
how war strikes straight to the heart.
Write: how still it is here.
Yes.

Translated from the Polish by Leonora Mestel

GEORGE THEINER

From 'Helping Those Who Have Been Silenced'

Since the political and cultural clampdown which followed the invasion of Czechoslovakia in 1968, all but a handful of the country's major writers have been prevented from publishing. They are not allowed to work on newspapers and periodicals (the leading magazines such as *Literární listy*, *Host do domu* and *Tvář* were in any case banned in 1969), their novels, stories and poems are not published, their plays not performed, they have been forbidden access to the theatres, film studios and universities. In true Orwellian style, the Husák regime has converted them into unpersons.

Or at least, it has tried to do so. Seemingly defenceless against the might of a totalitarian state, constantly harassed by the secret police who carry out frequent house searches and interrogations, the writers and poets have refused to admit defeat. Over five years ago some of them – Ludvík Vaculík, Václav Havel, Pavel Kohout, Ivan Klíma, Alexandr Kliment, to name but those who are known abroad through their books and plays which continue to appear in London, New York, Paris, Vienna, Munich and Zurich – started to exchange manuscripts they had written 'for the drawer', giving them to each other to read and comment on. This form of 'self-publishing' (*samizdat*) quickly caught on and gained popularity, so that today there are well over 100 such titles circulating in typescript, the operation having been given the name of *Edice Petlice* or Padlock Publications. They include both poetry and prose by top Czech authors, volumes of plays and literary criticism, philosophical treatises and historical essays. There are also two volumes of *Czechoslovak Feuilletons*, short pieces by some 50 distinguished writers, collected by Ludvík Vaculík, and *Views*, a similar anthology edited by the playwright Václav Havel.

George (Jiří) Theiner (1926–1988) was born in Czechoslovakia and came to London at the age of 11 to escape the Nazis. In 1945 he returned to Czechoslovakia, but his refusal to join the Communist party led to him being forced to work in the Silesian coalmines as part of a forced labour unit. After the Soviet invasion in 1968 he returned to England with his family and devoted his life to translating and promoting Czech literature. He worked as assistant editor of *Index on Censorship* and translated many great Czech writers, including Miroslav Holub and Václav Havel. He was a frequent contributor and good friend to *Modern Poetry in Translation*.

GEORGE THEINER

Letter to Daniel Weissbort, 15 September 1968

Vienna, 15th Sept. 1968

Dear Danny,

Just a few lines to let you know that we've
left Prague and are on our way to London. We have
been through a ghastly time and I feel that I've had
enough of Central Europe, however much I had hoped
that life might soon become quite tolerable in Prague.
August 21st has effectively dashed all such hopes
and it seems that my old dream of living in England
is now to be fulfilled, almost you might say against
my will. Life is a paradoxical business, isn't it.

Shortly before our Russian friends and allies
marched in to help us suppress all those wicked
anti-socialist forces and counter-revolutionaries
I had translated a few recent Holub poems, as well as
a new Kolář. I did not manage to send them off to
you and am therefore doing so now, in case you can
still use them for MPT 5. Your letter, dated August
19th, reached me after a fortnight, and I no longer
had the time /or indeed the composure/ to do anything
about your queries. Perhaps you can get Láda Smutek
at Dilia to deal with them.

I hope all is well with you, Jill, and the
children. We look forward very much to seeing you
before very long.

Advice for Sycophants

Did you excuse crimes and give praise to treason?
Blame it on the Party
Did you keep silent when even the grass cried out?
Blame it on the Party
Did you write when even the ink turned red?
Blame it on the Party
Did you believe when not even midnight gave credence to her eyes?
Blame it on the Party
Were you always ready to reap your rewards?
Blame it on the Party
Did you consider executions to be a necessary evil?
Blame it on the Party
Did you go whoring when even whores were loth to spread their legs?
Blame it on the Party
Did you serve when even bitches crawled under the table?
Blame it on the Party
Did you climb, twist and turn, ooze honey?
Blame it on the Party
Did you accept honours when even stones spat with disgust?
Blame it on the Party
Did you condemn when even the rope was ashamed to serve as a noose?
Blame it on the Party
Did you bark when even the basest mongrel had lost its voice?
Blame it on the Party
Did you inform when even stool pigeons found it beneath their dignity?
Blame it on the Party
Is there blood on your hands?
Blame it on the Party
Did you lick spittle and lie, were you greedy and sly?
Blame it on the Party
Did you not know what everyone knew?
Blame it on the Party
Did you force even children to whisper?
Blame it on the Party

Did you trample on the handcuffed?
Blame it on the Party
Did you spit on the dead?
Blame it on the Party
Did you intoxicate yourselves on other people's tears and sweat?
Blame it on the Party
Blame everything, absolutely everything, on the Party, you musicians of the night
Blame it on the Party

Translated from the Czech by George Theiner

Jiří Kolář (1916–2002) was a poet, translator and painter, whose later work was often experimental, blending visual arts and poetry. This poem was published by *Modern Poetry in Translation* in an Czech issue printed only months after the Soviet invasion of Czechoslovakia. In the editorial Ted Hughes and Daniel Weissbort write that, 'The Western poet perhaps envies his brother in the East, for while he sings of comparative comfort, comparative freedom, comparative despair, the reality of the threat and the disaster is not his.'

IVAN HARTEL

if I don't recant, someone else will

and so I stand once more
your guns pointing at my breast
inquisitively
steadily
once more the old comedy
is being played out
unfair play
once more the water rises up my chest
and the rate abandons me
go on bidding higher
right up to the gleam on the wrath-raised sword
at which I will again
recant

(without finding out
with what your guns are loaded
& your brains)

thus graciously with a slice of bread
I will be sent back to my flock

and allowed to graze

Translated from the Czech by George Theiner

Ivan Hartel (1943–) studied nuclear physics in Prague until he left in 1968 and
moved to the UK.

ANTONÍN BARTUŠEK

Anniversary in Fribourg
(21.8.1969)

In Prague's Little City Square
the grey-white pigeons,
disturbed by distant gunfire,
have just flown up
to the dome of St Nicholas'.

Our alarmed eyes
suddenly beat their wings
violently against the cage of the foreign city;
up the steep tower of the cathedral
they rise in anguish to the blue sky.

Translated from the Czech by Ewald Osers

Antonín Bartušek (1921–1974) published two volumes of poetry shortly after
the war and then followed a prolonged silence during the period of Stalinism
and the years of the purges. He began publishing again during the Thaw in
the 60s. Ewald Osers describes this period of silence in an issue of *Modern
Poetry in Translation*: 'One by one the gifted poets of the nation fell silent and
publishers' lists and literary magazines were filled with the familiar jingles
hailing the war-winning, world-liberating exploits of the Soviet Army.' The
more liberal years of the Thaw, culminating in the Prague Spring, were
curtailed when the Warsaw Pact countries joined in a Soviet invasion of
Czechoslovakia on 21 August 1968, the date to which this poem refers.

From the Introduction to Poetry International, 1967

However rootedly national in detail it may be, poetry is less and less the prisoner of its own language. It is beginning to represent, as an ambassador, something far greater than itself. Or perhaps it is only now being heard for what, among other things, it is – a universal language of understanding, coherent behind the many languages, in which we can all hope to meet.

SARAH KIRSCH

The Chitchat of Crows

My guiding star is a planet
As big as a fist and my compass
Is lying on the bottom of the ocean
But hope wants to dance
Only the sparrow hawk above the lowlands
Can read thoughts.

Translated from the German by Anne Stokes

'Sarah Kirsch (1935–2013) began writing in the former East Germany. She took
the name Kirsch when she married East German poet Rainer Kirsch in 1960.
In the same year she adopted the name Sarah in commemoration of Jewish
victims of the Holocaust, thereby distancing herself from Fascism, and, more
generally, highlighting the fact that anti-Semitism was a feature not only of
West but also East Germany's past. A free spirit, often at the centre of
controversy because of the criticism of state policy implicit in much of her
writing, Kirsch felt compelled to leave East Germany in 1977 due to the
persecution she experienced after she signed a petition against the expulsion
of the non-conformist singer-songwriter Wolf Biermann.' AS

Doris Najera and Detective Ramirez

Doris Najera has arrived *sin anunciarse*
at the cramped office of Jorge Ramirez,
Private Detective:

sin anunciarse: without
previously arranging an appointment:
the phone's been cut off for nonpayment:

these are difficult times.

Doris Najera
brings in her pocket a handkerchief,
ten thousand dollars, *una pistola*, a lipstick case.

Una pistola: these are a difficult times.

Detective Ramirez
looks at her with surprise: Doris Najera
has arrived *sin anunciarse*.

Detective Ramirez is
or was drinking whiskey at ten o'clock in the morning:
these are difficult times.

Yes
these are difficult times, but
Doris Najera has come without warning:

like fate : *así la suerte*,
like death : *así la muerte*,
like love : *así el amor*.

Translated from the Mexican Spanish by Cutter Streeby

LUIS FELIPE FABRE

Infomercial
(for the times)

Madam Housewife: are you sick
of trying to scrub, day and night,

blood clots impossible to clean
from the clothing of your family?

Do guts smeared over the walls of your home
keep you from sleeping?

Have you found yourself
sleepwalking, exclaiming: '*¡Fuera , fuera mancha maldita!*'?

Buy now!
Lady Macbeth Stain Cleaner
and finally end these viscous nightmares.

Lady Macbeth Stain Cleaner

is composed of microorganisms: *carroñeros*:
they will do the dirty work for you
eliminating

the remains of cadavers
without damaging the surfaces they're attached to:
Scientifically proven!

Lady, you know: killing
is easy, the hard part comes later.

But now
Lady Macbeth Stain Cleaner offers
an amazing solution that will revolutionise domestic hygiene:

Say goodbye to the trace of brains in your favourite chair! Say goodbye
to those bloody carpets!

Now take down the number on your screen
or call 01800 666
and hurry with your purchase!

The Multifunction Applicator and a package of body bags:
¡ totalmente gratis ! Absolutely free!

With Lady Macbeth Stain Cleaner
you will sleep
like a real queen.

Translated from the Mexican Spanish by Cutter Streeby

'*¡Fuera, fuera mancha maldita!*' is a translation of 'Out, damned spot!'

The poems of Mexican poet, editor and essayist Luis Felipe Fabre (1974–)
come wrapped in a bloody context: Mexico's Narco War. This crackdown
against organised crime syndicates has helped Mexico to become one of the
most dangerous places in the world to live.

JOSEPHINE BALMER

Naso the Barbarian

I see a world without culture, a bleak world
full of sorrow. In this place men become wolves
with no fear of Law, justice conquered by war.
For here, now, few vestiges of Greek remain
and even these are tainted by Getic burr.
Here, I can find no one who retains Latin,
not even proper names or substantive nouns.
Yet though my voice is spent, our poet's coinage,
and my native speech bankrupt, impoverished,
I talk to myself, liquidate frozen words
for this doomed art, the currency of my verse.

And then, watching the tribesmen in the markets,
bartering for goods in their common language,
while I communicate by mime or gesture,
a thought occurs: who is the barbarian here?

Translator and poet Josephine Balmer's (1959–) sequence of poems *The Word for Sorrow* combines versions of Ovid's *Tristia* with imagined accounts of First World War Gallipoli, seen through the eyes of a soldier who had, as a schoolboy, owned the Latin dictionary she was using to translate Ovid.

PETER HUCHEL

Winter Quarters

I sit by the shed
oiling my rifle.

A straying cockerel
gently with its foot
impresses on the snow
an age-old hieroglyph,
an age-old rune,
gently on the snow
the tree of life.

I know the slaughterer,
and his way of killing.
I know the axe,
I know the chopping block.

Slant-wise across the shed
you will flutter,
headless torse,
but still a bird
that thrusts its twitching wings
abruptly against the faggots.

I know the slaughterer.
I sit by the shed
oiling my rifle.

Translated from the German by Christopher Levenson

Peter Huchel (1903-1981) served in the Second World War and was taken
prisoner by the Soviet Army. He worked on East Berlin Radio until 1948, and
from 1949 he edited the GDR literary magazine *Sinn und Form*. In 1961 he was
forced to resign and for nearly ten years he lived in isolation under Stasi (East
German secret police) surveillance. The famous singer-songwriter Wolf
Biermann dedicated a song 'Ermutigung' (Encouragement) to Huchel during
this period. In 1971 Huchel was allowed to leave the GDR.

ROBERT DESNOS

Tomorrow

I'd live a hundred thousand years, and still
Be staunch in hope's foreknowledge of the dawn.
Old Father Time, whom sprains and shocks make ill,
Can moan – the dusk is new, new is the morn.

Too many months by now we've been on guard.
Alert, we've kept our firelight and our flame,
Talked low and pricked our ears at noises heard
That soon fell silent, lost, as in a game.

Now from night's fastness we attest again
The splendour that accompanies the day.
Unsleeping, we are watchers for the dawn,
Proof that, at last, we are alive today.

Translated from the French by Timothy Adès

'Robert Desnos (1900–1945), was the most exciting and skilful French poet of
his time. He first delighted the Surrealists with his spontaneous super-
Spoonerisms by "Rrose Sélavy". He wrote magnificent poetry during the
Occupation of France in the Second World War, with pseudonyms or literary
illusions to beat the censor. Arrested in 1944 as a Resistance man, after a year
of slave labour he died at Terezin.' TA

Springtime

(The real 'last poem', 6 April 1944)

Rrose Sélavy, beyond these bounds you stray.
Meanwhile the waters and the earth ferment;
The rose on fortress-walls pours out its scent;
Love has its sweats and springtime is their prey.

The rose has torn the stone-limbed dancer's side.
While others plough and sow, he treads the boards.
The public, blind and deaf and dumb, applauds
This rite of spring, when he has danced and died.

The word that's writ in soot is wiped away
At the wind's whim by fingers of the rain.
Nevertheless we hear it and obey.

Down at the wash-place where these waters run,
A cloud portrays both soap and hurricane,
Retreating when the thickets bloom in sun.

Translated from the French by Timothy Adès

WALDO WILLIAMS

The Dead Children

See these bodies of children.
They died as night
fell. They got stones
in sling volleys and shelter
then. The sun's heat failed;
she, their mainsun,
failed, with her kiss
and coddle, because
of the world's stones,
because of its snake.

See how each side is
many cuts. See the thin
thighs, how huge the
knees. They didn't get
the failure of their
'Sandwich, mum'. Their pallid
faces stung; her songs
charmed only the snake-
bite out of the dark.
They died let down.

See these bodies of children.
White and black and
yellow. Scores. The brute
snakes quiet over
borders; where his cold
torque strikes, the air
quivers. Say who gave
it sway over the green
earth? – a mad con-
junction of stars: 'You
must! You must!' Damn
you who fire the star
that damns the earth.

*Translated from the Welsh
by Damian Walford Davies*

GUILLAUME APOLLINAIRE

My Lou I shall sleep tonight...

(from *Poèmes à Lou*, XXXII)

My Lou I shall sleep tonight in the trenches
Freshly dug and waiting near our guns
Some twelve kilometres away are the holes
Where I shall go down in my coat of horizon-blue
Between the whizzbangs and the casseroles
To take my place among our soldier-troglodytes
The train stopped at Mourmelon le Petit
And I stepped down as happy as I climbed up
Soon we shall leave for the battery but for now
I'm among the soldiery and shells are whistling
In the grey north sky and no one thinks of dying...

[...]

And thus we shall live on the frontline
And I shall liken your arms to the necks of swans
And sing your breasts belonging to a goddess
And the lilac shall blossom... I shall sing your eyes
Where a choir of lissom cherubs is dancing
The lilac shall blossom in the serious spring!
[...]

Translated from the French by Stephen Romer

'Guillaume Apollinaire (1880–1918) never saw the publication of his *Poèmes à Lou*. They were published 30 years after his death, a delay which was in part due to the explicit nature of some of the material, startling in its conflation of erotic conceit and martial imagery, the latter drawn spontaneously from Apollinaire's daily life as an artilleryman on the Champagne front.' SR

'Waldo Williams (1904-1971) is arguably the greatest Welsh-language poet of the 20th century on the strength of his only collection, *Dail Pren* (*Leaves of a Tree*, 1956). Quaker, pacifist, anti-imperialist, and (in poet Anthony Conran's words) "patron saint of the language movement", he remains a cultural icon in Wales.' DWD

CLEMENTE RÈBORA

Voice from a Dead Look-Out

A body pulp-smashed
Resurfacing with ripples of face
Over the stink of the air ripped by teeth.
Earth a fraud.
Fury-wired I won't weep.
That's for those who can, and for the mire.
But if you return
A man from the war
Don't go telling those who don't know:
Don't go telling this thing wherever man
And life are on speaking terms still.
But get hold of the woman
One night, after a maelstrom of kissing,
If you come back at all;
And hiss in her ear that no thing of this world
Will redeem what was lost
Of us, the putrefied of this place.
Grip tight her heart till you but choke her;
And if she loves you, you'll know that through life
Much later, or never at all.

Translated from the Italian by Cristina Viti

Clemente Rèbora (1885–1957) was an officer on the North-eastern front in the
First World War. He suffered severe shellshock in 1915 and was hospitalised
for 'nervous trauma' and diagnosed with a 'mania for the eternal [sic]'.
Translator Cristina Viti writes that 'the beauty of his writing springs from the
tension between high-voltage energy & huge compassion, humility'.

Peace is an elegy said over a young man

whose heart's been torn open

by neither bullet nor bomb,

but the beauty-spot of his beloved.

PAUL VAN OSTAIJEN

Dead Sunday

Sunday
r
o
s
a
r
i
e
s
the minutes it cannot fill

the TRAM still stopped   emptiness
                                               Sunday
                                               vacant space

people stand alone
              lost   dropped
                        rosary beads

the tram detonates the everyday   consecrated Sunday tolling
                                       mothballs and buttoned-down women

                                                      the sharp
                                                      edge of
                                                      dull
                                                      Sunday

No Destination

only

tightRope walkeRs

The Dull Dance of the trams   on

m____y____h_i_g_h_____s__t____rung_____nerves

my stretched-out nerves

dance   to   the   music
of withered dry
                              r
                                o
                                  s
                                    a
                                      r
                                        y
                                          b
                                            e
                                              a d s

minutes

David Colmer writes: 'Paul van Ostaijen (1896–1928) was a teenager living with his family just outside of Antwerp when the First World War started. The family fled first to the Netherlands, but soon returned to occupied Antwerp, where Van Ostaijen remained for the duration. He published his first collection of poetry during the war and was known in the city both as a dandy and as a Flemish nationalist. After the armistice he fled to Berlin to avoid persecution for his Flemish activism and remained there for three years, moving in Expressionist and Dadaist literary and artistic circles. *Occupied City*, the volume from which this poem has been drawn, was published in 1921, the year he returned to Belgium.

Occupied City shows Dadaist influence in both its typographical experiment and observational style, but was also, according to Dutch poet Alfred Schaffer, shaped by Van Ostaijen's experience of the desperate postwar conditions in Berlin in a more general sense, producing a work that is "held together by sound, rhythm and black humour" but dominated by "fear, disillusion, destruction and nihilism. [...] In one fell swoop, his poetry had grown up".

Over some 150 pages, Van Ostaijen describes events in Antwerp from the siege of the city with its shelling and bombing to the years of occupation and the Germans' withdrawal at the end of the war. The poet uses a multilingual collage of scraps of dialogue, lines from songs, signs, and newspaper items to evoke the chaos and life of a city at war.'

Mahmoud Darwish (1942–2008) was revered as the voice of the Palestinian people. He wrote 'A State of Siege' whilst he was himself under siege in Ramallah during the Israeli invasion of 2002 and this powerful sequence of short lyrics demonstrates his remarkable poetic range. Published to huge acclaim throughout the Arab world, its publication in *Modern Poetry in Translation* in 2004 was the first publication in its entirety in English.

MAHMOUD DARWISH

From 'A State of Siege'

On the morning after the siege has ended,
a girl will go off to meet with her lover
dressed in blue jeans and a floral-print shirt,
blithe and careless, like cherry trees in March.
This is our time now, my beloved, all of it,
so please don't be late! Get here before
the raven descends on my shoulder,
please get here before the apple is eaten.
She is waiting for hope as she waits for her lover,
and he may never, may never, arrive.

[...]

Our freshly-brewed coffee, the squabbling sparrows,
the grass dappled with shadows by trees in full leaf,
the sun skipping walls just like a gazelle,
the scudding white clouds in what's left of our sky,
and everything else we remember and love
but are forced to forget for a while
on this dazzling spring morning –
these small blessings make our lives worth living.

[...]

In a land preparing for its dawn,
in a while
the planets will sleep in the language of poetry.

In a while
we will bid this hard road farewell,
and ask: Where shall we begin?

In a while
we will warn the young mountain daffodils
their beauty will be eclipsed when our young women pass by.

*

I raise a glass
to those who share my vision
of a butterfly's joyful iridescence
in this interminable tunnel of night.

*

I raise a glass
to the one who shares a glass with me
in the pitch black of this night,
a night so thick we're both in the dark.
I raise a glass to my ghost.

*

Peace for the traveller on the other side
is to hear a traveller talking to himself.

Peace is the sound of a dove in flight
heard by two strangers standing together.

*

Peace is the longing of two enemies
to be left to themselves till they die of boredom.

Peace is two lovers,
swimming in moonlight.

*

Peace is the apology of the strong
to the weak,
agreeing strength lies in vision.

Peace is the disarming of arms
before beauty –
iron turns to rust when left out in the dew.

*

Peace means a full and honest confession
of what was done to the ghost of the murdered.

Peace means returning to dig up the garden
to plan all the crops we will plant.

*

Peace is the anguish
in the music of Andalusia
weeping from the heart of a guitar.

*

Peace is an elegy said over a young man
whose heart's been torn open
by neither bullet nor bomb,
but the beauty-spot of his beloved.

*

Peace sings of life – here, in the midst of life,
wind running free through fields ripe with wheat.

[Ramallah, 2002]

Translated from the Arabic by Sarah Maguire and Sabry Hafez

YVES BERGER

2nd March: Al Rabweh

The poet's earth is everywhere
beneath the dry autumn grass
around the tombstone
upright on its hill

A man-sized pyramid of glass
contains flowers mementoes
some sprigs of green wheat
sheltered from the pressing sky

Facing the palace of culture
flags threadbare by the wind
at the top of their mast
declare nothing

Further off an armed guard
carries out his chores
and some dogs search for food
on a garbage dump

The hum of motors
the call of solitary birds
the hubbub of the town
drifts over the hill

Here lie the son's bones
washed by the tears of mothers
Here once the sun has set
light glows from the rocks

Translated from the French by John Berger

Yves Berger (1976–) is a painter and poet. Since his first visit to Palestine in 2005 he has identified with the Palestinian people and their suffering. This poem is taken from a cycle of poems called 'West Bank Diary'. Al Rabweh is a hill on the outskirts of Ramallah where Mahmoud Darwish is buried.

On the Rim of Abu-Tor

On the rim of Abu-Tor an Arab boy is walking
    across his roof. A schoolbook in his hand,
he goes sure-footed right up to the edge.
    All around is quiet, houses anchored to the slope
like the ships of some giant.
    A brown cow lazing on the path
could be a rusted scrap from a stolen car.
    In front of the house a drainage stream gapes wide
moistens its throat as if waiting for its prey.
    Why do his confident steps cast such terror upon me?
Something intimately foreign creeping
    through me like the vine that weaves
entwined between our courtyards.
    He walks, and I dare not take my eyes off him,
as if my gazing were bidden to protect his soul.
    I tend to the flowers in my plot, I water them
but my heart is on watch for his every step
    dangling like my life before my eyes.

Translated from the Hebrew by Jennie Feldman

Dvora Amir (1948–) was born in Jerusalem. This poem was taken from *Documentary Poems*, a collection in which the poet relates to her immediate environment and daily life, above all life in a country haunted by terror and the persistent presence of the Occupation. Amir regards her poems as personal rather than political, offering insights into life in Israel, 'between tragedy and dark hope'.

    Abu-Tor is a mixed Jewish-Arab neighbourhood on the south-eastern edge of Jerusalem.

SAMIH AL-QASIM

End of Talk with a Jailor

From the narrow window of my small cell,
I see trees that are smiling at me
and rooftops crowded with my family.
And windows weeping and praying for me.
From the narrow window of my small cell –
I can see your big cell!

Translated from the Palestinian Arabic by Nazih Kassis

Samih al-Qasim (1939–2014) was one of the foremost Palestinian poets. He grew
up in the village of Rama and experienced the Palestinian tragedy at first
hand, achieving fame as one of the celebrated 'resistance poets' during the
1950s. He was an outspoken opponent of racism and oppression on all sides of
the Middle East conflict.

SAMIH AL-QASIM

Excerpt from an Inquest

– And what do you call this country?
– My country.
– So you admit it?
– Yes, sir. I admit it.
   I'm not a professional tourist.
– Do you say 'my country'?
– I say 'my country.'
– And where is my country?
– Your country.
– And where is your country?
– My country.
– And the claps of thunder?
– My horses' neighing.
– And the gusts of wind?
– My extension.
– And the plains' fertility?
– My exertion.
– And the mountains' size?
– My pride.
– And what do you call the country?
– My country.
– And what should I call my country?
– My country...

Translated from the Palestinian Arabic by Nazih Kassis

From 'At the Edge'

Last year I accompanied Elyse Dodgson on a trip to the Western border of Ukraine, from where her family emigrated in 1916. There is an industry in roots tourism in Ukraine and plenty of guides and experts to instruct in the myths and the possible realities of family history, but we travelled alone, unsure of what we wanted to find: the finding was to be in the looking.

In this respect, the history of one's own genetic material is much like any history: the finding is in the looking and the looking never stops. Like any history too, its absence hurts us. If violence is done to this past and a border set up between then and now, the effect on later generations is peculiar and profound. The choking of a personal and collective history is a desperate thing. Millions of families have broken with the past in the act of emigration, and millions more have been forced to renounce their history and heritage in war and migration. On this trip it occurred to me that history was still the privilege of the few; that every community should have the right to find out how their ancestors lived and how they died. This I noted down in my exercise book in a revolutionary and self-mocking bold script. For how is that possible?

The community to which Elyse's family belonged was destroyed by countless waves of emigration and then the Holocaust. The area in which they lived had perched on the border of different countries. Every war had brought a change in street names and rulers. The meagre sources of information were diluted with myth and prejudice, fear and corruption; neglected by people intent on surviving, and championed by the few: the quixotic, bloody-minded, pedantic, saintly few.

The villages change their names like floating islands: Otynia, Ottynia, Otyniia. Kolomea, Kolomaiia, Colomia. Nothing ties up. There must be an ur-name, which is shifted this way and that with every new invasion of peoples, until the original name is quite gone and the approximations proliferate. We find approximate names on a map before we go, and then we hear names that sound approximately close to these, and then we are in the villages and I feel some disquiet at the heaps of unresolved approximations. Even the name of the country

Ukraina, means 'at the edge'. Here we are at the very edge of the edge, stumbling on vague precipices. I note other certainties instead: a cherry tree by the village name on the road. We pulled up with a screech as we passed the sign and reversed at speed. Victor the driver took Elyse's photo beside the sign, and we ate cherries. It was a hot day and there was no traffic at all. The land was green and fertile. Storks flew over the flat places. There were one or two old houses in the village and the driver said he would stop and we could photograph one and call it Elyse's family home in the album. It is not a great place for certainties: I can see why this would seem a noble substitution.

Elyse's father was born in Otyniia. It was once a thriving town with a large Jewish population. No one knows how large. A Jewish gen site says that Jews formed half of a population of approximately 4000. Poles and Ukrainians made up the remainder. But other websites have other figures: 6000, 1000, 3000. Before its decline the town boasted charismatic rabbis and several synagogues, shops, a marketplace. Few records of the Jewish population survive as they were kept in synagogues and the synagogues have gone.

What I suspect is that this little town had a man who spoke impetuously, without weighing his words, and a man so burdened by his thoughts he did practically nothing and it was a crying shame. An untilled plot of land stood near his house. There was a good number of cheerful decent people, who abided approximately by their convictions and their consciences, and a few who were more slatternly with their morals. The children were always worse than their parents. The old were always right. There was never enough money to go around. There was one day a fond boy, and a mother scolding a child along the road, and saying to her in Yiddish: do you think you are the only person in the world?

Elyse Dodgson is the International Director at the Royal Court Theatre.

✧

If my voice should die on land

carry it to the sea's level, friend,

and abandon it there,

on the shore.

RAFAEL ALBERTI

If my voice should die on land…

If my voice should die on land
carry it to the sea's level, friend,
and abandon it there,
on the shore.

Carry my voice to the level shore
and make it master there
of a white ship of war –

oh voice of mine,
with its fluttering ensign –

on the heart an anchor,
on the anchor a star
on the star a wind
on the wind a sail!

Translated from the Spanish by Robert Hull

Rafael Alberti (1902–1999) is regarded as one of the major Spanish poets of the
20th century. His work was first published in the 1920s. In the 1930s Alberti
joined the Communist party and fought for the Republic in the Spanish Civil
War, fleeing to Argentina after the war and only returning to Spain in 1977.

HOMERO ARIDJIS

In a Valley I Saw the Dead Shades

In a valley I saw the shades of the dead
chasing beams of light in the morning.
Their feet trampling on dream's black apples
and hands passing through bodies and trees.
Busily the shades raced one after the other,
but as soon as convinced they had caught something,
the beams slid through their fingers
as if shades, hands, beams were nothing.

Translated from the Mexican Spanish by George McWhirter

Black Grass

Through the window I see your brother
out cutting the grass in the garden,
but he never finishes cutting
because when he has it cut over here
it has grown over there. It is black grass
sprouted from men's hearts
and it resembles grandfather's hair:
resistant to the scissors of wind.
Day and night I see your brother
out cutting death's grass for it.

Translated from the Mexican Spanish by George McWhirter

Poet, essayist, novelist and columnist Homero Aridjis (1940–) has served as
Mexican Ambassador to the Netherlands and Switzerland and is an activist,
campaigning on ecological and social issues. He set up the Grupo de los Cien
(the group of 100), a group of Mexican artists and cultural figures who engage
support for conservation and environmental projects.

The Black Stars

No one should sing any more of love or war.

The order the cosmos was named for is gone.
The celestial legions are a monstrous blur.
The universe besieges us, blind and violent.
The serene sky is interspersed with dead suns,
Dense deposits of annihilated atoms.
Only desperate weight emanates from them –
Not energy, messages, particles, or light.
Light itself collapses, from its own heaviness.
And all our human seed live and die for nothing.
And the skies spin round perpetually to no purpose.

Translated from the Italian by Marco Sonzogni and Harry Thomas

ULRIKE ALMUT SANDIG

here is the passage from the street back to winter

1938. the small, inconspicuous curtain of history:
a child-size gate in the iron railings, six steps
down to the dried-up river-bed close to the zoo.

waiting there two days, standing with stars, and
being inspected in broad daylight. later at last off
to the station and into the trucks, that's when the first fell

like flies, like chaff. and still later the little wood of
beech + beech + snow. That is where this story ends.
but here is the passage, here's where it all starts again STOP

Translated from the German by Karen Leeder

Ulrike Almut Sandig (1979–) writes about this poem: 'On 10 November 1938 in Leipzig several hundred Jews were gathered up in the walled-in riverbed of the Parthe and displayed to the townfolk. From there 550 Jewish men were taken to the railway station and loaded onto trains destined for Buchenwald and Sachsenhausen. The memorial stone on the banks of the river Parthe is made of green diabase, diabase being Greek for "passage, transit".'

MYKHAILO DRAJ-KMARA

Swans

On the lake where willows dream
The swans splash and paddle across
The waters in spring and autumn.
Their necks bend like reeds.

When the frost arrives and echoes
Over things like plate glass
And the surface slowly glazes
With mesmerised whiteness,

They destroy cynicism and despair
With their unconquered song
Each indefatigable singer

Lets the constellations guide them
From the absence of being and freedom
Above oceans of music and symphonic foam.

Translated from the Ukranian by Steve Komarnyckyj

Mykhailo Draj-Kmara (1889–1939) was a poet of the 'Executed Renaissance'.
Ukraine's literary elite was targeted in the 1930s by the Soviet regime and
hundreds of Ukrainian writers were executed or rendered inactive by the
Soviet police. The critic Yury Lavrinenko, who compiled the defining
anthology of their work, coined the term 'The Executed Renaissance' which
neatly expresses the energy of the literary revival they embodied and its
brutal curtailment. The poem published here probably led to Draj-Kmara's
arrest and subsequent death in the Soviet penal system.

Valerio's Story

Yes, Daddy, I do know the history of Italy well,
I know where the Gothic line was, I know our house
was in a high-risk zone, you've told me
one thousand times. I know that day Appelius,
the Genoese, said on the radio the war was over
and you tossed your hoe in the air, and you danced
into the fields as if you were thirty.

I also know it was a clear day and the river was dried-up
I can almost see your little clogs, your woollen shirt
and your shorts. It was the 2nd and 3rd of October, in 1944,
and, yes!, there were the Terzoni evacuees who wanted
to go back home. You attended to them, I remember,
bringing some pots and some sheets on your shoulders.

You told me one thousand times that the river was dried-up
and that a cow plunged down from the wooden bridge, in a moment
the water arrived as a storm, wiped the bridge away and dragged
the cow, who knows where, and you, thank Heavens, escaped by a miracle.
Dear Daddy, you've never forgiven those Germans
who on a day of October only because of desperation
caused the barrage to explode, they caused all the things of those unlucky
people to fly away, they had you grown-up in one moment.

I feel like crying, you know, if I think of you and of grandfather
going down to the river for three months in the suffused autumn light
but never up to the bank, never too close, looking
from the edge as if all at once the water would reveal something,
a bump behind a stone, a floating secret appearing from the bottom.
You had been enchanted by the voice of history, by the Genoese speaking
from the radio to the people in the fields. Then you would leave towards the city.

You know Daddy, there was De Gasperi that day, the 2nd or 3rd of October
who was already thinking of dividing Italy, and you came back
empty-handed, because your little brother had remained entangled
on the bottom of the river and you didn't know how to tell it at home.

Translated from the Italian by Stefano de Angelis

Alba Donati (1960–) lives in Florence. Translator Stefano de Angelis writes of
her work: 'An attentive and pugnacious memory is the central and unifying
element of her poetry. On the one hand it deals with commitment and social
consciousness which, through the past of her own birthplace, rediscovers and
at the same time redeems the traces of a communal life and authentic human
relationships that were first brutally devastated by the Second World War...'

RAÚL RIVERO

Stardust

Julia Roberts makes a mistake with me
I resist her gaze hour after hour
and other times I punish her:
her seductress face against the floor.
If she's going to tell me something, I pay no attention
if she bats her eyes or any of that
I block her with a sweep of my arm
and I let her kisses freeze to her lips
Julia argues with the walls
she suffocates the silence with her reproach
and I, with my disdain, mortify her.
I normally ignore her during the day
although to tell the truth I use her
with passion every night as a fan.

Translated from Cuban Spanish by David Shook

'Cuban poet and journalist Raúl Rivero (1945–) was sentenced to jail for 20 years for alleged political crimes in 2003. During his time in prison Rivero was permitted to write only love poetry, which was routinely censored, not so much for the actual content of his work but as an exercise in domination. Of the drafts he would show his captors each week, several would be indiscriminately censored and discarded, sometimes without so much as having been skimmed for content. Still, captivity proved unable to dim Rivero's wit: "Stardust", his poem about Julia Roberts, is proof positive of that.' DS

HUGO CLAUS

1965

(in reply to a newspaper survey about the previous year)

Year of atrocities, year of TV screens and stock reports,
Year of milk and honey if you're asleep,
Year that weighs on your stomach if you're awake,
Sweet year, good year for sleepwalkers,
Year that 25 billion Belgian francs went to NATO
     for tanks, flags and jets
      (mosquitoes in death's unbounded clouds)
Year of Mobutu, we send him assistance in dollars and cents
     knowing they'll blossom into percentages,
Year of Voeren, which people want to rescue for a language they
     only read in advertisements,
Year of freeways for ever hastier sheep,
Year of rot in Belgian skulls,
Year that licked at the trough of folklore,
Year (fortunately far from our piggy banks and our folk dancing)
     of the escalation there where children grey with fear
     dig themselves deeper into mud
     (Give them this day our daily napalm
     and later our canned food and later our prayers)
Year that freezes smiles.

That was the year I went to live in a village
with books, a woman and a child
that grows
while I tell stories about tigers in the East.

Translated from Dutch by David Colmer

Flemish poet, novelist and dramatist Hugo Claus (1929–2008) published
poetry for more than fifty years and his two-volume collected poems range
from image-laden experiment, through political and erotic poems, to almost
whimsical light verse. This poem documents the year in which *Modern Poetry
in Translation* came into being.

Bertolt Brecht and Margarete Steffin:
Love in a Time of Exile and War

Bertolt Brecht and Margarete Steffin met for the first time in October 1931. He was 33, from Augsburg, son of a well-to-do bourgeois family. She was 23, from a poor district of Berlin, an activist in the world of Communist music, poetry and theatre, daughter of a seamstress and a builder. The occasion was the rehearsal of a satirical review of which he was one the authors and in which she had a part. Soon after that she acted in his play *The Mother*, they became friends, lovers and collaborators in his work, and he began to pay for the treatment of her TB, which she would die of ten years later.

Steffin was a gifted linguist. Besides her native German, she had good English, French and Russian; and could manage effectively in Danish, Swedish and Finnish. She put those languages, together with her skills as a secretary and her ferociously independent critical mind, at Brecht's disposal.

Brecht has often been accused of using people, women especially; but his relationship with Steffin, his love for her and his work with her, should make us think more understandingly about what it meant, in those times, in the struggle against injustice and Hitler's fascism, to use and to be used. Both equally desired, and thought it their responsibility, to be useful to the cause. Brecht's poems to Steffin are poems of a love which is, in its mixed entirety, tender, sensual, solicitous, jealous, protective, unkind and kind. But at the heart of it, unchanging, was a loving and fighting collaboration, a commitment to serve, to use and to be used, in a matter which, quite rightly, they understood to be one of life or death.

And alone among the women Brecht loved and who loved him, Margaret Steffin could answer him in poems.

Before long they were swapping sonnets. They chose a phrase, the harmless South German greeting 'Grüß Gott', to express their secret closeness when they were in company. For them it meant: 'I am touching you'. In their letters it appears as the abbreviation: *gg*.

Cover illustration to 'The Constellation'

BERTOLT BRECHT

When we were first divided into two...

When we were first divided into two
And one of our beds stood here and one stood there
We picked an inconspicuous word to bear
The sense we gave it: I am touching you.

The pleasure of such speaking may seem paltry
For touch itself is indispensable
But we at least kept 'it' inviolable
And saved for later, like a surety.

Stayed ours, and yet removed from you and me
Could not be used yet had not ceased to be
Not rightly there and yet not gone away

And standing among strangers we could say
This word of ours as in the common tongue
And mean by it: we know where we belong.

Translated from the German by David Constantine

MARGARETE STEFFIN

Emboldened, putting off formal address...

Emboldened, putting off formal address
Now I am given to you and wish your good entirely.
Whatever I lack I shall be well unless
Your love should ever be withdrawn from me.

The little word that we decided on
And none but us knew touch was what it meant
Word of the irresistible seduction
For months my hoard of good in banishment

That word is an embracing and a kiss
I who must wait so long for you I kiss
The word in every letter you write to me

And when I read it all my tears mean
Is that now you are with me once again
And I want nothing. As though you slept with me.

Translated from the German by David Constantine

VÍTĚZSLAV NEZVAL

From 'Mother Hope'

Mother Hope
Trembles like an aspen leaf
For on the gateway
To the village
Where the terrified creak of the hinges
Sobbing together
A big poster
Announces
Murder
She trembles
For she's wearing a light dress
In the street
Where a small crowd of women gathers
Deeply absorbed in themselves
Her modest tear of sympathy
Is too shy to claim attention
For her husband seems no longer young enough
To compete with the men of Sparta
And her son has not yet grown out of short trousers
But time flies
Soon she'll lock up her lonely house
As if she were a widow
And what madness
For the first time in her life sobbing helplessly she'll clutch
       her young son to her breast
To stop him with her own body
From leaving
To become one of the little figures
In the monstrous shooting gallery
And he will have to push her away
So as not to die from weakness sadness love

Translated from the Czech by Ewald Osers

VASKO POPA

Cape of Good Hope
(for Breyten Breytenbach)

At a fair in South Africa
White racists exhibited
A black couple

They made them climb trees
And howl
Crawl on all fours
And eat grass

I was left with a choice
Adds my poet friend

Either I took off my white skin
And hung it on the nail
Or

Translated from the Serbian by Anne Pennington

'Vítězslav Nezval (1900–1958) was the most colourful and versatile of Czech poets between the wars. He was associated in his early work with the French Dadaists, and was an exponent of "poetism", described by the Czech critic, Karel Teige, as "airy and playful, full of fantasy, unfettered and unheroic, with a bias towards love".' EO

✧

I have experienced the spaces of hope,

The spaces of a moderate mercy.

IVAN V. LALIĆ

The Spaces of Hope

I have experienced the spaces of hope,
The spaces of a moderate mercy. Experienced
The places which suddenly set
Into a random form: a lilac garden,
A street in Florence, a morning room, a sea
Smeared with silver before the storm, or
A starless night lit only
By a book on the table. The spaces of hope
Are in time, not linked
Into a system of miracles, nor into a unity;
They just exist. Like in Kanfanar,
At the railway station; wind in a wild vine
A quarter-century ago: one space of hope.
Another, placed somewhere in the future,
Is already destroying the void around it,
Unclear but real. Probable.

In the spaces of hope light grows,
Free of charge, and voices are clearer,
Death has a beautiful shadow, the lilac flowers later,
But for that it looks like its first-ever flower.

Translated from the Serbian by Francis R. Jones

Ivan V. Lalić (1931–1996) was a Serbian poet, essayist and translator, associated with *Modern Poetry in Translation* from its first issue. Lalić said in later years that his childhood in the war had marked everything he had written since.

PAUL CELAN

Tenebrae

We are near, Lord
near and at hand.

Handled already, Lord,
clawed and clawing as though
the body of each of us were
your body, Lord.

Pray, Lord,
pray to us,
we are near.

Wind-awry we went there,
went there to bend
over hollow and ditch.

To be watered we went there, Lord.

It was blood, it was
what you shed, Lord.

It gleamed.

It cast your image into our eyes, Lord.
Our eyes and our mouths are open and empty, Lord.

We have drunk, Lord.
The blood and the image that was in the blood, Lord.

Pray, Lord.
We are near.

Translated from the German by Michael Hamburger

You seedheads sailing the stratosphere,

she commanded, close your parachutes.

You hailstones, stop hurtling.

You migrating birds and meteor-showers,

you grids and gyres of space –

listen to this mother's cry.

Paul Celan (1920–1970) was born in Czernowitz (now in Ukraine) to a German-speaking Jewish family. His parents were killed in the Holocaust and he spent 18 months in a labour camp during the war. After the war he lived in Paris but continued to write in German. He suffered from depression and committed suicide in 1970. Translator Michael Hamburger writes of his poetry: 'Much of the later poetry is virtually untranslatable because the increasingly personal vocabulary tests and dislocates linguistic conventions. The syntax is abrupt, halting and tentative, the diction full of ambiguities, new word formations, semantic leaps and twists. The poems...tell us something we want to know, but often cannot be sure of understanding, about the extremism of Celan's work, its groping towards religious and social communion, in the teeth of acute isolation, scepticism and pain.'

DANIEL WEISSBORT

From 'Ted Hughes and Translation'

...I am happy to be able, finally, to publish Ted Hughes's re-working – intended for a Hungarian issue that did not materialise – of a long poem by Ferenc Juhász, 'The Boy Changed into a Stag Cries out at the Gate of Secrets', which W.H. Auden (see his Foreword to *The Plough and The Pen: Writings from Hungary 1930-1956*; 1963) believed to be 'one of the greatest poems written in my time'. Ted Hughes's version is a virtuoso performance and of much interest, not only because it is so powerful a piece of writing, but also, I think, because of the intimations of his much later involvement in the translation of Ovid's *Metamorphoses*.

DANIEL WEISSBORT

From 'Hughes translates Juhász'

Ted Hughes had seen the Juhász poem [...] While I was visiting him in Devon, presumably to plan the forthcoming (as we thought) *MPT* issue on Hungary, he re-wrote the translation, working with great concentration and at great speed. I carried it off with me, but as the issue for which it was intended ran into difficulties and was indefinitely postponed, I eventually returned it to Ted. I did not photocopy it and Ted had on this occasion not made a carbon copy. The sole copy of the translation fortunately surfaced again, however, when he was going through his papers before they were shipped to Emory University, in Atlanta, where I discovered it.

'What is intriguing,' as I wrote in a note on a poem (see my *Letters to Ted*, Anvil 2002), 'is that [Ted Hughes] felt able to rewrite the English version without reference to any source text. It is interesting that he is able, in this situation, simply to write his own version, based on Kenneth McRobbie's, whereas in other circumstances, i.e. when faced by the poet himself or by the source text in a literal translation, he feels compelled to stay as close as possible to the wording and even syntax of the original.' I had in mind, in particular, two major translations by Hughes, his selection of poems by another Hungarian, János Pilinszky, which he did under the rigorous guidance of János Csokits, and the versions of Yehuda Amichai, which he based on literal versions by the poet himself, who was a close friend and 'the tone and cadence' of whose voice, 'speaking English', he was above all anxious to preserve.

I have corrected some obvious typos. Where Hughes has written an alternative word in the margin and deleted the original, I have altered the text accordingly. Where he has not deleted the original I have included both words. The lineation appears not to have been finalised and I have left it as it appears in the typescript. I have, however, somewhat regularised the punctuation.

Ferenc Juhász (1928–2015) was born into a peasant family, in Western Hungary. His earliest collections appeared in 1949 and 1950. Juhász was a prolific poet, much of his work originating in a folk-tale peasant tradition.

TED HUGHES

On 'the provisional tense'

Writing this sort of statement, I'm more and more doubtful about every sentence one is able to form. When you know a thing inside out, you might have something to say. But on the vague and idle acquaintance we have with most things, as I have with the translation business which *MPT* drew on, you can really only make the most provisional subjective comments of impression – as if the whole thing ought to consist of questions. Perhaps that's what I should have written. Would it look affected. But it would be more honest than what I've written. I ask myself at each sentence whether that is what I do truly think – and the answer usually is that what I'm doing is constructing an 'idea', improvising it, out of scraps and fancies that are no more really than suggestions. And in the act I suppress all the counter-suggestions that cast doubts, and imply a possibility of the opposite maybe of what I'm asserting. It's an uncomfortable business. I'm beginning to read literary articles with more and more amazement. There's a whole grammatical tense missing – the 'provisional'. The trouble is, too, that when I manage to erect a sentence out of all that, it looks like a ziggurat in a swamp, or a round tower in the desert. I'm really disgusted by my attempts. In verse, at least, you have that missing tense – in verse everything is provisional – and playful – and only being requisitioned for some other purpose than its own. Well. Maybe it's just the effects of lead-poisoning in childhood.

[From a letter to Daniel Weissbort, 28 July 1982]

From 'The Boy Changed into a Stag Cries Out at the Gate of Secrets'

The mother called after her son
from the far distance
The mother called after her son
from the far distance,
she went out in front of the house, calling
and she loosened her hair's thick knot
which the dusk wove to a dense, stirring veil,
a valuable robe sweeping the earth,
wove to a stiff and heavily-flaring mantle,
a banner for the wind with ten black tassels,
a shroud, the fire-slashed blood-heavy twilight.
She twisted her fingers among the fine tendrils
of the stars, the moon's suds bleached her features,
and she called after her son shrilly
as she called him long ago, a small child,
she went out from the house talking to the wind,
and spoke to the song-birds, her words overtaking
the wild geese going in couples,
to the shivering bulrushes,
to the potato flower in its pallor,
to the clench-balled bulls rooted so deeply,
to the fragrant shadowy sumach,
she spoke to the fish where they leaped playfully,
to the momentary oil-rings, mauve and fleeting.
   You birds and branches, hear me,
listen as I cry,
   listen, you fishes and you flowers,
listen, I cry to be heard,
   listen, you glands of the pumping soils,
   you vibrant fins, you astral-seeding parachutes,
decelerate, you humming motors of the saps,
screw down the whining taps in the depth of the atom,

all iron-pelvissed virgins,
   sheep alive under cotton,
listen as I cry,
I am crying out to my son.

The mother called out to her son
and her cry climbed in a spiral
within the gyre of the cosmos it ascended,
her limbs glancing in the lightrays
like the skid-scaled flanks of a fish,
or a roadside boil of salt or crystal.
The mother called out to her son,
   Come back, my own son, come back,
      I am calling, your calm harbour,
   Come back, my own son, come back,
      I am calling, your pure fountain,
   Come back, my own son, come back,
      I am calling, the breast where your memory sucked,
   Come back, my own son, come back
      I am calling, your almost sightless lamp.
Come back, my own son, for this world of spiky objects has put out my eyes,
my eyes are sealed under yellow-green bruises, my jaw contracts,
my thighs and my shins are skinned,
from every side things batter in on me like crazed rams,
the gate, the post, the chair try their horns on me,
doors slam against me like drunken brawlers,
the vicious electricity snaps at me,
my scaling skin leaks blood a bird's beak crushed with a rock,
scissors slither off like spider-crabs of nickel,
the matches are sparrowfeet, the pail hacks back at me with its handle.

Come back, my own son, come back,
my legs no longer lift me like the young hind
   festering blooms open on my feet,
    gnarled tubers screw into my purpling thighs,
the skin over my toes glazes to bone,
   my fingers harden, already the flaking flesh
shells off like slate from weathered geologic formations,
   every limb has served its time and sickens.

Come back, my own son, come back
    for I am no longer as I was,
    I am a used-up shadow from the inner visions
    that flare through the thickening organs
    like an old cock's crowing, on winter dawns,
from a fence of shirts hanging board-frozen.
I am calling, your own mother,
come back, my own son, come back,
force new order onto the anarchic things,
discipline the savage objects, tame the knife and domesticate the comb,
because now I am only two gritty green eyes
glassy and weightless, like the dragonfly,
whose winged nape and moth, that you know so well, so delicately clasp
two crystal apples in the green-illuminated skull,
I am two staring eyes without a face,
seeing all, and one with the unearthly beings.
Come back, my own son, come back into place,
    with your fresh breath bring everything again to
    order/into place.

    In the remote forest the boy heard.
    He jerked up his head in an instant,
    his spread nostrils testing the air,
    his soft dewlap throbbing, the veined ears pointing
    tautly to that lamenting music
    as to the still tread of the hunter,
    as to hot wisps fronding from the cradle
    of a forest fire, when the skyline trees
    smoke and begin to whimper bluely.
    He turned his head to the old voice,
    and now an agony fastens on him,
    and he sees the shag hair over his buttocks,
    and he sees, on his bony legs,
    the cleft hooves that deal his track,
    sees, where lilies look up in pools,
    low-slung hair-pursed buck-balls.
    He forces his way towards the lake,
    crashing the brittle willow thickets,
    haunches plastered with foam that spatters
    to/on the earth at his every bound,

his four black hooves rip him a path
through a slaughter of wild flowers,
sock a lizard into the mud,
throat ballooned and tail sheared,
till he reaches the lake at last,
and looks in at its lit window
that holds the moon, moving beech-boughs,
and a stag staring at him.
For the first time he sees the bristling pelt
covering all his lean body,
hair over knees and thighs, the transverse
tasselled lips of his male purse,
his long skull treed with antlers,
bone boughs bursting to bone leaves,
his face closely furred to the chin,
his nostrils slit and slanted in.
The great antlers knock against trees,
roped veins lump on his neck,
he strains fiercely, stamping he tries
to put out an answering cry, but in vain,
it is only a stag's voice belling
in the throat of this mother's son,
and he scatters a son's tears, trampling the shallows
to drive out that lake-horror, scare it
down into the whirlpool gullet
of the water-dark, where glittering
little fishes flicker their laces,
miniature bubble-eyed jewellery.
The ripples smooth off into the gloom,
but still a stag stands in the foam of the moon.

Translated from the Hungarian by Ted Hughes

Pascale Petit (1953–) was born in Paris and grew up in France and Wales. She
has published six collections of poetry. The poem on the following page was
written in response to Ted Hughes's version of Ferenc Juhász's poem 'The Boy
Changed into a Stag Cries Out at the Gate of Secrets' and was published in
the same year in *Modern Poetry in Translation*.

At the Gate of Secrets

(after Ferenc Juhász)

A mother calls out to her daughter.
Her cry climbs in a spiral.
Out of the front door she calls,
to the muscat grapes clustered like planets.
Her voice rises and keeps on rising.
It plays with the thistles
on the plateaux, and drifts
      towards the stars.

She unlooses the coil of her hair.
It falls slowly, like a universe unwinding.
Corkscrew curls tumble slow-motion
and bless her tired body.
Filaments stroke her face
like an infant's fingers.
Her grey sunken cheeks
shine in pearly moonlight
and heal for a moment.
A mother lets loose her hair
as she calls for her lost daughter.
Her auburn chevelure
swirls about her in the dusk
like a universe bursting into flower.

Her cry shakes the webs of spiders
and races icy rivers
    that scythe through rock.
Her cry overtakes the eagle ascending a thermal.
You seedheads sailing the stratosphere,
she commands, close your parachutes.
You hailstones, stop hurtling.
You migrating birds and meteor-showers,
you grids and gyres of space –
    listen to this mother's cry.

The daughter tilts her head and sniffs the air.
The velvet on her new antlers
steams in freezing solar wind
and hangs like loops
      of the Milky Way.
The points of her antlers
shine like translucent white karst
against the vaults of space.

Her mother's voice brushes galaxies
   ranged like mountains,
and echoes across the voids
   that smoke with stellar dust.
Her voice shoots through force fields
and reaches the outpost of matter.

My daughter, she calls, come back
   and take care of me.
Our limestone cottage is a ruin.
Every room awaits you.
The furniture attacks me as I pass.
Only you know how to herd the chairs
so they stop butting me with their horns.
The table legs kick me like restless colts.
Come and tame the cutlery.
It flies at me like crazed insects.
The doors slam into me like coffin lids.
When I bump into the mirror,
molten glass floods my veins
   with embalming fluid.

My eyes have been searching too long.
They glow bronze-green in their sockets
and see a thousand facets in every corner,
     like the dragonflies'.
My sight is fractured like theirs.
Each prism holds an image of you
   pulsing on my retina.

Listen – I've sewn you dresses
from threads of my memories,
in fabrics woven from my nerves.
They have the colours of my visions.
Day and night I sew
with these swollen and trembling fingers.
My hands work faster than time.
The clock winds backwards,
and your garments get smaller
until I'm making baby-lace.
And still the visions tell me to sew faster
and still you're in a filigree forest,
impaled on the thorn of my needle.
I look out through the broken window
and see the diamond-petalled stars
and you, busy in your astral garden,
tending the flowers of light
as you once nursed me, my kind daughter.

A girl pauses at the gate of secrets
and hears what she has always longed to hear.
Dear mother, she replies,
I cannot come now.
So fast did I journey through the dark,
I grew four legs.
My feet have turned to hooves.
So long did I wait for your embrace,
I lost the use of my arms.
I was naked, so my skin grew a pelt.
I do not need your clothes,
now each hair of my hide is frosted
with crystals from the stars.
My virgin womb closed.
My budding breasts shrank.
My balls swing like purses
which hold moons and suns.

My mind has sprouted a bone forest
and every bone-leaf is a shield
to protect me from your gaze.
In memory of you I grew
this crown of twin cemeteries.
Every leaf is a tombstone
carved with your name.
And every fork of my antlers
cradles a nesting nebula.

So do not call me now, my mother,
my lightning-flash antlers
would sear your womb.
My flint hooves would crack your pelvis.
The dessert grapes on your vines
would be clots of your blood
if I bit them now.
The lamps in your house would fuse
as I approached your horizon.
Mother, I cannot go back.
Your ceilings are too low.
Do not look at these synapse-trees
I carry through the night.
For my antlers soar like singing star-trees
and no human must hear them.
And I can no longer drink from my breakfast bowl
with my name painted on the side.
I must drink from the lake of pure light.

I do not understand you, my quiet
and gentle daughter. You sound
like the great stag of the oak forests.
Your voice is distorted, your words
muffled as earth on my shroud.
Even when you were home,
you hid in your tree-house.
How many times did you steal cake
and run away to the woods?
How many times did you return
and sulk in a hut of silence?

Then you'd creep upstairs
and play your flute. Every note
was a rung you could climb up.
You surrounded yourself with ladders of music.
When you finally left, the piano
punched a hole in the roof
trying to follow you. For years
the keys rained down on me.

The girl-stag listens carefully.
Her mother's voice is persistent as a cicada
on the terraces of her childhood.
Do not remind me of my home, little mother.
Everywhere I look at the hissing constellations,
I see the snakes of our derelict vineyard.
The butterfly-nebulae flitting around my horns
are suns devouring one another.
And I have not forgotten my friend
the jewelled lizard.
I have a stag's sight, and can see,
in the stellar debris,
his scales rippling with sapphire eyes.
I have a stag's nose
and can smell oxygen trickling
through the pores of antimatter.

I bleed from a billion wounds.
Every second I die.
Every second I rise back up
to run deeper into the forest,
through the root-doors
and light-rings of night,
away from your arrows, my huntress.
Sometimes your voice is so faint
I forget I am your daughter. And your voice
dips into the whirlpool
at the centre of my brain,
is sucked in and down my spine,
into my bowels
and out with my stools.

Come back, the mother begs,
you are my only daughter.
Come back from your den of splitting atoms,
    your lair of light years,
to the homely lap of your mother.
I promise to shelter you.
You do not need the star-forests.
You do not need muscles
whining like ultrasonic jets
as they pierce the locks of space.
Do not go through the gate
at the end of the garden of secrets.
I will never reach you there
with this mother's voice.

Only to die, can I return to you Mother.
Only then can you bathe me
as you did when I was a child.
Then you can scrape off my fur, my flesh.
The marrow from my bones
you can sluice with the hose.
My brittle antlers will lose their lustre
and shrivel back into my brain.
When I return, Mother, it will be
to join you in the grave
where we will torment one another.
And no one else will suffer
as you will suffer then, my mother.

Tara Bergin writes: 'It was during my study of Ted Hughes's translations of
János Pilinszky that I first came across Hughes's version of Ferenc Juhász's
poem "The Boy Changed into a Stag Cries Out at the Gate of Secrets". I was
struck by the fact that Hughes had made this version based solely on an
English one by Kenneth McRobbie and began to make a close comparison
between his and McRobbie's version in an attempt to find out what Hughes's
alterations told us about his own poetic sensibility.

   During this work I happened to take a train to London. A stag-party got
on at York, and the carriage became, for a short period, territory ruled by
them. Their terrible, eager, desperate faces produced in me feelings of
interest, pity and fear.'

Stag-Boy

He enters the carriage with a roar –
he clatters in wildly and fills up the carriages with heat,
running through the train, staining the floor
with hooves dirty from the street;
tearing at the ceilings with his new branched horns,
banging his rough sides against the seats and
the women, who try to look away: Gallant!
He sings hard from his throat,
his young belling tearing at his chest,
pushing at his boy-throat.

Stag-boy –

the train's noise hums in his ears,
sharp and high like crickets pulsing
in the tall grass,
and he wounds it with his horns,
maddened like a stung bull,
pushing up his head,
pushing up his mouth for his mother's teat:
Where is her beestings?
Where is the flowered mug she used to warm his milk in?

No good, no good now.

He's smashing out of the train door,
he's banging his hooves in the industrial air,
he's galloping through the city squares,
and drinking from a vandalised spring –

And still his mother walks through the house,
crying: *Stag-boy, oh stag-boy come home!*

(time passes)

ERNST JANDL

oberflächenübersetzung

mai hart lieb zapfen eibe hold
er renn bohr in sees kai
so was sieht wenn mai läuft begehen
so es sieht nahe emma mähen
so biet wenn ärschel grollt
ohr leck mit ei!
seht steil dies fader rosse mähen
in teig kurt wisch mai desto bier
baum deutsche deutsch bajonett schur alp eiertier

(surface translation – after william wordsworth)

my heart leaps up when i behold
a rainbow in the sky
so was it when my life began
so is it now i am a man
so be it when i shall grow old
or let me die!
the child is father of the man
and i could wish my days to be
bound each to each by natural piety

ERNST JANDL

die zeit vergeht

lustig
luslustigtig
lusluslustigtigtig
luslusluslustigtigtigtig
lusluslusluslustigtigtigtigtig
luslusluslusluslustigtigtigtigtigtig
lusluslusluslusluslustigtigtigtigtigtigtig
luslusluslusluslusluslustigtigtigtigtigtigtigtig

(time passes)

CHRIS McCABE

Ernst Jandl: The Biomechanical Magus in London

Lower Marsh still retains its resonances from the old world in its title. Back when Lambeth was a marshland. The concrete brutalism of the Southbank is yet to reach here. The market stalls riffle their plasticised sheets. A few years back I stopped, as usual, to look in the window of the second-hand book shop and saw Ernst Jandl's *mai hart lieb zapfen eibe hold* catching my eye with its azure-on-royal blue, the typography so rough-cut that it seemed to be shimmering. It had a sticky note attached with a handwritten price: £2.

This is my Jandl moment in London, but there were many London moments for Jandl. *mai hart* was published by Writers Forum in 1965, at a period when texture and design were prevalent in the press. Then came the accelerated upping of the pace of production led by Bob Cobbing, Bob Cob, the leader of the Koncrete Canticle. Make, xerox, staple, distribute. Start again. I heard recently that there's a student writing a PhD on the history of Writers Forum and, after talking to everyone associated with the press, has found that only half of the press's output (estimated at approximately 1,000 items) are known by title. The blue I spotted in the window on Lower Marsh was something of a European rare bird. Like Jandl himself.

Jandl lived for periods of his life in the UK and taught English in Austria. He was born in 1925, three years after *The Waste Land* was published, and died in 2000, in the year that looks like a cygnet (as the visual poem by Pierre Garner suggests). He translated Gertrude Stein, Robert Creeley and John Cage into German. This fluidity between languages is significant as his poetry doesn't so much bring English and German together as create an Anglo-Saxon mulch resonant with futuristic possibilities; English words appear barbed, like embankment bramble, from the sonorous fluids of invented phonemes.

Peter Finch would later tell me that he was introduced to Jandl on a London Street in the 1960s. This was most likely somewhere around Earl's Court, where Cobbing had his quickfire Xerox machines perched for public use. This is the kind of chance encounter that London allows: one of the best sound poets of an older generation shaking hands with the best of his. Finch later told me, as we sat in the grungy snug of The

Hole in the Wall pub on Mepham Street, just a few hundred yards from where I'd found *mai hart*: 'He was fond of the Brits and came here often during that period. I came across his amazing "Ode to N" on a Concrete Poetry anthology album. "Ode to N" with its multi-layered Jandl voices and almost choral approach to his take on how the world felt about Napoleon stunned me. It was a way of making poetry that I had never considered. I then heard his BBC recording made by George MacBeth in, I think, 1966, including the famous World War One war poem about the trenches. Sound poetry as theatre. He was, it turned out, a huge influence on Bob Cobbing who was working on his ABC In Sound during this period.'

I've arrived at Southbank Centre. Jandl came here in 1971 to take part in the Poetry International festival. His involvement is a challenge to the very idea of poetry in translation as many of his poems – like Kurt Schwitter's 'Ursonate' – are beyond translation: the meld of sound and guessed-at meaning is what the poem *is*, in any language. This is a very different approach to poetry to many of the other concrete poets that Jandl was grouped with in the concrete anthologies. Eugen Gomringer, for example, aimed to create a poetry influenced by the clarity and universalism of motorway signs: his 'silencio' could be as easily grasped by a teenager in Brazil as by a pensioner in Walthamstow. Jandl's approach was to perplex through sound and fragmentation – and why not? The century he had lived through was beyond perplexing.

Like Schwitters he was building up his own Merz-like oeuvre, a totemic hideaway in self-stylised language that might keep the barbarous world at bay but might also become a monster that could take the world on. This self-styled position of lone wolf meant he could even bare his fangs at the concrete poetry movement; he was an outsider within the outsiders:

> i love poetry
> i love pottery
> but I'm not
> a concrete pot

There is a wilfulness in Jandl, a refusal to be easily categorisable even within an outside movement. 'I don't want to be | as you would have me,' he wrote.

In the *MPT* Poetry International Programme for 1971, a slim gold folio-sized slab containing photos, texts and adverts (DIAL A POEM 01-836 2872... 'over 40,000 people have listened during the past 7 months') the pages containing Jandl's are between Auden's and Bunting's. Late Auden, with the face of a long soaked fingerprint and Bunting in his turtleneck, as if about to join a sea trawler. Neither of these fit with the cool Kraftwerk look of Jandl. White shirt, slim tie, black NHS-style glasses. His lips pursed, profile side-on. The first poem printed here, 'oberflächenübersetzung', is described as a 'surface translation' of Wordsworth's 'My heart leaps up when I behold'. Jandl retains the cadences of Wordsworth's poem but lacerates the meaning of the original into asyntactically-led soundscape of nonsense. When read aloud his poem sounds like Wordsworth's but the meaning is completely different: 'May deer love pour yew-tree hold'. Jandl, as a maker of new language systems, precedes Google Translate poems by forty years.

Michael Hamburger, who translated Jandl's poems for Dedalus Press in 1997, calls this hybrid language 'Anglo-Saxon or Jinglish'. Wordsworth's passionate but sentimental declaration that – if he doesn't take joy in a rainbow when he's old then he'd rather not live ('or let me die!') – becomes in Jandl: 'ear lick with egg!' Jandl deviously hollows-out the established canon of literature as a necessary measure from someone who's seen the effects of two world wars: the first on his parents, the second on himself. Jandl looks at the Wordsworth poem with the knowledge that neither country or honour are worth dying for – let alone joy. One can see this technique as taking *language* through the plight of the pristinely signed-up recruit who's taken to the trenches and knocked on the head with shrapnel, as happened to that other great modernist, Apollinaire, in 1916.

Jandl has that unearthly skill of being able to remove himself from his own personality to write the unsayable: 'i have collapsed into myself | it frightens me'. His poems retaliate on the century through use of his body in performance. Jandl had been in the army in the Second World War and had become a prisoner of war. In his poems we got both language under assault and language as able to make its assault, mimicking machine-led devastation.

He can be heard reading his poem 'schtzngrmm' on YouTube against a montage of 20th-century war footage: he sits in a studio reading like a newsreader, the camera intermittently cutting between him and the images of the trenches and bombings, and then to plastic tanks. The footage ends with an older Jandl saying 'schtzgrmm' shows that you can write a poem about war – in spite of the bitterness of it which transcends the gravity of the issue'. Elsewhere he called poems like this 'Sprechgedichte': poems to be spoken.

Gagged breath and winded grunts are distinct stylistic tics. Just look at the poems printed on the pages of the 1971 programme: vowels are pulled across whole lines ('bleeeeeeeeeeee'); a slim futuristic piece of gristle is formed in 'verscheuchung zweier farben'), consonants are made to sit side by side like joints antagonised with the removal of ligature ('nnnrrrrrrrrrrr'), and a shape redolent of Herbert's 'Easter Wings' is formed in 'die zeit vergeht' though the meaning is again completely destablised: 'lustig......luslusluslusluslusluslustigtigtigtig-tigtigtigtig'. The breaking apart of 'lustig' – meaning funny (haha) – into parts, allows for the repetition of 'tig' to stand for the ticking of a clock. The poem's shape becomes an hour-glass filling or the outward swing of a pendulum.

Even though I'm here at the Queen Elizabeth Hall, the building he read at in 1971 – a building as angular and challenging as Jandl's poems – this isn't his finest London moment. This was six years before when he was on stage at the 1965 Poetry Incarnation at the Royal Albert Hall. He's been forgotten amidst the personality worship of Ginsberg, Horovitz, and Mitchell. Jandl is the small crazed European chopping up words and lunging bodily into language like a biomechanical magus. He is wearing his trademark glasses and starched white shirt which I now see clearly for the inversion that it is: the Nazi-look repurposed by an artist fighting for the free expression that language can be used for. He is there to do business amidst the flowing gowns and curling cigarette fumes of the other poets. As he reads we hear the audience's joy rising with the broken words of his poems; they are whistling, whooping, then up on their feet: feeling their bodies lifted by this unique and urgent per-former. After engaging the audience with this assault-through language Jandl then raises the page he's been reading from into the air, holding it up to the audience like a small white flag.

Poet, playwright and essayist Chris McCabe works as the Poetry Librarian at The Poetry Library at Southbank Centre. He is the editor, with Victoria Bean, of *The New Concrete: Visual Poetry in the 21st Century* (Hayward Publishing, 2015).

Sentence

I stalk words
　　　　and I string them together without delay

I stalk nouns – I stalk adjectives
　　　　the adjectives set up the nouns

I feel sorry for my vigorous verbs
　　　　– they remain without subjects

If you have some extra nouns
Bring them – I'll buy them for a good price

Translated from the Western Armenian by Ralph Setian

Zahrad (1924–2007) was one of the most significant Armenian poets of his generation, although he lived in Turkey. He was born in Istanbul and briefly attended medical school before devoting his life to writing. The Chair of the Armenian Writers' Union called Zahrad 'the huge oak tree of diasporan poetry'.

ZAHRAD

The Woman Cleaning Lentils

A lentil–a lentil–lentils–a lentil–a pebble–a lentil–a lentil–a pebble
A green one–a black one–a green one–a black one–a pebble–a green lentil
A lentil next to a lentil, a pebble next to a lentil–suddenly a word–a word next to a lentil
Then words–a lentil–a word–a word next to a word–then a phrase
And word by word a witless wording–a wornout song–a washed out dream
Then a life–another life–a life next to a life–a lentil–a life
An easy life–a hard life–why easy–why hard
But lives next to each other–a life–then a word–then a lentil
A green one–a black one–a green one–a black one–a pain–a green song
A green lentil–a black one–a pebble–a lentil–a pebble–a pebble–a lentil

Translated from the Western Armenian by Ralph Setian

From 'The Wash House'

They knotted the roots and petals of wildflowers together,
waved their hands in some fashion or other,
and this droop of a girl sat up from the green.

A bride for the groom. She doesn't say much,
words stumbling out like young shoots.
'Don't remember,' she says,
so I show her where she used to be broom,
hitching herself from the dry soil under the cliff,
bees clamouring at each cup.

I show her where she was meadowsweet,
where she thickened the low field by the stream:
always thirsty, always twisting towards the white spurting water,
and insisting her roots in tough currents downwards,
wrangling the earth.

I show her where she was oak flower,
pouting in gangs between the spring twigs,
urging the green thud of water up through the trunk
and into the fizz of those thousand pink mouths.

'Next?' she says, wheeling hair round her finger,
but we are due back at the hall.
We stand for a few moments longer,
watch the fritter of blossom over the stream.

Anna Lewis (1984–) drew her sequence 'The Wash House' from the story of
Blodeuedd, found in the *Mabinogion*, the major collection of medieval Welsh
tales. In this poem Blodeuedd is created from wildflowers by magic, to be the
bride for a young nobleman.

VASKO POPA

Swallows' Language

A crippled old woman
Teacher of foreign languages
Keeps the window of her room
Open all year round

A swallow has built its nest
In the glass of her lampshade

The old woman listens to the twittering
Forges plans for the future

One day when they carry me
Out of this cage
My companion will go on
With my work

She'll teach much better than me
Old frog that I am

Translated from the Serbian by Anne Pennington

VASKO POPA

Anne Pennington

Until her last breath she enlarges
Her Oxford house
Built in Slavonic
Vowels and consonants

She polishes the corner-stones
Until their Anglo-Saxon shine
Begins to sing

Her death is like a short breath-stop
Under the distant limetrees of her friends

Translated from the Serbian by Daniel Weissbort, Anthony Rudolf and Peter Jay

Anne Pennington (1934–1981) was Professor of Comparative Slavonic
Philology at Oxford and a translator from many of the South Slavic
languages, but she was particularly well known for her translations of Vasko
Popa, with whom she worked closely. This fruitful relationship between the
translator and poet was fostered by *Modern Poetry in Translation*. Popa read
his tribute to Anne Pennington at the Cambridge Poetry Festival in 1981.

Mimi Khalvati (1944–) writes: 'I remember a very old and well-thumbed copy
of Hafez an Iranian friend showed me, interleaved with countless Post-it
notes in varying shades of yellow. These, she explained, marked the many
occasions in her life when she had consulted Hafez, as one would the I Ching,
on their auspices. Her life and Hafez's ghazals were forever inextricably linked.
Mine, without my mother tongue, forever diminished. I long to english the
ghazal and do what I might do if I were writing in my first language.'

Ghazal: To Hold Me

I want to be held. I want somebody near
                         to hold me
when the axe falls, time is called, strangers appear
                         to hold me.

I want all that has been denied me. And more.
Much more than God in some lonely stratosphere
                         to hold me.

I want hand and eye, sweet roving things, and land
for grazing, praising, and the last pioneer
                         to hold me.

I want my ship to come in, crossing the bar,
before my back's so bowed even children fear
                         to hold me.

I want to die being held, hearing my name
thrown, thrown like a rope from a very old pier
                         to hold me.

I want to catch the last echoes, reel them in
like a curing-song in the creel of my ear
                         to hold me.

I want Rodolfo to sing, flooding the gods,
Ah Mimi! as if I were her and he, here,
                         to hold me.

SORLEY MACLEAN

Dawn

You were the dawn on the Cuillin
stillness of waters between the islands
the sun on his elbow in the stream of gold
the white rose that breaks the horizon

Simmer of sails on the luminous frith
blue-green of the sea, the sky's electrum
new light shining in the braids of your hair
and the sun rising in your complexion

Jewel of dawn, jewel of night, your
tenderness, and your beautiful face –
though the day of my youthful morning
is pierced to the heart by a death-grey stake

Translated from the Gaelic by the author
here in a version by Cameron Hawke Smith

Scottish poet Sorley MacLean / Somhairle MacGill-Eain (1911–1996) was born
on the Gaelic-speaking island of Raasay. Despite having published a relatively
small number of poems (under a hundred), he is widely considered to be
unrivalled in modern Gaelic poetry, and he is a key figure in 20th-century
Scottish literature. Translator Cameron Hawke Smith drew on MacLean's
own prose translations of his poems, Scots verse translations and notes on the
poem to produce versions which conveyed the visual imagery of the original.

Carandasi

Tell me I am necessary for you like sleep...
and not like opium to carry forgetting,
or pleasant as a breeze
scented with jasmine.

Tell me what you see
behind my art, my bright cloth.
Look into my face and show it to me.

Tell me what you read in books
and hear in coffee houses,
wedding parties. Teach me.

When our tired, gladdened bodies
drift down onto the bed,
kiss me like a husband
and spread over me an endless blue wing...

This poem comes from a longer sequence called *The Courtesans Reply*, inspired by M. Ghosh's translation from the Sanskrit of *The Caturbhani*, four monologue plays written around 300BC on the life of courtesans in India. Shazea writes about this poem: '"Carandasi" begins and ends with a line from Mahmoud Darwish's poem "Two Stranger Birds in Our Feathers". The tenderness in his lines was the seed that grew into my poem.'

DAVID CONSTANTINE

Editorial to 'Getting it Across'

Michael Hamburger's association with *MPT* goes back more than forty years, almost to our very beginning. He is named among the advisory editors in the second issue, Summer 1966; and to the third, Spring 1967, he contributed translations of Ingeborg Bachmann's 'Leaving England' and Helmut Heissenbüttel's 'the future of socialism'. In May of this year he sent us four of his own poems and ten days later the translations of Robert Walser, which we publish here. My letter thanking him for Walser arrived at Marsh Acres the morning he died. We were away in France when he sent it; had we been home, I should have written sooner, emulating him, the promptest of correspondents. How can we thank the dead?

When we asked Michael for work or gratefully accepted what he offered, we never fitted him into any of our particular themes; but, as it happens, he is peculiarly in place in this issue called 'Getting it Across'. Poet, translator, literary critic, tirelessly going to and fro between the languages, could anyone have done more? I wrote about him almost twenty years ago: an introduction to a Bibliography of the Publications of Michael Hamburger. I have a horror of bibliographies, but his was curiously moving. There you saw it: proof of the love and labour, the going between, the getting it across. I called my essay 'Man of Letters'. For me he embodied that title, it seemed a high office, a profession you would be honoured to serve in. So Hölderlin styled himself in Lyons in January 1802 in revolutionary France when the police asked him what he did: 'Homme de lettres', and so they entered him in their records.

Michael died on the same day as Hölderlin, 7 June, having spent much of his life preoccupied with him. At the age of 16, after only seven years in England, only seven years speaking English, he was looking for a publisher for his Hölderlin translations. They came out three years later, in 1943; by which time Michael, the German Jew, was in British army uniform. The Poetry Society invited him to come and talk on Hölderlin, and read from his translations. He declined. His Company Commander ordered him to accept, for the honour of the regiment. But his nerve failed him, he hid in the audience and got two friends to read and talk for him. That invitation and the occasion, like the translation and the publication themselves, were an absurd and beautiful act of opposition, against evil. Michael commented: 'If I had asked myself why that war was worth fighting, I should have said, because such absurdities are possible in Britain, and there was nothing I wouldn't do to keep them possible.'

Poems are bread on the waters, messages in bottles, they may land anywhere. I found a copy of *Poems of Hölderlin* in Llangollen, only last year: nearly 100 pages of introduction, then 140 of poems, the German facing Michael's English, page by page. Quite something, in the middle of a war against the native land of poet and translator! German soldiers were sent to the front with a special edition of Hölderlin, the so-called *Feldauswahl*, in their packs. Like Michael's volume it came out in 1943. A friend found me a copy in Oxford in 1968. The Nazis hijacked Hölderlin for a while. You might say that Michael helped him shake them off. They rot in ignominy and his verse sails on.

I first met and corresponded with Michael because of Hölderlin. I asked him would he read my versions, and he did. I remember his kindness. He and I translated very differently, as we both acknowledged. It moves me to think of that now: very differently, and the beloved text in common between us.

Michael was famously lugubrious. Everyone who knew him has a story. Ours is this. Visiting us once, he cast his eye over our small son's cactus collection. 'Ah yes,' he said, in tones of glum satisfaction, like a preacher lighting on yet another proof of original sin, 'I see they've got the mealy bug.' Most things have, either the mealy bug or some equivalent, and Michael always spotted it. I liked him for that, for the exact tone of voice in which he said, 'I see they've got the mealy bug.' He reminded me of my mother, my grandmother, two or three of my aunts, with their heroically doleful Mona Lott catchphrase, 'It's being so cheerful as keeps me going.'

Michael kept going, against melancholy, against the usual ills. And against fashion, trend, the many spreading duplicities. It was easy to think he would go on for ever and would always be rooting out something else for us from the Aladdin's Cave at Marsh Acres.

The German word 'übersetzen' has a more literal or a more figurative sense according to whether that prefix 'über' is separable or inseparable. Separable, the word means to carry over or across, from one side to the other, it might be an object or a person. Inseparable, it means to translate. Celan, whom Michael translated and who was himself (like Hölderlin) a great translator, and a poet who strove desperately to get himself across, plays on that dual sense in more than one poem. He has the image of a ferry, that bears things – often terrible things – across. Saint Jerome is the usual patron of translators, but Christopher might be too, or Julian the Hospitaller, the one carrying you over on his shoulders, the other ferrying you across in his boat. And since translators and good literary critics enable the poets into further and further life, we might nominate Charon also, a sort of Counter-Charon, shipping the vital soul of the achievements of the dead across the river back among the living, for us to embody and continue the best we can.

PAUL CELAN

Psalm

No one moulds us again out of earth and clay,
no one conjures our dust.
No one.

Praised be your name, no one.
For your sake
we shall flower.
Towards
you.

A nothing
we were, are, shall
remain, flowering:
the nothing–, the
no one's rose.

With our pistil soul-bright
with our stamen heaven-ravaged
our corolla red
with the crimson word which we sang
over, o over
the thorn.

Translated from the German by Michael Hamburger

GEORGE SZIRTES

The Voronezh Variations

(for Veronika Bowker)

Raven: *vóron*; *nozh*: blade, winds me out, re-winds me:
The blade must fall, the raven's free yet binds me.
Returns, re-venues, misses me and finds me,
Vorónezh, ravensblade whose whim defines me.

*

Vóron, a raven, *nozh*, a snitch: ditched by
Voronezh, like unstitched leaves, reached by
Voronezh, rehitched, stitched up by the bitch
Voronezh, the raven with the snitch.

*

Ravensditch, Ravensbrück, Ravensbeak,
Let me go, let me come, or else you will seek
me in vain, Voronezh, having dropped my life
on a whim, raven whose beak is sharp as a knife...

*

Alternatively: Crow, the Crow's bright blade.
Will you crow now Voronezh, now I have gone..?
Will you drop me or gather me in your masquerade,
crow, joker, with your sharp beak of black crow-shade.

*

Thieving magpie, Voronezh, black and sharp as night.
Will you drop your loot or pick it up and punish
your son with it, as a raven or magpie might,
you who are only a joke yourself, Voronezh?

*

This is no joke, Voronezh. I am not Poe's Raven.
I will not come knocking for you to drop the latch
and lock me out. I have no knife to prise my way in.
but I will return Voronezh, sharp as a raven's snitch.

*

Let me go, return me to my lost home,
Voronezh, I'm still yours though you drop me
you black joke, Voronezh, you cannot stop me
singing, even under your crow-black dome.

GEORGE SZIRTES

The Voronezh Variations: Versions of a Mandelstam Quatrain

I was introduced to this particular Mandelstam quatrain by a friend, Veronika Krasnova. I do not read Russian and knew Mandelstam only from various translations into English. Veronika was keen to explain the many possible readings of it. It springs out of the poet's exile to Voronezh in 1935, the poem itself written in the April of that year. It is an extraordinarily playful quatrain playing chiefly on the name Voronezh that breaks down into 'voron' (raven), and 'nozh' (knife). The voice is ironic, almost clowning, yet remains deadly serious. The poem is elegant in form, the sound 'Voronezh' returning time and again as pun, as echo, as haunting, as threat. As Peter Zeeman puts it in his book on Mandelstam's later poems, 'it cannot be rendered satisfactorily in translation'.

That is true of poetry generally since poems depend on ambiguity and the power of suggestion for their full effect but – one might argue – it is particularly true of this brief, crammed and yet somehow lucid poem that is almost a squib. One might further argue that since we know that no one translation of a poem can ever be wholly satisfactory there might be greater satisfaction in reading more than one version of it and that, by reading the various translations, in effect superimposing them on each other, one might build up a stereoscopic effect, or at least help convey the variousness of the poem itself.

That is what I tried to do with the sometimes terrifying help of Veronika's copious notes and explanations. I decided to make several versions, some freer than others, but, since I don't think complexity of manner and therefore also of form is indivorcible from complexity and form of meaning, I wanted them all to be as formally elegant as I could make them, responding to the puns, echoes and ambiguities of the Russian with puns, echoes and ambiguities in English – and, since the poem was personal, allowing myself to introduce the name of Ravensbrück (Voronsbruck), the concentration camp where my own mother was interned and which she survived. The raven brought in Edgar Allan Poe too. The aim, as it developed, became to make a series of dark jokes as if by a kind of extended legerdemain. None of the variations is intended to be a straight translation of the poem, though the first is probably the closest.

A poesia
É a liberdade
Da linguagem
De cada
Um

Poetry
Is the Liberty
Of Language Of
Every
One

Event • Digging

One year — in a Northern Ireland Spring — the poet Seamus Heaney —
sat under a window writing — and by chance caught sight of his old man —
digging potatoes — from a plot in a field. The moment he cut down with his
      spade —
he groaned — as if in pain — as if a crop
of potatoes lay concealed in the field beneath his spade —
while certain crops planted in Heaney's darkness — were loosened, too.
His old man didn't know it — but immediately afterwards — his son dug up
another kind of potato — to form part of the English language.

He hadn't won the Prize yet — he'd only managed a batch of first-rate chips
which I sampled once in a *Selected English Poems* — they made a deep impression
      on me.
The workmanship wasn't bad at all— and just like one fellow worker admiring
      another —
I couldn't help curling my fingers — and rapping the book with my knuckles —
      as if giving Heaney
a pat on the shoulder — my old pal.
When it came to potatoes — what more could *I* add?

As luck would have it — on another day — when I was writing in Chinese
intending to start — with some verbs — unclear in their meanings
there came a sound — not from my pen on paper —
but from outside my window. What interrupted me
was a young construction worker
who quietly mounted the scaffolding. As he climbed — he grabbed hold of my
      window-sill
and began scrubbing at blobs of cement — splashed on the windows by a summer
      construction project.

The buildings opposite had already been done — this was the final job —
to return everything in the surroundings — to its original state.
He scrubbed conscientiously — like a bird preening feathers —
deftly he handled — his cotton rag — chisel and mallet — and stretched out
      his neck to blow away any last traces.

Not a speck of dirt escaped his notice.
Often he pressed his palms against the pane — I distinctly saw —
the lines — on those palms — looking just like the surface of peat —
       but with moisture under them.

He was like a man who lights lamps — after he'd cleaned one pane till it shone
       brightly — he'd get to work on the next.
The meaning of his work was crystal-clear — to prevent truth — from remaining
       concealed —
I do much the same thing — from a host of clichés and stereotyped expressions
I accept and reject — weigh up carefully — reorganise — till at last they are
       polished to a shine
and the radiance of words — grasps things with insight.

In sunlight that gradually became clearer, his face
smiled a slightly apologetic smile at me.
His labour only relates to surfaces — but compared to driving piles
       deep into the ground
the intensity of such labour —is by no means less.
Only by standing firmly — does he manage to avoid falling from the fifth floor.
What he digs is another kind of hole — the depths belong to others.
What he plants is a different tree — the fruit already belongs to somebody else —
but this was none of his concern — his job was done —
he removed the dirt — and cleaned up the surroundings — that was all.

As he wiped the glass — he wiped me too, sitting behind the glass.
When I lifted my head out of words and phrases — and gazed at the reality outside
I realised that the beauty of the world — was not something I needed to rack my
       brains trying to imagine —
all I had to do was look.

I finally wrote down a verb — it had nothing to do with the labour outside my
       window
it did not involve glass — it involved Seamus Heaney.
Suddenly I recalled a poem he wrote — about potatoes, I thought
and so taking advantage of the bright light — I again dug out
my *Selected English Poems* — from a stack of books
and from 10,000 miles away — in urban Kunming —
crossed the border into Northern Ireland — on this radiant Tuesday.

The spade — that drove deep into the core of my being —
       was not the English language
but Heaney's father — on the ridge of a field outside the windows of his home
repeating without interruption that action —
digging.

Translated from the Chinese by Tao Naikan and Simon Patton

'Yu Jian (1954–) came to his voice as a poet of urban sprawl. He wanted to write directly about life in his urban Kunming, but he had to find a way to make the everyday poetically engaging. He found this in his almost paralysing sense of language as a chain: one idea attracts a cluster of synonyms that build up like water in a blocked hose until a move is eventually made to the next idea.' SP

SUJATA BHATT

Another Daphne

Und die verwandelte Daphne
will, seit sie lorbeern fühlt, daß du dich wandelst in Wind.

RAINER MARIA RILKE

And Daphne, newly transformed –
Daphne, who feels herself greenish,
laurelish
through and through
a glistening pliancy –
that Daphne has had a change of heart
and now she wants you, whoever you are,
to become the wind itself –

*

Who knows what Daphne really wanted –

Meanwhile, the girl who couldn't say love
has started writing poems,
love poems –

'Oh my!' she says,
'Maybe I'll keep writing love poems now.'

The wind in her hair,
the wind fragrant with roses and leaves –

And there, a song thrush – and there, a blackbird,
and look, swallows – today the swallows fly higher and higher –

*

Shall we change the story?

Remove Cupid's arrows,
          and let Daphne be free to choose –

                    *

          The girl says, *beautiful*.

                    *

'What about the crows?' her lover asks.
'Have you never seen crows fighting?'

And he shows her
          how they fence with their beaks –
'Like this,' he says, 'like this.'
And he shows her how
their heads dart out at each other –
'They love to argue,' he says, 'these crows
                    with their crow language.'

                    *

'Birdsong,' she says, 'birdsong.'

Sujata Bhatt (1956–) wrote this poem in response to one of Rilke's *Sonnets to Orpheus*, 'O Desire Transformation'. Behind both poems stands the myth of Daphne, who was pursued by Apollo and metamorphosed into laurel. Whilst Rilke's poem embraces this transformation, 'Another Daphne' sounds a melancholy note, and emphasises the human in the exchange, as translator and scholar Karen Leeder notes in her introduction to this poem in *Modern Poetry in Translation*.

✦

And as for him, he turns from rock, is enclosed

within the rock, is resurrected, vanishes

on the road that leads through his body

from fullness into wholeness.

ZSUZSA BENEY

The Translator

He steps into the poem. Rock. It closes
behind him, he too becomes rock.
He becomes absorbed in the cell
Of the bones, in their vaulted arcades.

But while he freezes, the clay about him
roasts at white heat, eventually melts,
and from the glowing magma there blossoms
a whole new framework, the rose in the desert.

And as for him, he turns from rock, is enclosed
within the rock, is resurrected, vanishes
on the road that leads through his body
from fullness into wholeness.

Translated from the Hungarian by George Szirtes

Zsuzsa Beney (1930–2006) was a Hungarian poet, essayist and surgeon. She
continued working as a surgeon until her 70th birthday. Her poems are
contemplative, often preoccupied by suffering and the borders of existence
and non-existence.

GIUSEPPE BELLI

The Good Life

Mi gram when late at neet comes home t'owd man
drops the clothes she's knittin' us, poor owd pet,
sets us table an' warms room best she can,
an' we eat a few spuds, what we can get.

Nah'n again we'll 'ave us an omèlet,
an' if tha wer to 'old it up to t' sun
just like an ear, light'd shine reight thru' it:
a few crusts to nibble on, supper's done.

Then me, wi' t'owd man an' mi sister Grace
a couple o' hours o' suppin' pass,
while gram cleans up an' puts things back in place,
til we can see to t' bottom of us glass.

Next a quick piss and an 'ail mary,
an' straight up to bed in peace an' plenty

Translated from the Roman Italian dialect into Yorkshire dialect by Paul Howard

The Romanesque sonneteer Giuseppe Belli (1791–1863) wrote 2,279 sonnets.
Translator Paul Howard writes that the beauty of Belli's sonnets is that he
uses the classical sonnet setting, but sends them up by couching them in
dialect. In his translation of 'The Good Life' Howard has given the poem a
Shakespearean scheme, but used Yorkshire dialect with its varied assonance
as an equivalent for the coarse double consonants of Belli's Romanesco.

WOJCIECH BONOWICZ

Night

The poem
first shuts you inside.
It doesn't want
you to look around, search
for different words
in different poems.

You sit cornered in the stone,
a scrunched
sheet of paper.
Defenceless and resigned,
you don't breathe. The poem
won't allow.

Inside the stone you can't
fidget or use
a bed a watch a map
and all the rest
of your imagination.

The poem
has its own imagination,
erected in yours,
then shut inside
to free itself.

You have to wait
in the corner of the stone,
where the golden dust
of hope occasionally glints.

In the end the poem
will open itself. The stone
will let you out: a sheet of paper
that will begin to breathe.

Translated from the Polish by Elżbieta Wójcik-Leese

Note on Paulo Leminski's Concrete Poetry

Central to Paulo Leminski's (1944–1989) poetry are two formative movements: the scholarly *Poesia Concreta*, or Brazilian Concretism, developed in São Paulo (1950s–60s); and 1960s–70s counter-culture.

In Concretism, the poem is designed for both eye and ear. Material forms on the page, their de- or re-construction, and their spatial arrangement become meaningful. Concrete poetry draws on 'ideogram', and non-verbal communication, the poem as an object in itself, not necessarily an interpretation of external objects or subjective feelings.

In letters, Leminski refers to himself one of 'the last Concretists and the first I know not what'.

The two poems published in this anthology, 'Poetry is the Liberty of Language of Every One' (p. 163) and 'Things don't start…' (p. 174) were translated from Brazilian Portuguese by Jamie Duncan.

Wojciech Bonowicz (1967–) does not shy away from questions of philosophy and religion in his poetry, but as translator Elżbieta Wójcik-Leese notes, the poems are 'modest, human-sized personal revelations, which frequently set off to examine our understanding of suffering, evil and death – and leave us with even more questions'.

as coisas   não começam   com um conto   nem acabam   com um

não começam   com um conto   nem acabam   com um   things

com um conto   nem acabam   com um   things   don't start

nem acabam   com um   things   don't start   in a story

com um   things   don't start   in a story   nor end

things   don't start   in a story   nor end   in one

don't start   in a story   nor end   in one   as coisas

in a story   nor end   in one   as coisas   não começam

nor end   in one   as coisas   não começam   com um conto

in one   as coisas   não começam   com um conto   nem acabam

as coisas   não começam   com um conto   nem acabam   com um

não começam   com um conto   nem acabam   com um   things

com um conto   nem acabam   com um   things   don't start

nem acabam   com um   things   don't start   in a story

com um   things   don't start   in a story   nor end

things   don't start   in a story   nor end   in one

don't start   in a story   nor end   in one   as coisas

in a story   nor end   in one   as coisas   não começam

nor end   in one   as coisas   não começam   com um conto

in one   as coisas   não começam   com um conto   nem acabam

as coisas   não começam   com um conto   nem acabam   com um

✦

The dead and I

we swim

through the new doors

of our old houses.

TOMAS TRANSTRÖMER

The Journey's Formulae
(from the Balkans, 1955)

1

A murmur of voices behind the ploughman.
He doesn't look round. The empty fields.
A murmur of voices behind the ploughman.
One by one the shadows break loose
and plunge into the summer sky's abyss.

2

Four oxen come, under the sky.
Nothing proud about them. And the dust thick
As wool. The insects' pens scrape.

A swirl of horses, lean as in
grey allegories of the plague.
Nothing gentle about them. And the sun raves.

3

The stable-smelling village with thin dogs.
The party official in the market square
in the stable-smelling village with white houses.

His heaven accompanies him: it is high
and narrow like inside a minaret.
The wing-trailing village on the hillside.

4

An old house has shot itself in the forehead.
Two boys kick a ball in the twilight.
A swarm of rapid echoes. – Suddenly, starlight.

5

On the road in the long darkness. My wristwatch
gleams obstinately with time's imprisoned insect.

The quiet in the crowded compartment is dense.
In the darkness the meadows stream past.

But the writer is halfway into his image, there
he travels, at the same time eagle and mole.

Translated from the Swedish by Robin Fulton

Tomas Tranströmer (1931–2015) was a psychologist and poet, and recipient of
the Nobel Prize in Literature in 2011.

HILDE DOMIN

Cologne

The submerged city
for me
alone
submerged.

I swim
in the streets.
Others walk.

The old houses
have big new doors
of glass.

The dead and I
we swim
through the new doors
of our old houses.

Translated from the German by Tudor Morris

Hilde Domin (1912–2006) was born into a Jewish family in Cologne and
studied law, sociology and political science. She emigrated in 1932 and spent
years in Italy and England, before eventually moving to the Dominican
Republic in 1940. She only returned to Germany in 1954, many years after the
war and settled in Heidelberg.

LEAH GOLDBERG

The Girl Sings to the River

Where is the angry river now
Taking my eyes, my face away?
My house is far where pine-woods sough;
Sad are my pine trees as they sway.

'Come,' sang the exulting flood before,
And called my name, and I was blind.
Lured by its music to this shore,
I left my mother's house behind.

And here I stand, her only child,
Tender in years – and the waters rise.
O why is the river, raging wild,
Bearing away my childhood eyes?

Translated from the Hebrew by Robert Friend

'Leah Goldberg's (1911–1970) poetry was a stream fed by many sources. Born in Kovno, Lithuania, her early background was Russian. In her teens she began to learn Hebrew, which became her adopted mother tongue.' RF

CARMEN BUGAN

Why I Do Not Write in My Native Language

The first time I found the country code for Romania in the telephone book I understood how far away from home I was. Because the 1989 Revolution began very soon after my family and I arrived in Michigan, the lines were busy and the connection was bad: there was white noise between the words, as if they needed time to go across the ocean, only to get stuck in our throats. I had the feeling that I had arrived at that place 'far away' from which I was never to return. That experience of distance has deepened over the past fifteen years. Now I can say that in writing poetry too, I have arrived at some 'far away' place, from which I will not return.

Like most people in my native country, I started writing in my youth. Perhaps my poetry-writing would have stopped at some point in late adolescence if I had not begun to write to my father's photographs. My father protested publicly against the Ceauşescu government in 1983 and was condemned to ten years in prison for 'propaganda against the socialist regime'. (He had spent seven years in prison for protesting against the incoming communist government in the 1960s, before he married my mother.) Writing about my father gave me a kind of certainty that he was still alive and it was something that my mother, my brother and sister, as well as our larger family, very much liked. Our collective grief was being given words which eased the pain.

In 1985, after my sister, my brother and I were denied access to the schools we wanted to attend and my mother was being pushed from one menial job to the next (at one point being even refused the job of feeding cows at the collective farm nearby), she was 'advised' to divorce my father to prove to the Party that she would not 'pollute' her children's minds with 'anti-communist propaganda'. My father was brought across the country, from the Aiud prison to our town. We saw him being taken from the black van into the courtroom. He was handcuffed, his feet were in chains. Many people found out about this 'public trial' and a crowd began to chant his name under the windows of the court-room. After the divorce was finished, my mother and the three of us children got separated from each other: we were all dazed. I don't remember which buses each of us took home but my mother asked me to wash the windows in the kitchen. I wrote about the divorce with my fingers on the dust of the window. Then she asked me to put it on paper. I guess that might have been one time when I knew that writing was 'important' for keeping the day alive in our minds. So I tried to be as faithful as I could to the experience and to what I was feeling. I must have been fifteen years old. When we left the country, my little notebook, with what might be called the root of my book *Crossing the Carpathians*, was confiscated.

My experience of writing poetry in English can best be explained by telling you about the making of the poem about my parents' divorce. In Romanian, years ago, I called it 'Divortul' or 'The Divorce'. When I began dreaming in English and when the words started to come to me in English, I felt an undercurrent of newness inside. There was freedom and exhilaration: my tongue was slowly getting untied and I wanted to see what it all sounded like in my new language. First I wrote what I remembered of the poem in Romanian and then I tried to translate it: it was called, successively, 'The Courtroom', 'An Oath of Love' and finally 'The Divorce'. Many of the first English versions had too many explanations in them: why my mother was forced to divorce, what happened in the courtroom – as though the whole history of the country needed to be told just so that the poetry itself could come through. Then, as I got more settled in my 'far away' place, I learned how the narrative could be put into images which conjure back the narratives. And so it happened with many other poems, until the English language began to thrill me with its sounds and the Romanian words never returned to translate the poems back. Lately I think that it would take much effort to put the culture I am writing from now into the Romanian culture I had left just before the Revolution. And if I tried to write in Romanian now, it would be more like going back home on an old (linguistic) map.

But there is more to it than that. People ask me so often why I do not write in Romanian that I think about it long and hard. First, I do not want to write in the language in which my family suffered inter-rogations, prison visits, threats of all kinds. I certainly do not want to remember all the times when we wrote to each other and burned our words: we were surveyed twenty-four hours a day for the last five years that I lived in my country and everything we said was recorded by microphones set up around the house. I hated subtexts, lies, the fear of words. Now I belong to those people who write in a learnt language. And I belong to those who strive to define their responsibilities as people who were born in one country and live quite willingly in another. This might seem to many the kind of thing one 'grows out' of. But the reason why one writes in one's native language, from exile, is that the native language has beauty and truth in it. Poets write in their native language to remember the warmth of their home, the customs of their villages and towns, their happy youth. They want to recreate a sense of home, a warm cocoon around the icy experience of exile. But my exile is my cocoon. I like it here in English more than I like remembering kids calling me 'daughter of criminal' in my native language: that never sounded safe or good or home. When I stopped looking behind my back to see if anyone was following me to harm me, I stopped looking at writing poetry in my native language. I think the poems themselves make my choice seem less harsh or less impertinent. In my situation it is not that bad to be on the side of forgetting.

Carmen Bugan (1970–) was born in Romania and emigrated to the US with her family in 1989, following her father's imprisonment for protesting against the Ceauşescu regime, and educated in the US and UK. Her books include two collections of poetry, *Crossing the Carpathians* and *The House of Straw*; a critical study, *Seamus Heaney and East European Poetry in Translation: Poetics of Exile*, and a memoir, *Burying the Typewriter: Childhood Under the Eye of the Secret Police*.

José Rosas Ribeyro (1949–) belongs to a group of Peruvian poets who came to prominence in the 1970s. Formed by the events of the 60s, including the military takeover of 1968 that was initially seen by many as Marxist and liberating, his poems occasionally resemble those by American and English poets of the time in their subject-matter, loose structure and deliberately non-poetic language.

JOSÉ ROSAS RIBEYRO

My Grandfather

My grandfather, alcoholic and asthmatic,
felt persecuted in the old streets of Liverpool;
he wandered about beneath the heavy grey cloud
with a smile on his round face
wearing out the cuffs on his white shirt.
He was a lover of the mystical. His weakness and strength
that set him apart and burdened him
with a purely metaphysical solitude.
My grandfather: a Peruvian in exile everywhere (I remember
a photo of him sitting on deck in a white suit
with a friend and a small dog).
He read the Romantics in English
and backdated newspapers in Spanish. He strolled around
reciting Shelley and Keats aloud or scribbled
in his thick notebook, his journal,
bits of poetry and various other illegible things
in both languages which along with some 18th- and 19th-century books were all he
        left us;
He makes me suffer
The faculty of imagination is the great spring of human activity
and the principal source of human improvement.
When, when shall I be master of myself?
(His handwriting was elegant; for him everything was
a matter of the moment.)
Belisario – his name, a family one
handed down from father to son – spent his summers
in Supe frequenting consulates and brothels
or dubious bars. My grandfather, a rotten businessman,
was driven out of various companies through irresponsibility.
Most nights he almost suffocated with the asthma
and died at forty-odd
in his sleep.

Translated from the Peruvian Spanish by C.A. de Lomellini and David Tipton

DAN PAGIS

Instructions for Getting across the Border

Fictitious man, get going. Here's your passport.
Remember, you are forbidden to remember.
These are the particulars you must answer to
(your eyes are already blue).
And don't try to escape
with the sparks and the smoke
through the locomotive chimney.
You are a man, and you'll sit in a coach. Relax.
After all, the suit's respectable,
the body patched,
the new name ready on your tongue.
Get going.
Remember, you are forbidden to forget.

Translated from the Hebrew by Robert Friend

INGEBORG BACHMANN

Exile

I am a dead woman walking
no longer registered anywhere
unknown in the prefect's domain
superfluous in the golden cities
and in the flowering countryside
wiped-out now for a long time
with nothing granted me

Only sound and wind and time
I who cannot live among men

With the German tongue
surrounding me like a cloud
above me like a roof
I stray through all tongues

O, how black grow
the sounds of the wind
the few alone fall

And the body is borne aloft to brighter regions.

Unattributed translations from the German made for the Spoleto Festival

Memories of Ingeborg Bachmann
and Modern Poetry in Translation

When Helga and I left London in 1961 most of our friends still lived there. These included Ted Hughes and Daniel Weissbort, two of the closest. Many years were to pass before our house in Wales had a telephone; we kept in touch with old friends by fleeting visits to London and by occasional letters. In 1965, from letters, and from the press, we became aware of the invasion of London by exotic poets and of a sudden fever of poetry readings. In letters, talk of *MPT* now took its place alongside news of pregnancies and children. And gossip, such as Danny's account of an evening on which Ted had rescued Voznesensky from the clutches of Ginsberg and Ferlinghetti.

MPT, beginning almost as a *jeu d'esprit* reliant upon friends and friends of friends, soon – conceived at an opportune moment – found itself the hub of a wide circle of writers. At some early stage I must have offered to translate some German. Ted sent a copy of Enzensberger's *Gedichte. Die Entstehung eines Gedichts* (1962). Some of the poems in that volume must have been recommended to him. I translated several, but as I worked on them my enthusiasm waned. If I got so far as sending versions, they were not published. What I did turn to were poems from Ingeborg Bachmann's *Die gestundete Zeit* and *Anrufung des Großen Bären*, two volumes of which Helga had copies. Some of these translations appeared in the third issue of *MPT*, others in the later 'Special Issue' and in *Delos*.

Danny or Ted must fairly early on have made contact with the National Translation Center at Austin, Texas, a well-endowed foundation. I was put in touch with the director, Keith Botsford. From him I heard that the Board, although for the greater part poets, was more partial to translations of old classics than translations of modern poetry. But Keith Botsford was a persuasive man and game for most things. He wrote to offer me $500 to complete a translation of all Bachmann's published poems. With this promise I was able in 1967 to take three months' unpaid leave and spend a summer travelling with Helga across Europe in an old Rover with four children ranged across the back seat. I must have been given Bachmann's address by Ted, who had written to her about my translations. I wrote to arrange to meet in Rome in September. So it came about that Helga and I called on her in her flat in Via Bocca di Leone. We for our part, while we knew much of her writing, had at that time no inkling of the extraordinary path of Bachmann's life up to that point. On her side, I could not help sensing a certain bemusement at a visitation from the provinces by this modest couple with their four small daughters in tow.

I completed the translations and sent copies to Texas and to Bachmann. I did nothing more about them at that time. After Bachmann's death, Michael Schmidt at Carcanet, who had been given a copy of the translations by Danny, was eager to publish them as a book. He tried hard, without luck, to obtain copyright permission. His letters to the agent met first with obstruction (the translations were 'too literal') and then with refusal to reply. I in the meantime had entered more deeply into the absorbing habitat of old Welsh manuscripts, where the hazards were fewer and more tractable.

The poet Ingeborg Bachmann (1926–1973) was born in Austria. Karen Leeder writes: 'Although she published only two collections of poetry before being overtaken by a crisis which led her away from the lyric genre, she is one of the most significant German poets of the 20th century. Bachmann's arrival on the poetry scene with her first collection, *Die gestundete Zeit* ('Mortgaged time') in 1953 was a major media event. At the age of 27 she was awarded the coveted prize of the 'Gruppe 47', and a year later the news magazine *Der Spiegel* ran a title story and cover photograph of her. Her initial celebrity had as much to do with her exoticism as with the sense that she gave voice to a particular historical moment. She challenged the expansive consumerist thinking and security of the restorative programmes of the 1950s, by illuminating an altogether darker side of progress.'

Bachmann's work was published repeatedly by *Modern Poetry in Translation* right from the early years of the magazine: in 1967 a large selection of translations by Daniel Huws, Michael Hamburger and others was published alongside some translations made for the festival in Spoleto, Umbria. A special poetry 'Festival dei Due Mondi' took place in Spoleto in 1965 and Ted Hughes attended, along with Ingeborg Bachmann, Miroslav Holub, Evgeny Evtushenko and Pablo Neruda.

From 'Contribution to the Debate on National Poetry'

Let the poet draw on the best of himself, that which reflects the essential values of his country, and his poetry will be national. Better yet, it will be a message for all, a fraternal message crossing all frontiers. What is important at the outset is what Césaire calls 'the right to initiative', in other words, freedom of choice and action.

Black Africa was systematically deprived of that freedom, for colonisation laid hands on its material wealth, dismembered its old communities, and made a clean sweep of its cultural past in the name of a civilisation conveniently called 'universal'. It must be added that this 'universal vocation' did not mean making the Peul, the Fouta or the Baoule of Ivory Coast a citizen enjoying the same rights as a good peasant from Beauce or a Parisian intellectual. It was merely a matter of permitting a certain number of Africans that veneer of education necessary and sufficient to the production of a herd of local bureaucrats prepared to carry out all tasks.

Of course there was no question of learning the local languages in school, or of using the imposed language to teach the true history of the great empires of the continent. *Our Ancestors the Gauls...*, etc....

This was the situation at the time that the modern African poets found themselves forced to resort to the colonists' own means of expression.

One can straightaway see the dangers.

1. The African creator, deprived of his language and cut off from his people, runs the risk of becoming the mere representative of a literary current (and no less gratuitous) of the conquering nation. His work, the perfect illustration of the policy of assimilation in its style and inspiration, will no doubt earn the warn approval of a certain type of critic. In reality, this praise is calculated above all to serve the colonising power which, when it cannot maintain its subjects as slaves, turns them into intellectuals subservient to Western literary currents. This is, in fact, another form of retrogression.

2. Originality at all costs is also a danger. Under the pretext of being loyal to 'Négritude', the African artist may allow himself to 'inflate' his poems with words borrowed from the native tongue and to seek out the

'typical' at every turn. Believing that he 'revives the great African myths' with excessive tom-toms and tropical mysteries, he will in fact reflect the reassuring image that the colonialist bourgeoisie wants to see. This is the surest way of creating a 'folkloric' poetry, whose appreciation is limited to certain circles that talk about 'Negro Art'.

One hardly needs to underline the fact that the true African poet, conscious of his mission, refuses both assimilation and facile Africanism.

He knows that by writing in a language which is not his brothers', he cannot truly interpret the deep song of his country. But, by asserting the presence of Africa with all its contradictions and its confidence in the future by struggling through his writing to end colonial rule, the Black artist who writes in French contributes to the renaissance of our national cultures.

Thus it does not matter whether his firm and open song explodes in alexandrines or free verse, provided that it breaks the ear-drums of those who do not want to hear him and that it cracks like a whip over the selfishness and conformity of the social system. Form exists only to serve thought and the only heritage that matters is the tenderness of a poem by Éluard, the radiant lucidity of Nâzim Hikmet, the 'unbound storm' of Pablo Neruda.

Translated from the French by Paol Keineg and Candace Slater

David Diop (1927–1960) was born in Bordeaux of a Senegalese father and a mother from the Cameroon. He was one of the founders of the literary magazine *Présence Africaine* in 1947 where this prose was originally published in 1956. He was teaching in Guinea when he was killed in a plane crash: all his manuscripts, including a new collection of poems, disappeared with him.

DAVID DIOP

Testimony

I was not born for profit-making plantations
I was not born for reptiles' kisses
I was not born for publicising alcohol
I was not born for citadels of sand
I was not born to manufacture death
From the Asian jungles to the Niger River
I was not born to act in minstrels' shows
I was not born for the automatic military salute
Oh that call that comes to me from the sky
The dark caravan of receding despair
And now the moist wing of Victory
Brushes my waiting heart as it whirls downward
I was born to break with stones
The tough shell of our false paradise
To cry Africa's impatience to the vast red sky
To caress the mobile bronze of Black women
And to live to live the anxious nights of Freedom.

Translated from the French by Paol Keineg and Candace Slater

GABRIELA MISTRAL

The Foreigner

She talks with an accent of her savage seas
that have who-knows-what kind of seaweed and sand;
she says a prayer to God without form or weight
looking old, old, as if she was going to die.
That garden of ours, which she made odd to us,
has produced cactus and grasses that scratch you.
Her breathing is the breath of the wilderness,
she has loved with a passion that makes her blanch,
which she never mentions and which would be like
the map of another star if she told us.
She will live among us for eighty years, but
she will always be as if she had just arrived,
speaking a gasping, whining sort of language
that only little animals understand.
One night when she is suffering more, she will
die among us, with only her destiny
for a pillow: her death will be hushed, *foreign.*

Translated from the Chilean Spanish by Arthur McHugh

Gabriel Mistral (1889–1957) was the pseudonym of Lucia Godoy y Alcayaga, a Chilean writer. She was born in a village in the High Andes. She worked as a schoolteacher until her poetry made her famous, and then she was able to influence education policy in Chile and Mexico. She was a recipient of the Nobel Prize in Literature in 1945.

Soleïman Adel Guémar (1963–) was born into a Berber family in Algiers. As an investigative journalist in the 90s he was subject to increasing violence and threats. He came to the UK in 2002 and applied for asylum and he and his family now have indefinite leave to remain in the UK. Translator Tom Cheesman writes: 'Adel Guémar's poetry is unavoidably political. It can be as brutally cruel as his country's experiences, but its mainstay is a passionate belief in human rights and dignity.'

SOLEÏMAN ADEL GUÉMAR

False Departure

1

must I eat great mouthfuls of dust
again – standing in for you –
in order to tell those masks
of absence and ugliness
cradled by sluts and marvels
what they don't want to hear
or go away – but where to? –
in order to put an end
to your cat-startled poses
to be made numb for ever

2

I'm going away to where the sun
shines less gently than here
but the very greyness tunes
the strings of sad guitars
born under the wandering star
damned to the end of time
for having committed dreams
deep in overcrowded dead-ends

tell me to wait a little longer...

all it needed was a No
to the high officials
in the watchtowers above!

3

act as if everything was possible
for the child who used to wish
that Algiers would be the loveliest
of all the brides

Translated from the French by Tom Cheesman and John Goodby

OVID

From Tristia

I

My friend, until you have been cursed
to wander, kinless, foreign lands where range
barbarians so foul the farmer goes
with a machete strung across his back
simply to milk his kine, you cannot know
time's secret ministries: how it can crawl
like a disease that steals
so sly upon a man he barely feels
its subtle victories; or like an army
marching at half speed. It's true: I have bogged down
in this forgotten outpost. Do not upbraid
narrowness of theme: I never wrote
to better purpose than when I implore
Augustus to be merciful.

II

I have bogged down here: a spit of land, a fistula
in the oxter of an Empire I once served.
In winter, the ocean freezes. Brigands
drive chariots over the ice, terrorise
farmers, raze the homesteads. Women
and livestock are seized while men are lashed
to stakes, compelled to watch their crops destroyed.
Leander would have found apt use
for such a frozen waste: he would have walked
the Hellespont's vault of glass, but those old
tales are not told here. Confined to bed,
I draft my epitaph: *Time that mocks*
bright blades with rust makes soft the bones
of him that lies here: Naso, who died for love.

III

Tristis lupus. I fall asleep among the men
and hear the voice of Erisychthon carry
over the trembling water. Hear him hawk
his trembling daughter, watch him cadge
a plate of food. Hear him howl
as wolves, grown fearful, leave off hunting
to watch each other starve. I need
no oread to tell me exile is
a parable of my oppressor's anger:
when I imagined Scythia,
the permafrost where Hunger
scavenges, I knew how finely calibrated
a deadfall I had found. Fate licked her teeth.
I woke among the keening wolves.

IV

The gods flee to the stars where they become
daft stories poets use
to show their mastery of form;
an exercise in rhyme.

Perhaps a corner yet remains in Rome
that holds in reverence the name
of one who versed with bite:
wherever poets meet

let the best chair stand empty;
let them remember
Naso, who would not stoop to wring
old metre from a heathen tongue,

who shamed the gods with his inventions
and found men less forgiving.

V

My favourites? Those who shamed the gods.
My favourite theme? Divine punishment
carried over, as when, naked at the window,
Arachne translates Jove's assembled rapes
enraptured by her own accomplishment.
A tapestry like that will make her name.
Poor girl. Let's watch until she disappears:
it won't take long (though longer than you'd think),
Minerva jealoused her the day she was born.
Close by, a well trimmed taper sobs
over a rack of shuttles and pins. I note
the bunched back; the way she shows
an almost human eagerness to clinch
her theme; the dwindling spinnerets…

VI

I watch you wave and when you disappear
become a house where nobody lives,
an old façade decayed, a pillow bereft
of the smell of your hair. A stranger asks
but nobody can place who lived in that
boarded-up ruin children say is haunted,
where manuscripts lie strewn about the floor;
where lemon trees have overrun the orchard;
where, in the quartered fields, stogged wheat
reeks like a byre and rape holds sway.
You wave your arms and crows
scatter like crows. And that's the pose
in which I've held you (waiting, open armed)
for seven years. And I'm still here.

In a version by Paul Batchelor

In AD 8 Augustus Caesar relegated Publius Ovidius Naso to Tomis (now
Constanța in Romania). Ovid spent his time in Tomis writing *Tristia* ('The
Sorrows'). Paul Batchelor writes of his version: 'Realising how much the Ovid of
Tristia was a persona made me less inhibited about trying on the mask myself'.

DIMITRIS TSALOUMAS

Rain I

Lately there's been someone at my door
Or so it seems, a discreet tap-tapping.
But all my likely visitors have left
With the first rains. Sometimes I think
A southerly is trying at the openings;
Others I suppose it is only the rain,
The rain's particular cacophony.

Again tonight – until I ask, 'Who's there?'
And think I hear the answer: 'Me.'
I open – and blame my ears. Another time
Say who you are, my friend. I want
A clearer voice than the rain in the guttering.
Don't make me open my door again,
Without a word, only for the desolate night.

Translated from the Greek by Helen Constantine with the author

Dimitris Tsaloumas (1921–) arrived in Australia from the Greek Island of Leros at the age of 30 in 1952. For ten years after his move he did not write, and then began writing again in 1963. Helen Constantine writes: 'This voluntary exile has not been particularly easy for Tsaloumas. He has lived in a state of perpetual conflict, often attended by guilt and a feeling of divided loyalties, and has always given the impression of someone at odds with the society he lives in.'

Rain II

Listen! Like a presence again
Outside my door, like a murmuring
This time, like conversation.
And I see my mother on the doorstep
And a forgotten brother of long ago.

Mother, we were lost, we were lost
But how tonight in such rough weather
And wherever did you find the child
In times like these, in such upheaval?
Not on the carpet with all that mud.
Leave your shoes on the step.

The child said nothing; but the mother found the house
Tidy; and she was glad.

Then we went down into underground places,
We lost each other on dark streets
While the sirens were sounding in panic
And I was pushing blindly at the doors of strangers
Feeling for my door in the dark.
But how can you enter without a key?
Who would open his door to me?
I sit here now and rack my brains
On the thought of that lost key.

Translated from the Greek by Helen Constantine with the author

From 'The Poet, neither Guide nor Prophet'

3. No people has ever lived without poetry. But often this people's poetry has been rejected, not acknowledged. Those who bewail its lot in mouldy lines flatter and betray its source. Instead of listening to it, they become its self-appointed spokesman and write whatever comes to mind. In such cases, it is not poetry which dies, but we ourselves who die to poetry and life.

To listen to time.

To listen to the earth.

There is no poetry that emerges from a void. It can be born of silence. From a wound. From a badly battered land and people. The poem scorns geography. It is the sun's hand and the sky of pregnant countries. The sea speaks and the wave turns in the hands of the child who tears the veil. The poem is a roadblock on the linear way. The poem spells out the star and urgent future.

'The poem of the future is a rebellious country.'

(Adonis)

4. The poem includes within itself all meanings: those most essential, the least immediate but most urgent.

The poem is not an equation that explains the world, but a new relationship between men and it.

Nonsense is a plausible seduction: nothing is clear, so do not ask the poet to be clear, like a sportswriter. When an author is asked to be clear, one demands that he changes not his style, but his ideas. (Abdelkébir Khatibi).

We do not seek hermeticism.

But poetry is merely the reflection of complex depths. Life in all its plenitude is not clear, the relationship between two human beings is not necessarily clear; love is not something clear. Therefore let us stop asking the poet to be clear.

5. Poetry takes words to their limits, where it rediscovers the virgin nature of the verb. To rediscover that virginity is to shatter language. Revolutionary poetry cannot be conceived of through an established language; but demands the creation of a new form of expression. Words are words. Precisely words. Dangerous. We become involved

through words. For the moment, we are still the concubines of words. We wait for the word to triumph.

6. *'To understand a poem is above all else to hear it.'* (Octavio Paz). To hear it with our eyes. To interiorise it, to act in such a manner that it lives within our body and our present and future memory. To live the poem. You cannot explain a poem. It is open to all possibilities, to all ways of hearing. It needs accomplices.

...

8. Why listen to the people?

No individual can consider himself the centre of the universe. So, the false poet, as Octavio Paz says, speaks of himself, nearly always in the name of the others. The true poet speaks to others in speaking to himself. He speaks *with* others. When it vents its joy or anger, when it thrills to life's call, the People is the only, supreme poem. The poet remains attentive to every creative possibility of a developing people. To speak of woman, sex, factories or earth are only some of the ways to participate in a country's growth and development. It is everywhere, within each of us. There is not a 'popular' poetry as opposed to poetry per se. There is only one poetry; and it so happens that the people possess it. But it is silent. It listens to time and what time says. It is the poem.

Translated from the French by Paol Keineg and Candace Slater

Tahar Ben Jelloun (1944–) is a Moroccan writer who has spent much of his life in Paris, after he was arrested and imprisoned in a military camp for participating in student riots in 1966. Although his first language is Arabic, he writes in French and has achieved fame as a French novelist. This prose was written shortly after he moved to France in 1972.

MARINA TSVETAEVA

From 'Poem of the End'

1

A single post, a point of rusting
   tin in the sky
marks the fated place we
   move to, he and I

on time   as death is
   prompt   strangely
too smooth the gesture of
   his hat to me

menace at the edges of his
   eyes   his mouth tight
shut   strangely too low is the
   bow he makes tonight

on time?   that false note in
   his voice, what
is it the brain alerts to and the
   heart drops at?

under that evil sky, that sign of
   tin and rust
Six o'clock. There he is waiting
   by the post.

Now we kiss soundlessly, his
   lips stiff as
hands are given to queens, or
   dead people thus

round us the shoving elbows of
   ordinary bustle
and strangely irksome rises the
   screech of a whistle

howls like a dog screaming
    angrier, longer: what
a nightmare strangeness life is
    at death point

and that nightmare reached my waist
    only last night
and now reaches the stars, it has
    grown to its true height

crying silently love love until
    – Has it gone
six, shall we go to the cinema?
    I shout it: home!

2

And what have we come to?
    tents of nomads
thunder and drawn swords over
    our heads, some

terror we expect
    listen   houses
collapsing in the one
    word: home.

It is   the whine of a cossetted
    child lost, it is the
noise a baby makes for
    give and *mine*.

Brother in dissipation, cause
    of this cold fever, you
hurry now to get home just
    as men rush in leaving

like a horse jerking the
    line   rope down in the dust.
Is there even a building there?
    Ten steps before us.

A house on the hill   no higher   a
    house on the top of the hill and
a window under the roof   *is it*
    from the red sun alone

it is burning?   or is it my life
    which must begin again? how
simple poems are: it means I
    must go out into the night
                  and talk to

who shall I tell my sorrow
    my horror greener than ice?
– You've been thinking too much.
    A solemn answer: yes.

3

And the embankment   I hold
    to water   thick and solid as
if we had come to the hanging
    gardens of Semiramis

to water   a strip as colourless
    as a slab for corpses
I am like a female singer holding
    to her music. To this wall.

Blindly   for you won't return
    or listen, even if I bend to
the quencher of all thirst, I am
    hanging at the gutter of a roof.

Lunatic. It is not the river
    (I was born naiad) that makes me
shiver now, she was a hand I held
    to, when you walked beside me, a lover

and faithful.
           The dead are faithful

though not to all in their cells; if
    death lies on my left now,
it is at your side I feel it.

Now a shaft of astonishing light, and
    laughter   that cheap tambourine.
– You and I must   have a talk. And
    I shiver: let's be brave, shall we?

Translated from the Russian by Elaine Feinstein

Marina Tsvetaeva (1892–1941) was one of Russia's greatest poets. She grew up in Moscow's wealthy bohemian circles, but revolution and civil war intervened and she spent much of her adult life in exile and desperate poverty. She returned to the Soviet Union in 1939. It was a terrible mistake: her husband was shot, her daughter imprisoned and Tsvetaeva, unable to earn a living to support herself, committed suicide.

Poet Elaine Feinstein's translations of Tsvetaeva (in collaboration with scholar and translator Angela Livingstone) were some of the first translations in the English language and they appeared in *Modern Poetry in Translation* when Tsvetaeva's work was still heavily censored in Russia. They had a profound effect on writers and readers here.

From 'Marina Tsvetaeva'

It is more than a quarter of a century now since I first began to make versions of the poems of Marina Tsvetaeva with the help of Angela Livingstone's word for word literal translations and notes. I had no earlier experience as a translator, little Russian, and no clear idea of why I was so drawn to a poet whose exile, neglect and suicide were tragedies out of all proportion to the difficulties of my own life. Yet there was something in me that responded to her story when I first read an account of her in the pages of Boris Pasternak and Simon Karlinsky. I fumbled towards an understanding of what we might have in common: disorganisation perhaps; an otherworldly eccentricity. Vera Traill, who became a close friend of mine in Cambridge, once offended me greatly by complaining of Tsvetaeva's housewifely ineptness while eyeing my disordered kitchen.

In the late 60s, I had published only one book of poems and felt very much an outsider in a world of English poetry which was then predominantly male. In the English tradition, women poets from Christina Rossetti to Stevie Smith were spinsterly figures, often devoutly Christian, and even when I admired them, they hardly related closely to my own life. As I began to work on 'Poem of the End', I recognised something in Tsvetaeva's work I could not find expressed elsewhere: an unguarded passion, and a desperation that arose from it, which was willing to expose the most undignified emotions. Even as I struggled to find ways of channelling such intensity into a workable English idiom, I was beginning to be seduced by her example. I wanted to take the same risks in my own writing.

For Tsvetaeva, her own life was the material of her art. She even said: 'I don't love life as such. If I were taken beyond the ocean into Paradise and forbidden to write I would refuse the ocean and Paradise.' And the extravagance of that hyperbole connected to something in myself. Yet these were the last days of what used to be called The New Movement; naked autobiography was thought to be embarrassing or even indecent; any propositions had to be hedged with a 'perhaps' or 'probably'. [...]

Tsvetaeva's assurance that what she was doing was *important* made her a source of strength for many women poets. For all the sadness of her own death in Yelabuga, they sensed that she fought to stay alive, and was an exhilarating counter-force to the allure of Plath and Sexton. For the centenary of Tsvetaeva's birth a number of women poets gathered in the Purcell Room in London's Festival Hall to read their very different versions of her poems. It was an extraordinary occasion, the packed hall offering evidence of her power as an iconic figure even among those to whom the Russian language was completely unknown. Afterwards, we all talked about the nature of her influence. I remembered she had once remarked scornfully that although she knew she would be the most important person in the memoirs of those men who counted her among their friends, 'she had never counted in the masculine present'. But it was felt that even though, unlike Akhmatova, she was more commonly the lover than the beloved, her amazing stamina and dedication went beyond her need to be needed. We marvelled at the toughness with which she was able, as her daughter wryly noted, to 'subordinate any concerns to the interests of her work, I insist, *any*'. [...]

When I first came to work on the first translations from Tsvetaeva, I was already impatient with the forms of current English poetry. I had begun to look across the Atlantic to William Carlos Williams, to Charles Reznikoff, to Black Mountain poets such as Olson and Ed Dorn (who was a visiting lecturer at the time I was teaching at the University of Essex). I was part of a group of *English Intelligencer* poets who followed Jeremy Prynne; they came and sat on my Trumpington floor in the 60s. From these I drew techniques which helped me to find equivalents for the movement of Tsvetaeva's poetry: em spaces rather than dashes, for example. More important for my own development as a poet, though, were my attempts to preserve her stanzaic structure. Since then, I have never written completely open verse; what I wanted was to feel the rush of rhythm flowing down the page, the checks and constraints of the shape of the verse structure. [...]

Not many of us will be tested as Tsvetaeva was tested by poverty, isolation and desperation. In our own smaller lives, we learn what we can. In my own development, I know exactly how much I learnt from her technically; for instance, the use of personae, particularly from classical mythology. Like characters in fiction or drama, personae allow poets to penetrate other lives without forfeiting their own patterns of feeling. [...]

It's hard to predict, but I shall probably not do many more translations. The pressure is elsewhere: in the work of understanding, and confronting the passing of time. Even if I do, it is unlikely I shall once again have the good fortune to find such a life-transforming figure as Marina Tsvetaeva.

RIDHA ZILI

Ifrikya the centre of my being

Hard black bread
I gnaw you every morning
and grow drunk on that white
wine
which tastes of death
throughout the day and night
I drink you
I drink to my fill
to quiet my colonised rage

Ifrikya

I live with your hope
the men sow seeds
the bagpipes play at night
the snakes sing like
sirens

Hard black bread
I gnaw you every morning
I am proud of this wine
which moistens my eyelids
I grow bored on my hard bed
dreaming of the sun
the sea
like a fly in the vast desert
ignorant of this world
Hard black bread
I gnaw you every morning
you are harder
than during the time that I gnawed stones

Let
each of you know
your children have no honey
you always sigh
let each of you know
unhappy men
the snow which fans its wings
and sleepless nights
have no sadder hue
than the funeral flowers
of weightless silence

Hard black bread
I gnaw you every morning
so that my heart aches
My veins burst with blood
storms and floods
my joys are torrential

Give me back
the velvet love
of a sky I can touch
the twinkling stars
dancing tiptoe

Dead or alive
Ifrikya
I want to return to you
Ifrikya
native land
Ifrikya centre of my being.

Translated from the French by Paol Keineg and Candace Slater

Ridha Zili (1943–2011) was a Tunisian poet and photographer, who wrote all his poetry in French, despite his schooling in Arabic. *Ifrikya* is the Arabic name for Africa.

YANNIS RITSOS

Return

The statues left first. The trees soon after,
the people and the animals. The place
was utterly deserted. A wind came. Newspapers
hurried along the streets, and thorn-twigs.
At night the lights came on of their own accord.
On his own, a man came back; he looked round,
took out a key, and pressed it to the earth
as if passing it to an underground hand
or planting a tree. Afterwards he climbed
the marble steps and looked out over the city.
One by one, cautiously, the statues returned.

Translated from the Greek by Robert Hull

Yannis Ritsos (1909–1990) was a poet and activist. Arrested after the Greek
military coup in 1967, he was exiled to Leros. His poetry was often banned and
even publicly burnt.

The Tower of Steps

You bridge the town below with the town above.
Your steps are made of spears
that pierce the spines of some stars, true,
but mostly the spines of dragons.

At the bottom, a golden barrel
stuffed with comets, words,
and tears, mostly tears.

The green eye of the moss
lights your way
and silence alone is your fortress.

Whoever enters through your narrow door
will walk the green path forever.

Someone pulls the curtains
on the tower of Sibiu
and I'm facing the tower of Manhattan
where the poet returns each winter
to unspool memories of a feverish childhood.
The only stairs in the stairless hotel:
a crucifix.

Translated from the Romanian by Mihaela Moscaliuc

Liliana Ursu was born in Sibiu, Romania and has been widely translated into
English. Mihaela Moscaliuc notes how the poems are 'often anchored in the
landscapes of her native Romania, in the soul and history of places such as
Brașov, Sibiu or ancient monasteries'.

LILIANA URSU

Between the Wheat Wells and the Bridal Mirrors

In the Main Square, where rope-makers sell rope
and shoe-makers shoes,
the shadow of the three moons floating evenings above town
is caught in the butterfly net of children,

while furrier Brid fills his well with wheat.
The same happens in the Little Square
where Nicolaus the Goldsmith places the clean fruit of his work
in the cabinet under the three moons floating evenings
above town

Who will spark the blades and kitchen knives
now that the sharpener's house has been demolished
and Sibiu shimmers with June bugs.

Luckily, the poet has a working room for bridal mirrors
and a net for catching beautiful dreams
not too far from the Bark Mill.
Each night, down in the Golden Valley, he flies kites made of poems
penned with his friend, J G Bayer, hat-maker and illustrious orator.

Translated from the Romanian by Mihaela Moscaliuc

Joan Ariete is a Filipino poet from Pampanga who writes in Kapampangan
and Tagalog.

Why I Left

People ask me
why I left the sweeping green
and brown of my dew-blessed land.
Pampanga, where men get drunk half-naked
and rage at the relentless sun
that burns their hearts,
their wavering resolve.
Where at dawn they wake up to menthol cigarette smoke,
and the crackling laughter
of wives who dye their hair a shameless burgundy.
Where shoeless children play,
dragging calloused feet through puddles of wasted time.

I will not lie.
Leaving Pampanga is a badge I wear,
a row of shining medals on my chest,
a scar on my cheek.

I packed a bagful of clothes
and my dripping pens.

When my country failed me,
I failed it in return,
and loved it even more.

People ask me
why I left the sweeping green
and brown of my dew-blessed land.
I will not lie.
We are a nation of emigrants:
the only truth I have,
and the only truth there is.

Translated from the Kapampangan by Shon Arieh-Lerer and the author

DENISA COMĂNESCU

Return from Exile

Eleven years, four months and seventeen days.
A short exile?
This notebook isn't the same as then.
I've filled quite a number.
Some were large, bound between gilt covers,
others small, light, made of Bible paper.
At night I touched them in secret,
fingered their membrane-like pages,
each time more urgently, with such
insistent, insatiable desire.
During the day, I didn't dare go near them.
They might as well have been a stranger's.
Later I gave them to friends:
For you, for your new book of poems, I'd tell them.
This brought luck to some, or so they'd pretend.

Then you arrived,
after eleven years, four months and seventeen days.
In the morning, fearless in the light that seems to banish death,
we fill membrane after membrane, simply and naturally.
When I turn a page covered with writing,
Orpheus averts his eyes.

Translated from the Romanian by Adam J. Sorkin

Denisa Comănescu (1954–) is a poet and translator, and Editorial Director of Humanitas Publishing House in Bucharest. She was a founder member of the Civic Alliance in 1990, and Secretary of the Romanian PEN Center from 1990 to 2004.

Seamus Heaney (1939–2013) sent three 'freed' speeches for the 'Freed Speech' issue of *Modern Poetry in Translation* from Virgil's *Aeneid*, titled: 'Aeneas', 'The Sybil' and 'Anchises'. He began translating *Aeneid* after his father died in 1986. The text was, according to his daughter, Catherine Heaney, a touchstone for the poet and something he returned to again and again. Heaney's translation of Book VI of Virgil's *Aeneid* was published in 2016.

VIRGIL

The Sibyl

From Virgil's *Aeneid*, VI, *ll.* 112-139

Meanwhile the Sibyl,
Resisting possession, storms through the cavern,
In the throes of her struggle with Phoebus
Apollo. But the more she froths at the mouth
And contorts, the more he controls her, commands her
And makes her his creature. Then of their own accord
Those hundred vast tunnel-mouths gape and give vent
To the prophetess's responses:

'O you who survived,
In the end, the sea's dangers (though worse still await
On the land), you and your Trojans will come
Into your own in Lavinium: have no fear of that.
But the day is one you will rue. I see wars,
Atrocious wars, and the Tiber surging with blood.
A second Simois river, a second Xanthus,
A second enemy camp lie ahead. And already
In Latium a second Achilles comes forth, he too
The son of a goddess. Nor will Trojans ever be free
Of Juno's harassments, while you, without allies,
Dependent, will go through Italia petitioning
Cities and peoples. And again the cause of such pain
And disaster for Trojans will be as before: a bride
Culled in a host country, an outlander groom.
But whatever disasters befall, do not flinch.
Go all the bolder to face them, follow your fate
To the limit. A road will open to safety
From the last place you would expect: a city of Greeks.'

Translated from the Latin by Seamus Heaney

TADEUSZ RÓŻEWICZ

Chestnut

What is sadder
than to leave the house
of an autumn morning
when nothing speaks of an early return

the chestnut in front of the house planted
before my father's time blooms in our eyes

mother is small
you can carry her in your hands

on the floor stand pots
in which preserves
like goddesses with sweet mouths
retain the flavour
of eternal youth

the soldiers in the corner of the drawer will
still be lead to the end of time

and almighty God who mixed
bitterness with sweetness
hangs on the wall helpless
and badly painted

Childhood is like a worn-out face
on a gold coin which rings
cleanly

Translated from the Polish by Geoffrey Thurley

NINA CASSIAN

I wanted to stay

I wanted to stay behind in September
on the desert, this faded beach.
I wanted my meals to be
the ashes of my false cranes.
To hold the heavy wind in my hair
like water asleep in fishing nets.
Alone by the muscular sea,
I wanted to smoke a cigarette that
glared more than the moon.
I wanted to watch time move –
one hand in the trees and
the other in greying sands.
But it seems I'm meant for stage goodbyes.
I'm meant to wrench myself from places
when my soul isn't ready,
just as I walk away from love
while I still love.

Translated from the Romanian by Laura Schiff and Virgil Nemoianu

Nina Cassian (1924–2014) left Romania in 1985. Her satirical poems about Ceauşescu were found in a friend's flat whilst she was abroad. Fearing for her life she claimed asylum in the States. She wrote many books of poems in Romanian, and was an active translator as well as a poet. In later years she also wrote in English.

Tadeusz Różewicz (1921–2014) was a poet, playwright and novelist, a prolific writer and constant innovator who had a formidable influence on a whole generation of Polish poets. He was widely translated and acclaimed for the 'new' poetic language he forged, which was 'simple, direct and austere, admirably suited to "shout in a whisper" the fears and anxieties of 20th-century man' (from the introduction in *Modern Poetry in Translation*).

Forlorn cuckoo,

your call

keeps us awake

BEWKETU SEYOUM

In Search of Fat

A multitude of thin people, all skin,
call out like rag and bone men,
'Where's our fat?' They rummage
every mountain, stone and huddle-huddle,
search in the soil, search in the sky.
At last they find it, piled up on one man's belly!

Translated from the Amharic by Chris Beckett with the author

Elegy

The fall of every leaf diminishes me,
so when I hear a rustle
I send my eyes out of the window
to look at the trees in the yard.
Alas! where there were woods,
now I see flag-poles standing.
Men have swept nature's nest away
to build their cities.
The melody of the nightingale
has lost its immortality
and I am sitting on a dead land,
writing my elegy in the sand.

Translated from the Amharic by Chris Beckett with the author

'Bewketu Seyoum is a young Ethiopian poet, journalist and satirical novelist. He performs around the country to great hilarity and acclaim. An article he published in 2011, suggesting that religious conservatism was holding Ethiopia back economically and socially, earned him a severe beating by a group of angry deacons!' CB

BEWKETU SEYOUM

Meditation on the Garden

Bunch of grasses,
untrimmed,
you appeared out of my yard
suddenly
and illuminated my spirit,
leading it to hope.

Bunch of grasses,
untrimmed,
you showed me
that the colour of hope is green.

Bunch of grasses,
you appeared suddenly,
as if you had descended with the dew,
you baptised me.

Then I said: 'He who was clad in flesh
and came into the world
but passed in vain,
failing to appease my pain,
He has come back,
clad in grasses,
and hurled away my burden!'

Translated from the Amharic by Chris Beckett with the author

Recalling Rocco

'You have such a beautiful face,' the Tuscan filmmaker said to the old man, continuing to film him after the interview was concluded. He was right. Giuseppe, in his 90s, has a fine face, expressive, strong-boned; it reveals his tough peasant life. In the interview he'd talked about his friendship with the great humanist poet, Rocco Scotellaro (1923–53), who wrote about the impoverished land and people of southern Italy in the 1940s and who at the age of 23 became the first Socialist mayor of his birthplace, Tricarico, in Basilicata, and who was dead by 30.

This September was my second visit to Tricarico. In 2013 I accompanied *MPT*'s then Editors, David and Helen Constantine, for a reading at the *Centro di Documentazione di Rocco Scotellaro e la Basilicata del secondo dopoguerra*. *MPT* had published some Scotellaro poems in 'The Big Green Issue' (2008) and in a pamphlet (2009), both translated by Allen Prowle. Allen and I then collaborated for several years on a longer collection, *Your call keeps us awake*, published by Smokestack Books (2013). That night the great convent hall was packed and the audience spilled out into the courtyard and the rain. Later, local people crowded round us, each with a personal, affectionate story about the poet, as if he'd died only the week before, not 60 years ago. Scotellaro's fiancée, who has kept all his letters and has never married, has only now agreed to talk publicly about him, for this documentary film *Appunti per un viaggio in Lucania.*

As I'd also participated in the film, I was invited to attend the interview with Giuseppe. He sat on the front steps of his small terraced house in the old Arab quarter of Rabata. Inside, the room contained a round wooden table covered by a white tablecloth with four chairs, a comfortable sofa and a large flat-screen TV on the wall. How had his life changed since the old days? 'You'd never throw away bread then, children were dying of hunger. There was no running water.' He pointed down at the narrow cobbled street. 'And this was a dirt track, filthy with shit from the animals brought down to the fields at 3.30 every morning.' Both he and his wife, Antonietta, had worked the fields. It was a hard life. She lost two babies and the couple are childless.

Giuseppe had known Rocco since he was eight. He pulled a cracked black and white photo of his friend from his wallet. It had always been with him, even when he went to work for six years in Germany. 'Rocco was one of us,' he said. 'We were uneducated but he never looked down on us. He'd play *morra** with us and he loved to dance. And, of course, he was always by our side for the land occupations.' At one point he went silent, trembling with emotion, remembering the 'betrayal' when Rocco's political opponents charged him falsely with corruption and he was temporarily imprisoned. Did Rocco know who was responsible? 'He invented a song,' Giuseppe said, 'which he'd sing in public meetings in the town square. It was in dialect. It was oblique but it showed up each of his enemies. He could do that with words. After all, he was a poet.'

*an illegal game of chance played for drinks

ROCCO SCOTELLARO

The Full Moon

Our beds fill with the full moon,
mules pass by on shoes of soft iron,
a dog gnaws its bone.
Under the stairs, you can hear the donkey,
its shudders and scratching.
Under the other stairs
my mother has slept for sixty years.

Translated from the Italian by Allen Prowle

Rocco Scotellaro (1923–1953), socialist mayor of Tricarico, worked tirelessly for land reform. He was imprisoned on false charges by local landowners and died of a heart attack shortly after his release, aged only 30. His poems express his allegiance with peasant life and his intimate knowledge of the conditions peasants endured.

ROCCO SCOTELLARO

Forlorn Cuckoo, Your Call Keeps Us Awake

All round the brown mountains
your colour has crept back,
our old September friend.
You've settled in among us.
When, fleeing the burnt stubble
of our fields, castaway crickets
screech at the doors,
our women have heard you quite close.
From the vaulted ceilings hang
strings of dried figs and green tomatoes;
there's a sack of hard wheat,
a heap of felled almonds.

Forlorn cuckoo,
your call
keeps us awake:
Yes, we'll trudge back along the paths
and, tomorrow, get down to work,
when water streams yellow again
under the furrows,
and the wind billows
our coats in the cupboards.

Translated from the Italian by Allen Prowle

YI LU

Evening Construction Site

workers flip over from the slope
look straight at me with hunger and fatigue

concrete mixers stained with wet mud
stones   grains of sand   reaching a pedestal that sees no daylight

inside naked cables
rubber tubes expose red and blue cords
like an artery unconnected

iron frame   cement components
like huge bones lying in disarray

a pile-driver stands
on a painstricken surface

a light bulb of 100 watts
the brightest silence

translated from the Chinese by Fiona Sze-Lorrain

Yi Lu (1956–) was born in the southern province of Fujian, and is by age
considered a 'second-generation' woman poet in modern China. A theatre-set
designer by profession, she is a private poet associated with neither a
movement nor a school of thought.

EUPHRASE KEZILAHABI

Sorting the Rice

News came from Arusha
and we started sorting the rice of *ujamaa*.
Eyes to the front, eyes to the side, separating the stones,
making a little tomb of tiny stones.

And picked out the broken grains one by one,
our fingers busy like sewing machines.
Day and night – our eyes started hurting –
making a little white anthill of specks.

The pebbles and bits were so many.
We started cooking after a long while of working.
When we sat down to eat
we still found stones and broken grains.

When will we eat without the stones, without the broken grains?

Translated from the Swahili by Annmarie Drury

Euphrase Kezilahabi (1944–) was born in Tanzania and his poems engage with
nation-building and its conundrums. 'Sorting the Rice' (1974) is concerned
with the realities of post-colonial governance: *ujamaa* was the socialist
programme initiated in 1967 by Julius Nyerere, Tanzania's first president.

The Spirit Lord's Bearkill

The highest god, father mine
created me, the shyback oathbear.
I roam the sacred sootbarked earth
where the underlings dwell.
I wade through thickest kneehigh moss.
And found a moor's sunwarm edge.
I chased after sleep, sound enough for neckchopping
I chased after sleep, sound enough for shoulderchopping.
One forepaw I used
for a pillow, tenflapped, trimmed with flaps
which my mother, the Moosj woman, had sewn.
The other forepaw I used as a cover
cut out at the neck, trimmed with swans
which my mother, the Moosj woman, had sewn.

Sleep, sound enough for neckchopping
I chased after.
One earlet of mine eavesdropped on the land
sacred land god dwelled in
heard the true oath's swearingvoice.
One eyelet of mine is overcome by seven jolts of deepsleep.
On my flankerman's flank a deepthroated
throatthunder is rumbling.
The bear's three three leaps I leap
the bear's four four leaps I hop.
I turn around
I twist
my sinewy necknape.

Look how I'm hunted by the whitehorsed man!
The white horse came to a halt at my side.
The sublime flaming sword of Torem appeared
the sacred flaming sword of Torem appeared.
A painsnouted horsefly stung
the sacred bear's little mortal spot.

And I saw:
When I, sacred bear, had my four buttons unbuttoned;
when I, sacred bear, had my fur stripped off.
Into a threeribbed birchbark cradle
am I laid,
in a fourribbed birchbark cradle
do I wake up.
Just look!
I reach the lodge door
streaming with molten gold.
The many village women arrive.
The many village men arrive.
They play watergames.
They play squirtgames.
I am carried through the lodge door
streaming with molten gold.
I may watch the girls' endless pastime.
May watch the boys' endless pastime.
When I am let go
on my way to the great god
I come into the jangling of great money
on my way to the little god
I come into the jangling of little money.

Magibearheyhey!

Translated from the Vogul by Dorothea Grünzweig and Derk Wynand

The Mansi people, or 'Voguls', are part of the Ob-Ugrian group of peoples.
Their homeland lies in West Siberia, beyond the Urals and along the Ob River.
Today some 5500 Mansi remain but their culture suffered under the Soviet
regime and is dying out. Ecocide, especially by oil companies, urban migration
and Putin's repressive policies towards non-Russian cultures have all contributed
to this decline, which one Finnish anthropologist has called genocide.

The texts of their songs were recorded towards the end of the 19th century
by Finnish, German and Hungarian researchers. The songs were accompanied
by a harp of reindeer strings, called 'goose' or 'crane' or 'singing wood' and
they included prayers, magic spells and bear songs.

The belief system of the Mansi includes a vast number of deities and
spirits like the *Moosj*, the forest spirits. The god Torem occupies the highest
place in heavens.

HARRY MARTINSON

Cable-Ship

We fished up the Atlantic cable between Barbados and Tortuga,
held up our lanterns
and patched over the gash on its back,
fifteen degrees north and sixty-one west.
When we put our ears to the gnawed part
we heard the murmuring of the cable.
One of us said: 'It's the millionaires in Montreal and St John's
discussing the price of Cuban sugar
and the lowering of our wages.'

We stood there long, thinking, in a lantern circle,
we patient cable-fishers,
then lowered the mended cable
back to its place in the sea.

Translated from the Swedish by Robin Fulton

The swamp mosses drink of the stream...

The swamp mosses drink of the stream
until it is more and more low-voiced.
It sinks its watery clucking
to a summer whisper, drowned out by midges.
It soon changes to sign-language,
which every tussock knows.
Soon its hidden meaning blossoms up
in moist buckbeam.

Translated from the Swedish by Robin Fulton

Harry Martinson (1904–1978), orphaned at the age of six when his father died and his mother left for the USA, was a sailor for seven years. Thereafter, back in Sweden, he became one of the best-known writers of his generation, winning the Nobel Prize in 1974.

African Anthem

Rainbow, rainbow
Where have you been?
My mother needs a sash
To match her skin.

A shower of colours
To catch her eye,
A garment of light,
Across the sky –

Shining like her face,
Streaming from the sun,
Seven different colours,
To reflect my special one.

One colour's not enough –
Nor one without the other.
All of them must be
Worthy of my mother.

Rainbow, rainbow
Where have you been?
My mother needs a sash
To match her skin.

Translated from the Tigrinya by Charles Cantalupo

Reesom Haile (1946–2003), poet and scholar, came from a traditional farming family in Eritrea. He left his country for twenty years and, returning in 1994, found its languages and poetry 'a bit battered, but well, considering they had been targeted for extinction. But we carried our languages and our art in our memories and our voices and we used them as effectively as we used our weapons to defend ourselves throughout the struggle.'

JACQUES RÉDA

The Fête

Here's a village where they don't much die, it seems
from the look of the tiny graveyard, its tombs
discreet along the walls, as on feast-days
the old leave space for the young who will dance
and maybe lay out a grand night-time picnic.

I'd be happy in this village where they don't much die,
where dead, you're one of the crowd, smartly dressed
as the living make merry, tipping back wine.

Its hollow is sheltered by trees from the past
on a plateau, an ocean floor, you can tell.
Where stone – tomb, hearth – is decked with shells,
where sky lets its blue marine-mammal belly
rest, as if time weren't yet on its way
with rivers and roads from village to village,
with people all rushing to be there next day
for the fête.

Translated from the French by Jennie Feldman

Jacques Réda (1929–), poet, essayist and prose writer, lives in Paris. He says of
his work: 'The topography of the soul – to use a catch-all term – attracts me
as much as that of towns and landscapes. Writing is another way of changing
without necessarily being elsewhere or in a different era: becoming, there and
then, someone else – but only provisionally, since he too will want to change.'

EUPHRASE KEZILAHABI

Thread

Put your left arm on the table
then bend at the elbow
so your fingers touch your cheek.
Allow me to fasten a thread of life
between your thumb and shoulder
so your head becomes an imaginary calabash of my lute
and your heart the thrumming of existence on our journey.
Allow me, then, to play my lute near your ear
and sing you a song of love in old age.

When we started off, I loved the gap between your front teeth.
Now I love the more, the bigger spaces
that I can't fill with any gold of my acts.
Then, your face was uncreased
and your smile with its tiny pools made me crazy.
Now when you spit, the saliva ends up on your chest
but your face wears lines etched by authentic love.

Let's totter ourselves fashionably away,
heads down, counting footsteps of those who've already passed,
each tap of our sticks telling again the love we share.
We're not threatened or harassed by passers-by.
Although we can't thread a needle
to mend our meannesses,
the good things we created with this thread of life
are garlands enough to see us to the grave.

Translated from the Swahili by Annmarie Drury

✦

a lone fox, resembling a thin, peeled

shred of bark...

SHINJIRO KURAHARA

A Fox

In winter twilight in the quiet mountains
a lone fox, resembling a thin, peeled shred of bark,
climbs up
a three-forked, bare tree.

He gives off a strong odour of iron,
closely watching the invisible hunter
climbing up the foothills.
He recognises, too, the sound of his footsteps:
dirty desire.

The fox slowly climbs down from the tree,
and disappears into the four-dimensional desolation,
where the moon-coloured vixen waits for him.

Translated from the Japanese by William Elliott and Katsumasa Nishihara

A Footprint
(Dictated in his last illness)

Long ago
a fox ran along a clayey river bank.
After an interim of ten thousand years
a footprint
turned fossil
remains.
Look at it and you'll see what the fox was thinking while running.

Translated from the Japanese by William Elliott and Katsumasa Nishihara

Shinjiro Kurahara (1899–1965), poet, short-story writer, lover of antiques, left
six volumes of poetry, but is now almost forgotten in Japan.

JÁNOS PILINSZKY

'Creative Imagination' in Our Time

The task set by the title of this lecture surpasses my powers. I can offer only a series of reflections, without a knowledge of deeper interrelations.

If I understand him correctly, Baudelaire makes a sharp distinction between fancy and imagination. It is in the more dilute medium of the surface, in the loose combinations of fantasy that fancy wanders imprisoned. As opposed to this, the 'creative imagination' – insofar as it is combinative and analytic – strives beyond the recognitions gained through analysis, to reach that ultimate, unanalysable simplicity to where the imagination can *find its way home* only at the cost of unquestioning submission. Artistic creation, in a literal sense, is nonexistent. But the submissive imagination may establish contact with that absolute freedom, love, presence, and familiarity with which God chose the world.

In short, what we call 'creative imagination' is nothing else than the sacrifice of the imagination, *passive creation* (next to it, fancy is imagination's venial sin, its chronic childhood disease).

As my choice of words should have revealed by now, for me, art is fundamentally religious in origin, and I feel that each professedly religious work – even a masterpiece – is in a certain sense a paraphrase. (More specifically: once all art is truly rooted in religion, religious art cannot be said to exist, least of all religious literature, given the proximity of sacred texts.)

But then what is the inevitably religious in art?

With our Fall, I believe, not only did our intellect grow dimmer, not only did our will become disposed to viciousness, but our imagination fell into sin with us, flawing, as it were the world's reality, its incarnation, that final consummation and perfection which in creation was originally and naturally entrusted to our imagination.

Our Fall reduced the reality of creation to the irreality of mere existing. *Since then*, art has been *imagination's morality*, its contribution, its toilsome work toward the fulfilment and restitution of the reality and incarnation of creation. 'Et incarnatus est', *since then*, could be the closing phrase, the authenticating seal of every masterpiece.

The fulfilment of this incarnation is absolutely spiritual in nature, and, like prayer and love, freely penetrates the most diverse stations of time. It has a preference for the past, and even there, for the tragic the irreparable, the outrage, the 'insoluble'. It prays for its dead by incarnating them.

Much has been written on the kinship of mysticism and art. Actually these two are the same by being perfect opposites. They are the perfectly coinciding branches of the same road, the same love; ascending from and descending to the same world in the dynamic equilibrium and unfathomable peace of devoted submission and liberated ecstasy. Jacob's ladder, with God's angels ascending and descending, is the common, and only, means of the imagination's finding the way home.

If we now consider our time, we find that the fate of our imagination is rather disquieting and tragic. I would not go as far as to say it has renounced for good its laborious mission, but it has certainly strayed on the wrong path, on the road of heresy. It yielded to its original weakness when it began to covet the certainty of science. Since then, the imagination has led a mirror-existence, hoping to experience in the certainty of style that which should be attained only in the self-forgetfulness of submission, 'with downcast eyes'.

Scientific thought in art – in a strange way – with or without meaning to do so, inaugurated a mirror-age, an age of narcissistic elements. Since then we speak of good stylists. A whole new epoch arrived, placing the stylistic certainty of appearances before the self-forgetful incarnation of the world. We have tried to move into this mirror all the virtues of great literatures, from controlled beauty to controlled ecstasy. Since then, we see all and know all; what's more, we see and know better; but would that we were blind and alive – with our backs to the mirror.

When the soul grows tired, and with it, the imagination, we objectify the world in a style, somewhat as love, grown tired, objectifies the other person in sexuality. In opposition to the always creative shouldering of the world's weight, the spirit of worldliness, corporeality, in a word, materiality, gains the upper hand, heralding the vain rule of an incarnation superficially and for the moment freed, secured – and aggravated.

But, paradoxically, it is we, and we alone, who have become truly blind, just as jealousy's thirst for certainty in the end sees nothing of the other person, corporeality nothing of the body, worldliness nothing of the world. We have lost sight not only of reality, but finally of our chief ambition – experiencing our presence in the world. The modern theatre is an eloquent example of this.

One fine day we awoke to find that what happens on the stage is *nowhere present.* As if the event had lost its predicate. All mimicry – adjectives, nouns, and participles – became useless with the disappearance of that which could realise and establish the event with the powerful verticality of the *hic et nunc.* The theatre of the absurd sought a way out of this totally horizontal drama. Its failure, however, is clear. If, in a de-sacralised and deincarnated world, I choose the verticality of the verb, this event will coincide with the moment of suicide and assassination, with its dimensionless abyss. Hence, just as the theatre of mimicry seeks its *verbs*, the theatre of the absurd is forced to steal its hard and painful adjectives from here and there, to gain some kind of life. Both suffocate in the same lack of air. One wanders in the wasteland of its adjectives without ever really happening, and the other, aside from happening, has no other possibilities. The only difference between the two is that – in their attempts to deceive – one is 'vertical', and the other, 'horizontal'.

We had wanted to be present at all costs, and it is our very presence that we have destroyed.

It is true that in the mirror everything is more intensely together. What falls outside it appears to be nothing. However, it is precisely this nothing which is alone valuable. And since exactly this sole value has turned into a desert, all the riches and surprises of the mirror mean nothing to us.

However, the mirror has a great and disastrous advantage: it is infin-itely manipulable. In our days art protests against the various kinds of manipulation without noticing that art itself had been guilty of this much earlier, and that its mirror-existence gave rise to its unhappy resilience, unfortunate liability, its flair for each and every illusory rebirth.

The question remains: can we break the mirror on our own? I do not know. It is unlikely. I only know that God, from time to time, bleeds through the fabric of history, and by the grace of the situation man again becomes submissive. Auschwitz today is a museum. The dents and scratches we can find on those objects piled up in showcases are the hieroglyphics of our century, our life. An eternal lesson. Those who 'wrote down' these signs probably never lived to compose their sentences. More evidence of how far real things fall outside the calculable borders of personal achievement. Real value (beyond the chaos of publications, amidst the eternal peace and silence of communication), is a table fully laid, where everyone is welcome, and everyone can eat his fill without taking from anyone else. In the divine context: most of the time it is one person who lives out the value, and someone else who writes it down. Does it matter? It is God and He alone who writes, on the fabric of events, or on paper.

I am thinking aloud. Just as there is no individual redemption, there is no collective redemption either. Still, the interpersonal character of an act of kindness, universal in its immediacy, is the concretisation of everyone's everpresence in the 'other person'. Similarly, in the drama of the imagination, there is no way out without the shouldering of the most extreme failings. If the destined pace of today's 'religious artist' is at all determinable, it can only be the position of infinite patience and brotherly sharing. And perhaps it is because all of us, without exception, have arrived at the farthest possible distance from there, that we have come closest to the realisation of an 'evangelical aesthetics'. In our days it is impossible to mistake God's incarnation in time with God's final coming. Our faith can in no way be a stranger to that deathly weakness for which the God of defeat alone can offer remedy, that doubtless human defeat in which there was included, as it were from the beginning, the unsurpassably intimate, divine equivalent of resurrection.

For us it is not difficult to see that everyone, at all times, is working on the same harvest, even the literature of deincarnation and manipulation, if for no other reason than to speed up the drama – the drama of our imagination, of our incarnation – toward the outcome.

In 1967 I bumped into André Frénaud on the Boulevard St Germain and we sat down for an espresso. There we sat at the café table, both of us in grey and neatly combed, like two inspectors of flour mills, while outside uncombed crowds freshly risen from their beds undulated by, half-naked and in fantastic costumes. It was then that I truly understood that the literature of the mirror – to stay faithful to glass as the raw material of the metaphor – finally and of necessity became the literature of the test tube when it chose the rigidifying intensity of the moment and was hopelessly left behind by the disproportionately more colossal possibilities of the avenue.

It is well known that Rilke on his deathbed dismissed with a single impatient wave of the hand all the creations of his pen – his works and his correspondence. It is also well-known that all his life (with a mortal presentiment and justness, as it were) he was especially drawn to plain, illiterate folk, and the peasant girl, the only person he allowed near his sickbed, did not have the slightest idea who it was she was tending in his last agony. This beautiful and tragic document attests two things for me. First, that the role of our imagination far transcends the bounds of art, and second, that it is not enough to love and praise simplicity, but we ourselves must find the way back into self-forgetfulness. But this moving document, which exemplifies the constantly recurring trial and encounter of consciousness, in Rilke, and unconsciousness, in the simple peasant girl, for me also represents in some way the two Europes.

While one half of our continent has been writing for centuries the drama of the individual, of freedom and complexity, the other half has testified through the ages about the hardships of community, of oppression and the simple human fate. I shall mention one example. The art of the West, leaving the potential universe of the static around the thirteenth and fourteenth centuries, has been painting, throughout the Renaissance and Baroque storm of movement, canvases full of the problematics of freedom, while in the East the icons remained static, and only the fluctuation of their intensity gave eternal evidence of all that was inexpressible in time.

It would be easy to conclude from this single example that for prolonged periods the West and the East have been interchanging the problematics of, respectively, freedom and individuality, with those of oppression and collectivism. But this is not true either, not in the past nor in the present. In the past century it was a Dostoyevsky in the East, and in our century, a Simone Weil in the West, who wrote the most authentic accounts of the individual and the human masses. The truly 'obedient ones' know and instructed at all times about all things. Only on the surface are there two Europes (more precisely, three: I would say Central Europe is the third, the locale of the dramatic confrontation of the other two.) In reality, the drama of the imagination is one and indivisible. And while on the surface – with the postponement of salvation – there is a welter of the most diverse variations and improvisations of errings and errancies in the interplay of the mirror and our everydays, deep down the unity is unbroken, in the love of justice, of carrying the burden, in the continuity of awe and submission. True, this unity and continuity is only occasionally called art, only occasionally literature. But does it matter? In the true history of the imagination, silence is at times more important than all written sentences.

And here, finally, I have in mind that imageless imagination, that ultimate and inexhaustible source, that brotherly silence of the imagination, which no amount of noise can suppress.

Translated from the Hungarian by John Bátki

This lecture was delivered by Pilinszky at the international conference on poetic imagination held in Poigny in October 1970.

JOHN E. SMELCER

Spring on the Yukon

An old man standing on a riverbank
watching icebergs float downriver,
like polar bears swimming to the sea.

Smiling, he waves goodbye to them.

Farewell winter!
Farewell cold and darkness!

Welcome, welcome
summer.

Owl and Mouse

Owl swooped down and caught
an unwary mouse at midnight.

As Owl flew away Mouse pleaded,
'Please don't eat me. I don't want to die.'

Owl replied without sympathy,

'You can't always get what you want.'

Today, only about two dozen elders still speak Ahtna Athabaskan. John Smelcer is the one living tribal member who can read and write in the language. His poems/ translations make up most of the literature of what survives of an entire culture. In 1997 Ted Hughes published a small selection of them, entitled *Raven Speaks*.

237

From 'From Minorities to Mosaic'

It is just as well that in 'Little Gidding', Eliot's interlocutor, impelled 'to purify the dialect of the tribe', is a 'familiar compound ghost' who must at the very least have Virgil's Latin and Dante's Italian as well as Eliot's English in mind. The association of *minority languages* alone with *dialect* and *tribe* would otherwise be ringing alarm bells. Twenty-five years of working with European minority language-groups, including my own, the Welsh, have made me over-sensitive to the terms used. There are no absolutely neutral ones. The French state prefers *langues régionales* since to speak of a minority in France suggests conflict. Basques and Catalans, when speaking French, prefer *minorisée* to *minoritaire* so as to emphasise that they are not minorities by virtue of some natural law but have been minoritised by the structures of state power. Numbers count but are not what define the minorities. Catalan-speakers are more numerous than Danish-speakers, Welsh-speakers outnumber Icelandic-speakers by nearly two to one.

Where once there was a clear distinction between *official* languages and the rest – often degraded to the category of *dialect* or *patois* – now one can find varying degrees of co-officiality on defined autonomous territories within the state. *Lesser-used languages* was a clumsy English translation of *langues moins-utilisées*, the European Commission's attempt to find a neutral term that has now largely been overtaken by the Council of Europe's *regional or minority languages*. These include cross-border minorities – those who speak the language of an adjacent state but have minority-language status in their own states – such as the Finland-Swedes, or Hungarian-speakers in every country bordering on Hungary. These have their problems too, but not always the same ones as the free-standing minorities.

In continental Europe the distinction between long-established autochthonous languages and recent immigrant languages is well understood. Speakers of immigrant languages have different aspirations and a home territory elsewhere. But this has been less understood in the UK where *minority language* has often conflated Scottish Gaelic and Welsh with Bengali and Gujarati, to nobody's benefit; but more than a decade of devolution and the most recent Welsh Language

Act is fast changing that perception.

In the cultural and literary spheres – and this is particularly true of the Celtic languages because of the antiquity of their literature – majority cultures have often found it possible to romanticise and discriminate at the same time. The classic text for Welsh is the opening passage of Matthew Arnold's lectures *On the Study of Celtic Literature* where the poet stands on the Great Orme at Llandudno. Looking east the view towards Liverpool is busy with commercial activity but a little prosaic. But looking west he sees 'eternal softness and mild light...... Wales, where the past still lives, where every place has its tradition, every name its poetry and where the people, the genuine people, still knows this past, this tradition, this poetry, and lives with it and clings to it.' One can understand that what David Jones called the 'bland megalopolitan light' required as its obverse, a twilit Innisfree, an unchanging, poetic area of retreat and escape from what Arnold in 'The Scholar-Gypsy' called 'this strange disease of modern life'; but the implications of this perception for the living Welsh language were not good and the word *clings* is a signal of worse to come.

Arnold's lectures which led to the establishment of the (now en-dangered) Chair of Celtic at Oxford for the study of the ancient liter-ature, went on to urge that 'the sooner the Welsh language disappears as an instrument of the practical, political, social life of Wales, the better, the better for England, the better for Wales herself. Traders and tourists do excellent service by pushing the English wedge further and further into the heart of the principality; Ministers of Education [and let us remember that Arnold was an Inspector of Schools] by hammering it harder and harder into the elementary schools.'

While few would associate themselves today with the violence of those images, the underlying perception of minorities and their languages as representing some ancient, ethnic essence, unchanging yet doomed to extinction, dies hard and is endlessly reproduced in the tourist images of most minority-language areas. The implied contrast is with a plural, open, developing civic and modern culture, often perceived as the universal culture (though always language-bounded), to which minorities may be interesting contributory currents. But *every* language is a cultural crossroads of some kind, not a cultural island, and that is where we come to literary translation...

The image that we come back to time and again when looking for a way to describe this variety of compatible elements is the mosaic. Gradually the majority / minority dichotomy may be overcome, and literary translation will play its part in the process, but that time is some way off – and still a long way off for those institutionally weak minorities marginalised in centralised states such as France and Greece.

Ned Thomas is a Welsh writer and literary critic and the founder and Honorary President of the Mercator Institute at the University of Aberystwyth.

a thousand fingers invoking God...

GERÐUR KRISTNÝ

Ægisiða

Oystercatcher scurrying
over the sand
made by the master's hand
– like you

And now it's said
you've gone
to a better place

I doubt that
for there was nothing wrong
with this one till now
when the grasses huddle
fearfully on the bank

– a thousand fingers invoking God

Translated from the Icelandic by Victoria Cribb

Gerður Kristný (1970–) is a full-time writer of poems, stories, plays and biography. Her recent poetry has reworked Eddic mythology into contemporary poetic shapes.

Somewhere, a birch wood is being stolen now...

Somewhere, a birch wood is being stolen now,
Somewhere, skies are stolen,
Somewhere, a dream...
Somewhere, they are stealing eternally
And the light cowers
In the yellow arms of the lamps.

Translated from the Armenian by Armine Tamrazian

Razmik Davoyan (1940–) is Armenia's most prominent living writer, with seventeen collections of poetry and many works of prose and children's literature to his name.

LAL SINGH DIL

Nadeen

I have fallen in love
With this flower smelling of the earth
With the colour of this trowel.
The handle's smoothness
That has come through a repeated clasp of the hand
Is more beautiful than any work of art.
The veinous hand that remained
The trowel's friend through the rainy season
Looks like the furrowed brow of a warrior.
And this warm stale smell
Rising from the shrivelling flowers!
I feel like bursting into song
For these fading colours.
Even though the sun has shone for them
The great rains have washed
The winds have kissed their faces
What if the trowel worked against the sun
Insulted the winds
Rebuked the soft heart of the rain!
I may be a wheat stalk
Or this flower
That grows as a weed
I would love the sharp sweep of the trowel.
And all the pain within these flowers,
Expressing which this heartless trowel too
Is crying with these weeping colours.
Don't let its tears fall to the Earth
The girl's back will break with their weight.

Translated from the Punjabi by Trilok Chand Ghai

LAL SINGH DIL

The Outcasts

Cleaning up the mangers
Gathering cow-dung
Or wheat spikes:
They work very hard
These gentle outcast daughters.
Spiky straw, hot plates,
Sharp-edged vegetable cutters,
Needles –
As if all these had been trained
To hurt their hands and feet.
This iron basin,
Resembling the helmet
On her soldier husband's head,
That one of them always carries on her head
Makes her look like a warrior
I have seen her dance
I have seen her sing
Ouf! When they cry
It seems colourful walls were soaking:
Who can watch this?

Translated from the Punjabi by Trilok Chand Ghai

Lal Singh Dil (1943–2007) grew up facing the isolation, indignities and insults
heaped upon the 'low castes'. He became a part of the Naxalite movement in
Punjab hoping that the revolution would bring about social and economic
equality, liberating him, and millions like him, from the curse of social
exclusion and economic deprivation. But the revolution never happened, the
movement died down, and he lived and died excluded and marginalised.

KO UN

Places I want to go

Thirty years ago
I had places I wanted to go.
I was everywhere on a map
of a scale of 1,000,000: one.
Twenty years ago
I had places I really wanted to go.
The blue sky that kept returning to me through the bars of my cell window
was my road.

Thus far I have managed to plod here and there.

But I have set a few places aside.
After I have quit this world
the places I want to go
will keep on waiting for someone to come.

I had places I wanted to go.
When flowers fell,
when flowers fell in the evening,
I straightened up,
closed my eyes.

Translated from the Korean by Brother Anthony of Taizé and Lee Sang-Wha

Ko Un (1933–) is South Korea's foremost poet. He became a leading
spokesman in the struggle for freedom and democracy in the 1970s and 1980s
and was often arrested and imprisoned.

ŪṆPOTI PACUṄKUṬAIYĀR

Should clouds refuse to rain because they have in the past...

Should clouds refuse to rain because they have in the past,
the land stay barren since it once put forth,
there would be no life. So, if we approach you,
my King, in your beautifully-constructed chariot,
it's sad for you to not reward us now
as you once did. Unlike have-nots
those rolling in it should be charitable.
And you're different – you give away
even the as-yet-unconquered wealth
of your enemies... O Lord,
succour those poets
who beseech you.

Translated from the Tamil by Vidyan and Thirunavukkarasu Ravinthiran

This lyric is taken from a Tamil anthology of four hundred poems, compiled
between the first and third centuries C.E., which contains work by many
different writers, some female and some anonymous.

HOMERO ARIDJIS

In its warmth Summer is a nest...

In its warmth Summer is a nest
a kingdom that kindles drowsily
a green and living creature

beasts rendered holy by the sun's insistence
mountains stirring with bodies and with dreams
plants of the air with foliage
rocking an insect on their crowns

branches that rise and settle trembling
sunned and on the river shadows cut by sun
densities that blueness penetrates
open here an eye and there a blossom

in the deepest root and the highest ear of corn
an intense struggle
a hungry generation
are happening like a grateful gesture

each creature each shadow every echo
rise into the day beginning
a trembling song of thread-thin hymns

Translated from the Mexican Spanish by Michael Schmidt

✳

dreams are never fulfilled

and feelings only give rise to grief…

KRISTIINA EHIN

Cows come from the sea...

Cows come from the sea
on this morning at the beginning of time
blue-green cows
udders full of salty sea milk
and the Sea Mother drives them ashore
with a switch of sea-grass

Sea Maidens come keep the cows
and keep yourselves
from lecherous herders by night
In autumn may a hundred blue-green cows
be back here in the bay between mottled stones
May their horns glisten in the mist
and may your eyes sparkle
But keep your hearts clear and cool
like the morning dew

You will never get used to the life of human women
it puts fetters on the heart
dreams are never fulfilled
and feelings only give rise to grief
People are beautiful but cruel
They keep to their kin like insects
they gather the gold of dreams by night
squander it all away in the morning

To become someone's own means being
dangerously close to a human star

But your eyes are like the sea of the world
stars drown in it

Sea Maidens come keep the cows
But keep your hearts clear and cool
like the morning dew

Translated from the Estonian by Ilmar Lehtpere

JOSÉ WATANABE

The Arrangement

I don't know whether the rancher did it intentionally
but he gave me his chair and let me observe this admirable arrangement:
the nightjar
is perched on the bull's back, confidently, knowing
that from the horns to the haunches
of the bull there runs an aggressive pulsation.
But with the nightjar there
it would appear that the bull is at peace, at ease, he hears
the soothing sound of the bird's claws scratching his hide,
he feels
the little tongue
that cleans the blood from his sores
and the fluttering wings that sweep away the dust
and the beak like a nurse's delicate instrument
probing for
the larvae that burrow beneath the skin.
And so the therapeutic bird obtains its food.
That's the commonplace exchange
but the nightjar gains more: on top of the bull's back
it enjoys
a vast tenderness that no one suspects, the paradox
of the animal kingdom.

Translated from the Peruvian Spanish by C. A. de Lomellini and David Tipton

José Watanabe (1946–2007) was born in Laredo, a large sugar cane farm in northern Peru. His father was a Japanese immigrant and his mother a Peruvian of Andean origin. In a very intimate way, Watanabe fused his two deep cultural backgrounds in a brief but intense poetic work. He was also involved in the film industry as a screenwriter, production designer and art director.

Kristiina Ehin (1977–) was born in Rapla, Estonia. She has published five volumes of poetry in her native Estonia. Her work has been translated into twelve languages.

How the Mole Came to Be

A peasant wanted to steal his neighbour's field. He buried his son in the ground, after telling him what to say to any question he was asked. The magistrates came to the field with the defendant, and the man who wanted to seize the other's property said: 'Black earth, speak, whose are you?' 'I am yours, I am yours,' they heard a child's voice cry from the earth. The real owner, when he heard that, gave in and the magistrates decided in favour of the unjust man. When they had all gone, the father took a spade and hurried to dig his child out. The child wasn't there! The father called him, and the child replied, but from further and further away. He had become a mole.

Translated from the Serbian by Anne Pennington

Aquarium

My sister in the aquarium
withdraws among the weeds.
Day and night we look for her, where she is,
aunts, children, grandchild,
look for her in the slimy, strange
leaf-foliage tomb-graveyard.

She squats on the bed. Debris.
She shudders. Wakes. Starts.
Lights a cigarette. Speaks. Talks to us. To nobody.
Like a fishbird
her fins flutter, crumple:
she shudders and throbs. Her fishbird eyes
aren't casting about for our eyes, they just
bore holes. It doesn't matter where,
as long as there is a hole in anyone, anything,
against us, against me, against her,
a hole, at all costs.

Translated from the Hungarian by Peter Jay

VALERIO MAGRELLI

I was lying on an outpatient's bed...

I was lying on an outpatient's bed
hidden behind a screen.
'Antigone', 'Yes', 'You there?', 'Yes, here'.
The bones of the back, the backbone.
And they start talking to each other,
the two old folk, the two old voices.
Because a voice grows old,
even in sounds you find the bone of time,
even in breathing. They sighed and inside
the sound, the sound echoed itself,
an echo preceding the words themselves.
Something wrecked and unhinged, the marrow
stripped from the spinal column and
unsheathed like a glittering sword,
voice-carcass,
backbone of the voice.

Translated from the Italian by Jamie McKendrick

Valerio Magrelli (1957–) was born in Rome and teaches French in Italian
universities.

CESARE PAVESE

Donne Appassionate

At twilight the girls come down into the water
as the sea, outstretched, withdraws. Within the wood
each leaf twitches, and cautiously they tread back
across the sand onto the bank beyond. Only the surf
continues, away into the distance, its restless games.
The girls are afraid of the seaweed that lurks
beneath the waves, how it clutches both legs and shoulders:
so naked, after all, is the human form. Hastening upward,
they call to each other by name, keep their eyes peeled.
Even the shadows, in the dark depths of the seabed,
are enormous: they seem to flit this way and that,
as if magnetised by each passing body. The wood, then,
is something of a refuge in the setting sunlight
except the girls prefer to remain out in the open,
seated on a sheet laid cosily across the shingle.
So there they are all huddled, clasping that sheet
about their legs and contemplating the sea outspread
like a meadow in the waning light. Yet in a meadow
which of them would now dare to lie down naked?
From the sea weeds would leap, licking their feet
as an aperitif before swallowing the body whole.
Down in the sea sometimes there are eyes which flicker.
Out skinny-dipping on her own in the pitch darkness
which exists only between moons, some unnamed stranger
disappeared one night and she has never been seen since.
Big girl, they say; she must've also been dazzlingly white
or those eyes at the sea floor could not have reached her.

Translated from the Italian by Martin Bennett

Cesare Pavese (1908–1950), poet, writer, translator, was imprisoned and, in 1935,
sent into internal exile for anti-fascist activities. After the war he joined the
Communist party. Depression led to his eventual suicide.

Towards the Baths of Caracalla

Off they go to the Baths of Caracalla,
young friends astride Rumi or Ducati bikes,
modestly or insolently male,
hiding unconcerned or showing off
in the hot folds of their trousers
the secret of their erections...
With wavy hair, youthful
coloured sweaters, they cleave into
the night in a never-ending
carousel, invading the night,
splendid owners of the night...

Off he goes to the Baths of Caracalla,
body erect as on his native
Apennine slopes, among the sheep tracks
that smell of age-old flocks and holy
ashes of Berber villages – already impure
in his dusty loutish beret,
hands in his pockets – the shepherd, migrant
at age eleven, and now here, his Roman laugh
malicious and festive, still warm
with red sage, fig and olive...

Off he goes to the Baths of Caracalla
the old head of the family, unemployed,
whom rough Frascati has reduced
to a cretinous animal, a holy fool,
with the useless junk in the chassis
of his dilapidated body rattling
in pieces: his clothes a sack
that contains his slightly hunchback spine,
two thighs doubtless full of sores,
old baggy pants that flap below
pockets of a jacket heavy

with greasy packets. His face
smiles: the bones in his jaw
chew and crack his words
as he talks to himself, then stops
and rolls the old fag-end of a cigarette,
a carcass where all its youth
remains in flower like a bonfire
inside a bucket or bowl:
a person never born never dies.

Off they go to the Baths of Caracalla

. . . .

Translated from the Italian by N.S. Thompson

Pier Paolo Pasolini (1922–1975) was a communist, acclaimed film director,
writer and intellectual. N.S. Thompson writes: 'Pasolini was an inveterate
night owl, prowling Rome's streets and low life for sex. It is thought these
dangerous exploits led to his murder. He was found battered to death on a
beach.'

JACK MAPANJE

Kalikalanje of Ostrich Forest

'Kalikalanje, diminutive already
fried one; my name is Kalikalanje,

son of Kalanje and Likalanje, both
of Lanje, a village that has stood

by the woods of ancient *Ostrich
Forest* from the beginning of time.

How I came into the world, birth
elders amongst the Yao peoples of

Malawi, Mozambique, Tanzania
where my tale is told by the fire,

have numerous varying accounts.
Some claim, "Kalikalanje leapt out

of his mum's womb, of his own
accord, and landed straight onto

her frying pan, there to turn him-
self over and over again until her

groundnut oil fried him clean and
dry." Others attest, "We pulled out

Kalikalanje from his mum's belly
and placed him on her pan to fry

clean and dry." Yet others assert,
"We saw Kalikalanje kicking about

the grass and wattle beds of ancient
Ostrich Forest, we picked him up

and restored him to his mum's glory
though later he jumped onto her pan

to fry clean and dry." Some birth
elders dance before they declare,

"We *extracted* Kalikalanje, God's
diminutive already fried one, not

from his mum's womb, not from
his mum's belly, nor did we pick

him from grass and wattle beds of
Ostrich Forest, truly but truthfully

we *extorted* Kalikalanje from his
mum's knee, then he jumped onto

her pan to fry clean and dry." Some
among such elders fiercely protest,

"No, *we* extracted Kalikalanje not
from his mum's knee, but from her

big toe, then we gave him liberty
to jump onto his mum's broiling

pan to fry clean and dry." Others
contend, "We wrung Kalikalanje

not from his mum's knee, nor from
her big toe, but from her thumb;

then he leapt onto her pan to fry
clean and dry." The accounts of

the tale of my birth, the birth of
Kalikalanje, God's already fried

diminutive, are legion; and if some
should acutely contradict others,

that's the spirit of my tale; what
birth elders agree on wherever they

tell my story is: when I breathed my
first breath, at once I opened my

eyes and saw, at once I touched and
tasted, at once I heard and smelt,

at once I knew the past, the present,
the future; at once I began to talk,

think, imagine in my mum's tongue;
besides, at birth I did not scream as

foolish babies do all over the world;
after screaming with rapture at my

conception, I just thought it might be
prudent to merely chuckle at birth.'

'"Kalikalanje of Ostrich Forest" is based on the legend of Kalikalanje, a well-
known folk tale figure among the Yao and Nyanja speaking peoples of
Malawi, Mozambique and Tanzania. Essentially the hero/heroine comes into
the world already endowed with supernatural powers, which include knowledge
of past, present, future times and events. Kalikalanje loves fun, justice, freedom,
peace, truth and where these are absent he/she will play every trick available to
get them. To some Kalikalanje is a menacing trickster who must be eliminated
at all cost, though those who try, do it at their own peril. Each account of
Kalikalanje has its own emphasis, special slant or accent depending on the
moral needs of the community; but the tale is often told for sheer pleasure too.
    My account of the legend may be shorn of its original Yao or Nyanja flavour
through translation (for example the idiophones in the original languages
have been sacrificed in favour of clarity!) but I hope to have retained the
symbolic, social-cultural-political nuance that is generally embedded in the
tale, making it relevant to the world of persistent liars and impostors at the
time it is told – the story of Kalikalanje has timeless resonance.' JM

Jack Mapanje (1944–), poet and university lecturer, was arrested in 1987 and
spent three years, seven months and 16 days in prison on account of a collection
of poems which Hastings Banda, the President of Malawi, found offensive.

VALÉRIE ROUZEAU

01 43 15 50 67

By the time we've finished talking it has snowed
We'd laughed and sighed like a pair of sisters
Can you see this caribou when you look out it's a cloud
A moose an ermine little moving fox
It changes every moment changes to sky-blue sky
If the night has stars in it it's a promise of blue
Have you checked the great she-bears and chimney-stacks
We ought to see oceans more
We ought to recognise a giraffe at first glance
All white white white white where you are as well?
A squid a cuttlefish an octopush would nicely ink it in
All white white white without red rabbit eyes
We mustn't make each other late time's getting on I'd better go
There are some in dotty frocks and some in geometric shapes
And I almost forgot
Old things float up and new ones too
A slotted spoon a convalescence or a precious stone
Jewel of sleeping water there was a cat called that
It was
Drowned jewel
Clouds don't miaow though jewellery can trickle down
When we stopped our oneversation we came down as snow.

Translated from the French by Susan Wicks

Valérie Rouzeau (1967–), poet and translator, was born in Burgundy. She is the author of a dozen collections of poems, among them *Pas revoir* which, translated by Susan Wicks, was published by Arc as *Cold Spring in Winter*. Rouzeau writes of this poem: 'Before I got the poem printed in French, I checked the phone number was nobody's, which was the case. 01 stands for Paris, Île de France, 43 was my dad's birth year, 15 because it's the 15th poem in the collection, 50 is my mum's birth year and 67 is my birth year.'

TAKAGI KYOZO

Poor Harvest

This cold rain soon turns to snow.
How meagre these rice-shoots!
Yet we have to keep banging an old oil can
to scare off these shrill sparrows.
The sea sounds as if a storm's blowing up.
A flock of seagulls screeching overhead.
A father is reading with vacant eyes a letter from
his daughter working at a cotton-spinning mill.
The mother is trying to make a meal from bruised spuds
she scratched up in the fields.
But the fire will not burn, it only smoulders,
And the matches have all been used.
The house is full of smoke.
The bairn's yelling.
What a miserable evening!

Translated from the Tohoku dialect of Japanese by James Kirkup and Nakano Michio

James Kirkup wrote: 'Some poets are inextricably a part of their natural surroundings, of the place where they were born. We cannot separate the poet and his personal vision of what to some may seem a very narrow world. Yet great poems spring from the most unlikely places – Clare in rustic Northamptonshire, Norman Nicholson in Millom, Takagi Kyozo (1903–1987) in the harsh environment of northern Japan. Indeed, these three poets exhibit certain resemblances to one another. They were all three, because of physical circumstances or personal preference, on the fringes of those "movements" scholars strive to discern in the unclassifiable realms of poetry.'

Fruit has fed the worms,

roses have returned

to the nocturnal beehive…

Lean Months

And do you remember the long
    milkless midwinter days,
    the lean months' fry,
    salted chips soaked in a pail,
    the well house
        and the plain song of running water,
    boats in their cribs
        covered with canvas,
    sheep on the shore,
        and cold feet,
    and evenings long as eternity,
often then impatiently waiting
for fishing weather
and fresh catch for the pot.

And do you remember
    one evening at dusk.
    You stood on the beach with your foster-
        mother.
    Staring in fear at frozen rollers,
    out over the fjord,
    into the sky –
    you expected a small boat to round the
        headland,
    but it did not come.

And dusk turned to heavy darkness with
        storm sounds,
    silence
    and tears on a pillow,
    and you fell asleep in a bed too large.

And do you remember
                    your joy in the middle of night,
                    when you woke feeling on your head
                    the touch of a horny palm
                    and across your cheek
                    the soft warm stroke of the back of a hand.
Your foster-father had returned
– and kissed you as you put your arms around his
                    neck.
And there was still a chill in his sea-moist moustache.

            And next morning there was blue catfish
                    on a frosty front-door slab,
                    and the sun shimmered in
                            haddock-scale silver –
            and happiness in a poor man's house.

Translated from the Icelandic by Sigurður A. Magnússon and Mick Fedullo

Jón úr Vör (1917–2000) is accounted one of the bringers of modernism into
Icelandic poetry, particularly through the publication of his collection *The
Fishing Village* in 1946, a description of the poor and primitive life of fishermen
and their families in a village before and during the Depression.

Although born in 1904, Edvard Kocbek published most of his major poetry in
the 1960s. This makes him more of a contemporary of poets like Zbigniew
Herbert, Vladimir Holan, or Vasko Popa, than of his own generation. In all
these poets, the influence of modernism and its aesthetics collided with the
tragic history of their countries. Kocbek is one of the true witnesses of our
new dark ages. He died in 1981.

EDVARD KOCBEK

Landscape

The scent of wild animals
nears the houses,
pregnant women's
lips move,
ripe space smells
of oily stuff
and darkened corn.
Fruit has fed the worms,
roses have returned
to the nocturnal beehive,
the landscape has lain down
behind its image.
The silence rattles anciently,
memory weighs anchor,
moonlight plays
with a peacock's tail.
Things grow bigger
from their presence,
drunkards cannot drink enough thirst,
animals cannot reach the bottom
of their innocence,
the wind feeds on precipices
and darkness on thieves.
The world is riddled
with homesick pains,
I turn in a charmed circle
as in wedding dreams,
I cannot recollect
a formula to set me free.

Translated from the Slovenian by Michael Scammell and Veno Taufer

JÁNOS PILINSZKY

Knocking

We slept. In my dreams I was a tree,
then nothing, then such a child
as knocks on a grown-up's door.

Meanwhile you too were a tree. A child's skirt.
Not a door. Knocking. Knock.
Together we knocked. I no longer know
whether on the same door? This much is certain:
a cherub's thrashing-about would be like this.

Translated from the Hungarian by Peter Jay

FADHIL ASSULTANI

A Tree

I remember now, in my forties,
a tree
next to my home
beside a brook.

I remember now our secrets:
how she used to spread her shadows under me
bend her branches around me
and slip into my clothes
putting me on
as I put her on
together entering the brook.

I remember now, in my forties,
my stories to the tree about the gardenia
and about the girl
who left us
only shadows over the water.

And I moved away
how far did I move away?
But I still see her
stretch her branches towards me
in order to lift me – to heaven.

Translated from the Arabic by Saadi A. Simawe and the author

Fadhil Assultani (1948–), born in Hella, Mesopotamia, is an Iraqi poet and
the literary editor of *Asharq Al-Aswat*. He has translated Toni Morrison, R.S.
Thomas and others into Arabic.

✳

From the start we saw our editorship as something like an airport for incoming translations, an agency for discovering new foreign poets, and new translators, who then, if their qualifications were right, might pass inland to more permanent residences in published books.

Preface to Modern Poetry in Translation: *1983*

At this stage in MPT's long career, one feels tempted to look back over the unique tidal wave of poetry translation that swept through English (and through the other chief Western languages) in the 60s and early 70s. Where did it come from and what happened to it?

That boom in the popular sales of translated modern poetry was without precedent. Though it reflected only one aspect of the wave of mingled energies that galvanised those years with such extremes, it was fed by almost all of them. From other standpoints, other aspects might seem more significant. There are diagnoses to be drawn from the mass epidemic of infatuation with hallucinogenic drugs, the sudden opening to all of the worlds of Eastern mystical practice and doctrine, particularly of various forms of Buddhism, the mass craze of Hippie ideology, the revolt of the young, the pop music of the Beatles and their generation, the *Walpurgisnacht* of new psychotherapies. From yet other standpoints, all these must appear as the natural but minor harmonics of the real historical event – the shock-wave consequences of modern physics working through the old, anachronistic human system, and materialising in the new bomb and the imminent end of the world, which was dramatised and magnified by the confrontation of Russia and the United States. The stage was being set, in those days, by our dawning realisation – it had taken time – of what Hitler and Stalin had actually made of mankind, as if they had revealed it of our-selves, as if there had been some sort of mutation in humanity, though history reassured us, in depressing confirmation, a refreshed under-standing of the old evidence, that we had always shared these weaknesses, just as Hiroshima, Nagasaki and the war in Vietnam circumstantially confirmed that the guilt was indeed ours. It is easy to forget, in the crowded perspective of recent history, that these realisations took form as a shocking novelty. I call it the setting of a stage, but it could feel more like biological inevitability, an evolutionary first phase, an inescapable preparation for some final human confession and apocalypse. That historical moment might well be seen, by a detached Spenglerian, as a development from the spiritual plane, an unfolding from inwards, a millennial change in the Industrial West's view of reality that had roots far back in time. But all the immediate circumstances of it were, to say the least, unacceptable. And when the whole burden was touched off, as it was, by factors that seem almost coincidental, one can understand how the resulting euphoric madness came to have such pathos, and such universal appeal. It was a forlorn adolescent attempt to establish agape as a world republic. We were all taken unawares by a decade that became in many ways a poetic image simply for youth, which had behind it the magical power of sexual awakening, and the archaic biological imperative to love and embrace everybody, especially those with foreign genes, before it is too late.

The factors that touched off this conflagration were, of course, the surge of economic prosperity that rose out of the late 50s, as the West recovered from the Second World War, and the emergence of all western countries, and indeed of all the countries of the world from the Ice Age of that war and the Dark Age that had preceded it. That re-awakening of the world's countries, to themselves and to each other, after such nightmare experiences, was a stirring thing to live through. If the Modern Age burst from its crib in the 1914–18 war, it came to consciousness of itself in the 60s. It was forced into consciousness. One can easily understand the suddenness of the need to communicate, to exchange dreams and revelations and brainwaves, to find a shared humanity on the level of the heart. The flux of poetry translation followed inevitably. And not only on the level of the heart. The translation of poetry became important, almost political business. The political role of poetry in Russia certainly had something to do with this. In one sense, the transmission from Russia, which began with *Dr Zhivago*, was the carrier wave of the whole poetry translation phenomenon. As the alter ego of the Soviet global threat, modern Russian poetry can be seen lifting poetry translation to the crest of excitement. Through this circuit, the mood of doom found a strange kind of hope in the poetry of other nations, or perhaps simply in the poetry of humanity felt as a whole, as a single threatened creature. And perhaps this explains why poetry for those brief years became central to the exploration of drugs, of Buddhism, of imaginative systems from the childhood of the race, of the music and liberties of the young. One feels that only a giant collapse, a bankruptcy, a momentary utter fatigue of all other civilised promises, could have let this happen. It was indeed a confession of sorts, a moment of psychic nakedness. Obviously it could not last. Mankind readjusted, the ego recovered its resilience. Even if the money had not run out, it could not have lasted. As it was, in quite a short time, the main landmarks of the world's modern poetry became accessible to all, the glamorous, stormy affair with Russia entered its grim, realistic years of marriage, the Beatles generation began to grow deaf and grey, and to worry about its children.

Throughout all the confusions of that period runs one tenacious band. It was established in the late 50s before the mounting potential showed any very visible portents, and it is still unbroken now the uproar is well past. This band consisted and consists of the working translators. The best of them continue to be active – and most of them are still comparatively young. And though their popular audience has been absorbed back into the landscape, and publishers are more and more reluctant to cooperate, some of their finest achievements have appeared quite recently, and others are only now, in 1982, moving towards publication.

Probably one's own generation always seems to have played a key role of some sort, so I may be wrong in my impression that the main work of translating poetry was done – was certainly initiated – by the generation born five years or so either side of 1930.

In 1960, before things began to move, before the Beatles had lifted their voice, the translation of poetry seemed to lie in the hands of a few enterprising individuals who were merely following from other languages what they couldn't find lying around them in their own. Robert Bly was setting up The Sixties Press. But if you were aware of him at all, his rallying calls for recruits to the cause of Vallejo, Trakl, and others, sounded as much like a last stand as (what it was) the beachhead of an invasion. W.S. Merwin seemed to be toiling away in the traditional wage-earning task – translating Juvenal and Mediaeval French as readily as Éluard and Neruda – rather than embarking, as he was, on the immense map of adventurous foreign explorations which he has since filled in with such marvellous detail. At that time, one's own fascination with what they were doing carried no feeling of what was on its way. One was too aware, perhaps, of the solid wall of dismissal (and derision) that the poetic and critical canon of the 50s presented to such alien texts. But when the wave arrived, and the passionate international affair commenced, suddenly almost all the poets of this generations found that the dull isolations of the 50s had been imposed on them, and that they were all interested in the same thing: translating the poetry of other languages. Everything happened then at heady speed. And it was curious to watch those somewhat wartime-utility, old-fashioned personalities (the last of the old order) casting off ten years in style of dress and behaviour and taste in music, and immersing in the headlong element of joyful freedoms that had snatched up their translations (and everybody felt the pull). No doubt they were fore-runners anyway, a little ahead of their times, and naturally susceptible. In the long run, some of them became leaders of a sort, and took further than anybody else the determination to transform themselves and to enter the new world thoroughly adjusted – an attempt as evident in Merwin and Bly as it is in Ginsberg.

As these names suggest, the Americans performed the tendencies more wholeheartedly, but in the end the overlap of curiosity was pretty well complete, among English translators and American, though with a characteristic – and revealing – difference in their preferred fields of attention.

This seemed clear, at least, when we launched the first issue of *Modern Poetry in Translation*. Daniel Weissbort and myself had been talking for years about a magazine of this sort. In the end, as the boom neared its peak, with publishers calling for more, and almost every poet we knew busy with translation, it seemed easier to let the magazine take off than to keep it grounded. The sheer pressure of material forced the issue. Even so, in that maiden flight our material was of a particular kind.

From the start we saw our editorship as something like an airport for incoming translations, an agency for discovering new foreign poets, and new translators, who then, if their qualifications were right, might pass inland to more permanent residences in published books. We had a general notion of making familiar to English readers the whole range of contemporary possibilities in poetry – in so far as translation can convey any idea of such things. We weren't beyond the hope of influencing our own writers in a productive way. We even toyed with the fantasy of sending to every known poet – offering to their curiosity – a free copy of each issue. Acquaintance with the diverse poetries of the modern world, we felt, couldn't be bad, even if it only helped to confirm home-grown virtues. That fantasy evaporated with the first bills, but it was partly responsible for our format – a flimsy newspaper (the first issue was on ricepaper) that would never seem to demand more than a cursory scanning, and wouldn't much resist being thrown away. Functional, current, disposable – such were our key words. And our ambition was to build up, eventually, the complete picture.

The same approach determined the large amount of material we tried to pack in. We had some hope of shifting the contents from the fine arts category – and the highly-developed resistance it meets – to that of a bulk commodity, almost like news. We would have liked to hurry the response of our readers from insular wariness in the face of the foreign object (we always thought of an English audience) towards a casual, easy acceptance of the world's medley of poetic dialects. These ideas were probably indefensible, and they certainly lacked market research, but they did crystallise a vital opportunity in the air of time, and they served our real purpose – they were effectively creative in that they helped us to get the current flowing in volume, and kept it flowing with a momentum that occasionally moved large freight. The reservoir of material seemed inexhaustible – more like a sea than a reservoir, a living, evolving, circulating sea. And since we proposed to assemble each issue from the poetry of a single country, or of two or three related countries, we set out with what was virtually an infinitely long-term plan.

This wide-open hospitality to all Modern Poetry, which was the overall character of our policy, meant that the decisive thing came to be our personal taste in poetic quality, and in style of translation. Later on (after I had withdrawn from the co-editorship, which I did so there should be no embarrassing mistake about who was doing all the hard work), it was Daniel Weissbort's taste alone, or, occasionally, that of some guest editor. But in all the years since, Daniel Weissbort has held to the guiding principles we started with, refining them on the way in the perennial debate concerning the various virtues of the various methods of translation. Since our only real motive in publishing was our own curiosity in contemporary foreign poetry, we favoured the translations that best revealed the individuality and strangeness of the original. This usually meant a translation that interposed the minimum of the reflexes and inventions of the translator. The exemplary demonstration of this appears in Shelley's note to his translation of the opening chorus of Goethe's *Faust*.* We were happily resigned, that is, to all the losses sustained by the most literal translation of the verbal sense. This method can have some drastic results: where the original poem's centre of gravity, so to speak, lies in the verbal texture, the poem can easily disappear completely. (Pushkin is the famous case of how all-important the verbal texture can be.) But 'the most literal' covers a wide range between denotative and connotative extremes. Ideally, we would have

---

* Hughes is referring to the following note by Shelley: 'Such is a literal translation of this astonishing chorus; it is impossible to represent in another language the melody of the versification; even the volatile strength and delicacy of the ideas escape in the crucible of translation, and the reader is surprised to find a *caput mortuum*.'

liked to see at least some poems translated with the concern for both extremes served as meticulously and flexibly as in Bleek's translation of Bushman lore – though we understood the limited appeal of anything so raw and strange unless it has the guarantee behind it of a literary personality as solid, say, as Beckett's. We tried to avoid translators who claimed to produce a 'parallel equivalent' of some original's unique verbal texture. It seemed to us, in our purism, that a 'parallel equivalent' in the way of imagery, evocative effects, rhyme schemes etc, had to be a new thing, quite different from what we were after. However fine it might be in itself, in relation to the original it could only be the crudest of analogies, with the added crime that it seduced honest curiosity with a charming counterfeit. What we were looking for, naturally, was the best of both worlds, and as in the Bushman lore of Bleek we occasionally found it in the work of very modest poets. Most often, oddly enough, but perhaps inevitably, we found the closest thing to it in translations made by poets whose first language was not English, or by scholars who did not regard themselves as poets. Among the still-readable survivors of the translations made in the last twenty years, a surprising number have been made by such people. Our high principles were all very well in theory, and as touchstones, but in practice, of course, we had to compromise, and were quite ready to if the results seemed to us provisionally worthwhile.

What finally overwhelmed us into publishing our first issue was the translated work of a group of poets who seemed to us revelatory. A little earlier, Al Alvarez had brought back from Eastern Europe poems by Miroslav Holub (Czechoslovakia) and by Zbigniew Herbert (Poland). About the same time, Daniel Weissbort found poems by Vasko Popa (Jugoslavia) and Yehuda Amichai (Israel). I came across poems by János Pilinszky (Hungary).

Over the next years, other poets – Celan, Różewicz – would emerge through translation to join them, but these first few impressed us as a totally new phenomenon. And it is interesting to note, in passing, that Holub was translated by a Czech (George Theiner), Herbert by a Pole (Czesław Miłosz), Vasko Popa, in the translations we first saw, by himself (and Anne Pennington, who later translated him so miraculously, regarded herself as a scholar with no claim to being a poet or even a versifier). Yehuda Amichai seemed good in any translation, but the best, the most touching and haunting, were by himself. And we found Pilinszky in translations made by the exiled Hungarian poet János Csokits. To complete this list, Różewicz was eventually translated by a fellow-Pole, Adam Czerniawski, and Celan by Michael Hamburger. The 1930 generation of American and English translators, in fact, had very little to do with this particular invasion, except in giving them an appreciative welcome (and except insofar as Michael Hamburger was one of the earliest, as he has proved one of the most gifted and productive).

That group of poets all belonged to the 1920 generation, the generation that came of age during the war, and they belonged together in an obvious way. They seemed to us to be the serious voice of that historical moment. It was common in those days to hear how all poetry had died in Auschwitz, but theirs seemed not only to have taken full account of it and survived it, but to have created a new moral being out of the experience, already adapted to the worst imaginable future. And all these poets shared another characteristic: in literal translation, their work made English poems of great freshness, force and truth. Whatever the verbal texture of the originals might be, evidently their real centre of gravity was in something else, within the images and the pattern of ideas and attitudes. They also enjoyed, no doubt, a lucky combination of translators. But for us, as I have said, they more than justified the launching of *MPT*. They made it inevitable.

Since then, Daniel Weissbort has steered the magazine through 44 issues. The collected volumes now make a weighty Encyclopaedia of Modern Poetry in Translation – a mine that has not been neglected by anthologists, researchers, publishers, or poets. Just what we hoped it would be. Meanwhile the translators go on working at what is now a great series of naturalised poetic monuments. However fashionable support may come and go in the future, there seems to be no reason why that should not go on.

✳

Take your time Death

Take a seat on the crystal of my days…

MAHMOUD DARWISH

from 'Mural'

And I want
I want to live
I have work to do on the geography of volcanoes
From desolation to ruin
from the time of Lot to Hiroshima
As if I'd never yet lived
with a lust I've still to know
Perhaps Now has gone further away
and yesterday come closer
So I take Now's hand to walk along the hem of history
and avoid cyclic time
with its chaos of mountain goats
How can my tomorrow be saved?
By the velocity of electronic time
or by my desert caravan slowness?
I have work till my end
as if I won't see tomorrow
and I have work for today who isn't here
So I listen
softly softly
to the ant beat of my heart: Bear with me my patience
I hear the cry of the imprisoned stone: Set my body free
in a violin I see yearning's migration between peat and sky
and in my feminine hand
I hold tight my familiar eternity:
I was created then loved then died then awoke on the grass of my tombstone
whose letters from time to time refer to me
What's the use of spring if it doesn't please the dead
and show them the joy of life and the shock of forgetfulness?
That's the clue to my poems
at least the sentimental ones
And what on earth are dreams if not our only way of speaking?

Take your time Death
Take a seat on the crystal of my days
as if you've always been a constant friend
as if you were the foreigner among living creatures
You are the exile
you haven't a life
your life is only my death
you neither live nor die
you kidnap children between their thirst for milk and milk
You'll never be a child in a cradle rocked by finches
never will angels and stags tease you with their horns
as they teased us
we guests of the butterfly
You are the miserable exile
with no woman pressing you to her breasts
no woman to make during the long night
nostalgia Two
in the language of desire
and to make into One
the land and heaven which is in us
No boy of yours to say: Father I love you
You are the exile

You king of kings
There's no praise for your sceptre
no falcon waiting on your horse
no pearls embedded in your crown
You are stripped of flags and music
How can you go around like a cowardly thief without guards or singers?
Who do you think you are?
You're the Great Highness of Death
mighty leader of the invincible Assyrians

So do with us
and yourself
as you see fit

Translated from the Palestinian Arabic by Rema Hammami and John Berger

MIROSLAV HOLUB

Wings

> We have
> a microscopic anatomy
> of the whale
> this
> gives
> man assurance.
>
> WILLIAM CARLOS WILLIAMS

We have
a map of the Universe
for microbes,
a map of a microbe
for the Universe.

We have
a Grand Master of chess
made of electronic valves.

But above all
we have
the ability
to sort peas,
to cup water in our hands,
to seek
the right screw
under the sofa
for hours

This
gives us
wings.

Translated from the Czech by George Theiner

Birdsong on the Seabed

These days I am so very sad
Sad to the point of yawning –
Drowning down in dream.
Whirlpools softly spinning,
Oh, give in to the sea
To the moon, the water, the grief
Circling, I am falling
To the algae-blanketed seam
The muffled war-like ring
Of bells draped in weed.

Bird slides under the waves
Bends them by force of its wings

Amongst the glowing of stones
The ear-lobate curling
The waxy husk of shells
And the weed-serpent unfurling
Triton is swimming through,
Bird takes pains to hide
Wing-shovelling down
No nest-building on stone
Fish, no life amongst you,

But singing to the bed, to the boulder
In a watery Sodom-night
To the deafest fish of the deep
About the stars above streams,
The ancient skin of the oak,
About candlelight.

And about fire and brimstone
The *lampada*'s unending flame,
About the dust of moths

And brief moth-pain
And scorched moth-bone.

Bird slides under the waves
Bends them by force of its wings.

The bruise-blue salt corrodes the eye
Pain pecks at the beak.
Sing, perched on the bony arm
Of a drowned man, sing
Of his life's path, a candle he once lit.

Bird slides under the waves
Bends them by force of its wings.

Bird sings as if from the branch at dusk:
The shining garden, the sun
But the cold-blooded beasts believe
None of the tales of heat, none
But the shadowy seahorse believe –
When silent, willow o' the wisp
In the little round boat of a nutshell
Falls to the depths of the sea,
Then the sea-foal believes.

Is it worth singing where no one can hear,
Unrolling trills on the bed?
I am waiting for you, I lean from the boat –
Bird, ascend to the depths.

Translated from the Russian by Sasha Dugdale

Elena Shvarts (1948-2010) lived all her life in St Petersburg. A poet of faith and great visionary power, her work is notable for its inventive imagery and surging rhythms. In this poem the poet sings to the cold-blooded sea beasts of the warm land above, but none believe her song. The *lampada* is the light before an icon.

KANEKO MISUZU

Stars and Dandelions

Deep in the blue of the sky
Like pebbles under the sea
Waiting under night's waves
You cannot see stars in the day.

You can't see them, but they're still there.
Even these things you can't see, they're still there.

The withered dandelion, scattered its seeds,
And into a crack in a tile, shhhh, so quietly,
Hiding away until spring comes again,
You cannot see those strong roots.

You can't see them, but they're still there.
Even these things you can't see, they're still there.

Translated from the Japanese by Quentin Crisp

Kaneko Misuzu (*née* Teru) (1903–1930) was born in Yamaguchi Prefecture. Her hometown of Senzaki was a fishing village, overlooking the Sea of Japan. In 1927 she entered into an arranged marriage, which proved unhappy for her. Her husband forbade her to write poetry or continue correspondence with her friends and associates from the magazines. In 1930, she asked for a divorce with the single condition that she could keep her daughter. Her husband agreed, but soon changed his mind about custody of the child. As a divorced woman, at that time, Teru had no legal rights to the child. When her husband asked for custody and eventually said he was coming in person to take the child, Teru felt that her only recourse was a protest suicide. On 9 March, 1930, she took an overdose. She was 26 years old. Although popular in her lifetime, and compared by one enthusiastic editor to Christina Rossetti, after her death she was forgotten until her recent rediscovery in Japan about ten years ago.

KRYSTYNA MIŁOBĘDZKA

Four Poems

rush upon this house, pilgrimage high tide
bonnet dress rosary in nomine small shoes
Patris et Filii strong needlework
with the hand on the knob
rush upon this house, not peace, now and forever
record of this rush
ebb and flow, offering one's own self to the mouths
whom am I eating, who is eating me

door in this ascending descending staircase

face half-turned, half dark once in my
and already not in my direction

they are in this photograph!
motherfather   horseflowerbedashtree   peonies

assumed in me, in haven at last

the longer my looking, the shorter my seeing
I am that I am

path running through the forest, down the hill
forest in the forest, is in itself, opening its own

glassiness (hinterpane) of what I can see
of what I'm saying here

this will be that sky, under the sky an ash
this will be the ash, that first tree
this the ash after the ash
this the me after the me
empty space
show me that place
your place for a start, for a new

I'm starting

Translated from the Polish by Elżbieta Wójcik-Leese

Krystyna Miłobędzka (1932–) wrote in a recent script called 'lost along the way': 'Truthfully, my autobiography as a writer (and not only as a writer) looks like this:

> A crow settles on the tip of the thinnest twig, though the seat is
> neither comfortable nor safe, and the swinging itself is a mere
> trick to keep balance. It is scared. Pretends to be a lighter bird.

I am a creature that is heavy, awkward, hard of seeing, hard of hearing, hard of speaking. This creature wants to appear nimble and weightless to itself and to others. It pretends that it knows well how to live and write smoothly, without any effort. And yet, all the time, it is learning life and writing. It is scared of its own awkwardness, scared that others might notice. To talk about oneself and one's own writing is to talk about imperfection. I will remain this heavy bird.'

✵

My constituency is the nation of

the small townlands...

LIAM Ó MUIRTHILE

The Parlour

You had to get a key to open it. In the cool
Interior your blood was racing, looking for
The secrets of mantelpiece or drawer.

Once the door was quietly locked, I was shut in,
Back among the photographs of forebears,
Devoutly attending this most private altar.

That was where the priest robed for the Stations:
The hiding-place of accordion and saxophone,
Of cattle certificates and papal marriage blessings.

We spent one whole year hiding out on the farm,
Fleeing the polio that was rampant in the City,
Wasting the legs of children in the streets.

Now in that country parlour I am seeking
Something else: that tie we have with the past –
To bring back to the light its blinded citizens.

They all said I looked like my mother's father,
And here's his wedding: cold as the marble shelf
In his bone-collared, high-necked shirt, and my bent nose.

And here's Paddy 'The Russian' Murphy from Sliabh Owen
Who hadn't the remotest interest in farming,
Whose ear they held a gun to in the time of the Tans.

Not that he ever did any act of daring.
He was delicate, and more interested in poetry
Of the *Nation*'s kind from the nineteenth century.

The Kilmichael ambush happened at the far end of the parish;
I used to fancy it was my grandfather who provided
The Volunteers' bucket of tea the night before it.

It wasn't actually; he was too far away.
But people on the run often slept in the settle,
And once the house was cleared for a military court.

My small moments of history; my household gods; my myth,
Revisiting the parlour for my benefit, so now I know
My constituency is the nation of the small townlands.

Translated from the Irish by Bernard O'Donoghue

Liam Ó Muirthile (1950–), born in Cork, was associated with the poetry
magazine *Innti* and for many years wrote a column for *The Irish Times*.
Bernard O'Donoghue writes: 'Translation of Ó Muirthile's work seems to me
to be particularly vital because of his quiet, reasoned addressing of public
issues, perhaps attributable to his dual role as poet and journalist, and for his
demonstration that modern and international subjects can be treated in Irish
as much as in any other poetry.'

Gerontology or When You Get Old

My wife and I,
we often sit on a bench
outside the city and gaze.
Our canes
at our sides.

A flower quivers in the grass.
A snail wanders across the path.
And ants crawl up the tree.

The wind is blowing a little,
and it is very quiet.

But the other day
a tiny airplane landed.
It was just small enough
to hold in one's hand.
It rumbled a bit and came to a stop.
A toy gnome got out
and asked us
the way to Honolulu.
But we didn't know.
So the gnome got back in
and flew off
straight up into the sky from where he came.

If we
were to tell our neighbours,
they'd think we had lost it.
And we won't tell our doctor either,
definitely not him.
At most we'll say:

A flower quivered in the grass.
A snail wandered across the path.
And ants crawled up the tree.

Translated from the Franconian-German dialect by Shon Arieh-Lerer

Heinz Ehemann (1931–), born in Nuremberg, lives and works as a writer and a painter in Erlangen. He writes both in standard German and Franconian dialect. His dialect poetry book *A glanner Schbooz hoggd aufm Fensderblech* was published by Glock und Lutz in Nuremberg in 1976.

Georgi Gospodinov (1968–), is a poet, novelist and short-story writer well represented in English translations published by, among others, Graywolf Press, Arc and Northwestern Unversity Press. His stories have something of the narrative complexity of Borges. And in prose and poetry alike he asserts his love of life and the value of it in a homeland whose circumstances have changed drastically during the passage of one century into the next.

GEORGI GOSPODINOV

My Mother Reads Poetry

2 packs thin ready-rolled pastry sheets
2 coffee cups butter melted
a kilogram of apples
1 cup biscuit crumbs
1 cup ground walnuts
2 coffee cups sugar
1 packet cinnamon powder

Wash the apples, peel
and remove the seeds, grate
in large strips, mix
with the sugar, the ground walnuts
and the cinnamon.
Take a pastry sheet,
grease it
and cover it with another sheet.
Spread some of the apple mix
over them and roll
them together. Repeat
with the other pastry sheets.
Grease them and bake
over medium heat, until
the top crust is red,
and the bottom pink.

When you bake it, it's a strudel,
but for now it's still a poem.

Translated from the Bulgarian by Maria Vassileva and Bilyana Kourtasheva

HAI ZI

Sonnet: Crown

The girl that I love
The girl of river
Her hair turns into leaves
Her arms turn into trunk

Since you can't be my wife
you must be my crown

I'll share you with the world's great poets
wrap my harp and arrow bag with your leaves

The roof of autumn   the weight of time
Autumn is bitter and fragrant
It makes a stone bloom   like a crown

The roof of autumn is bitter and fragrant
The air is filled with the bitter fragrance
of laurels and almonds from a cleft-open crown

Translated from the Chinese by Chun Ye

Hai Zi (1964–1989) was born and raised in a farming village in Anhui Province. When he was 15 he passed the entrance exam to the prestigious Beijing University and at 20 he started teaching at China University of Political Science and Law. Between 1984 and 1989, he wrote about 200 poems and several epics. He committed suicide in 1989. He is now one of the most widely read contemporary poets in China.

It was your words

whitened the orange trees,

freighted their branches

with love's flowers, with snow...

NIKIFOROS VRETTAKOS

The Orange Trees of Sparta

It was your words
whitened the orange trees,
freighted their branches
with love's flowers, with snow.

I filled my arms with them.
I went home.

My mother was sitting outside
in the moonlight,
fretting over me.

This is what she said to me,
scoldingly,
sitting out under the moon.

It was only yesterday
that I washed your hair;
only yesterday
that I changed your dress for you.

Where have you been?
Who soaked your clothes with tears
and filled your arms with the blossom
of the bitter orange?

Translated from the Greek by Robert Hull

GUY GOFFETTE

From 'Elegy for a Friend'
(for Paul de Roux)

II

Always, still, tomorrow, these paltry
words, thrown off in passing, overflow us.
They pile up in the margins of our lives
smooth, unfevered

sand, to which no one pays attention
until the heart suddenly beats
its wings and begins to count its steps,
because everything has been said,

everything, and all that's left is to shut the door.
But suddenly it resists and creaks like
memory before a mountain of forgetting:
this pile of sand, this

silence that takes up all the space and screams.

Translated from the French by Marilyn Hacker

Guy Goffette (1947–) is, in Marilyn Hacker's words, 'one of the most unabashedly lyrical contemporary French poets'. 'Elegy for a Friend' is dedicated to the poet Paul de Roux, Goffette's close friend, who had suffered a stroke.

Nikiforos Vrettakos (1912–1991) was born in the village of Krokees, near Sparta, and published his first collection of poems, *Under Shadows and Lights*, in 1929, at the age of 17. That same year he moved to Athens to attend university, but left after a year to take a series of jobs as a clerk in various businesses. In 1937 he began a thirty-year career in the Greek Civil Service, also during this period seeing combat in the Greco-Italian War. In 1967, when the Colonels seized power, he went into self-imposed exile in Switzerland and Italy, returning to Greece in 1974. Vretttakos was considered one of Greece's most important poets. Some of his poems became popular songs in musical settings by Greek composers, including Mikis Theodorakis. He was elected a member of the Academy of Athens in 1987.

WANG WEI

Autumnal Dusk in the Mountains

On the bare mountain, rain has just passed.
The weather is gloomy. Autumn is on its way.
The bright moon shines between the pines.
A clear spring trickles over a rock.
Bamboos rustle. A woman returns from washing.
Lotuses stir beneath a fishing boat.
I long for the coming spring and rest.
The world and his wife can come and stay.

Translated from the Chinese by Julian Farmer

Wang Wei (699–761) was a painter, musician and poet of the Tang period –
and a devout Buddhist. He had the almost customary period of exile to the
provinces, but passed it well enough in cultivating his estate on the Wang
River. Returning to the capital, he managed quite astutely to combine his day
job with his deeper needs. Michael Foley, another translator of Wang Wei,
said of him: 'He is an inspiration to all those who gaze from office desks at a
patch of sky.'

When you return it's always...

When you return it's always
as though I saw you
for the first time:

my soul emits a silver dust
as catkins do
when spring winds first touch them.

Translated from the German by Martina Thomson

Paula Ludwig (1900–1974) was born in Vorarlberg in Austria – 'under a full moon,' as she put it, 'in a castle in the middle of a wood.' The castle was small and a bit of a ruin where her parents, who were poor, lived rent-free. Her father, a carpenter, had worked for a firm that made organ screens. He now made coffins. She had a child when she was 16. Deserted by its father she hid away in a small village and supported herself by peddling shoelaces. Towards the end of the Great War she made her way to Munich where she moved among actors, painters and poets and where her first slim book of lyrics *A Trace of Happiness* was published. In these, her best years, the years between two wars, she wrote the poems inspired by her passionate and fraught relationship with Yvan Goll. In exile (1938–53), most of it in Brazil, she suffered isolation and hardship; and returning then to Austria she could not reconnect with and develop the gifts of her earlier life.

PAULA LUDWIG

A day and a night it took me...

A day and a night it took me
to grasp it was you
who called me.

I trembled with the touch of your breath –
frailer than the graveyard crocus
in spring winds.

The burial-linen is still about me
the shock of resurrection in my limbs
my breasts pointed from the touch of angels.

Oh, hold me gently
softly restore my eyes.
In the darkness of your breath
let me slowly wake to life.

I was braced and big –
like a mountain range
my sorrows outgrew me.

But now I am weak.
Frightened, dumb
I stare at the face of redemption –

Translated from the German by Martina Thomson

PRIMO LEVI

Singing

...But when we began to sing
Our songs, senseless and good,
It seemed that everything
Stood as it once had stood.

The days were merely days.
Seven made a week.
Killing we thought was wicked.
Of dying we didn't speak.

The months sped by so fast,
With too many to come for complaints!
Again we were only young:
Not martyrs, the shamed, or saints.

We had these thoughts and others
As long as we could sing.
But it's all hard to explain,
Being a cloudlike thing.

[3 January 1946]

Translated from the Italian by Marco Sonzogni and Harry Thomas

YVES BONNEFOY

Threats of the Witness

1

What did you want to set up on this table
If not the double fire of our death?
Frightened, I destroyed in this world
The red, bare table where the dead wind speaks.

Then I grew older. Outside, the truth of words
And the truth of wind have ceased their fight.
The fire has drawn away, which was my church,
I am no longer even frightened, I do not sleep.

2

See, all the paths you went along are closed now,
No longer are you granted even the respite
To wander even lost. Earth, failing, sounds
With your footsteps which are going nowhere.

Why did you allow brambles to cover
That high silence you'd arrived at? The fire,
Empty, watches over memory's garden
And you, shadow in the shade, where are you, who are you?

3

You no longer come into this garden,
The paths of suffering and aloneness vanish,
The grasses intimate your face of death.

It does not matter to you any more
That stone conceals the dark church, and that trees
Conceal the dazzled face of a redder sun,

For you it is enough
To take a long time dying as in sleep,
And now you do not even love
The shadow you will wed.

Translated from the French by Anthony Rudolf

Each meal is a bowl of rust-coloured rice...

Yves Bonnefoy, born 1923 in Tours, the son of a railroad worker and a teacher, is a French poet among the most important of his generation. His *Hier régnant désert* (from which this poem is taken) was published by *MPT* with a facing translation by Anthony Rudolf as *Yesterday's Wilderness Kingdom* in 2000. Bonnefoy's influence extends beyond the world of poetry thanks to his essays on literature and art, his translations of Shakespeare's complete tragedies and his teaching at the Collège de France.

HÔ CHÍ MINH

Entertainment

(from *Prison Diary*)

Half a bucket of water a day:
it's up to us whether we drink it or wash.
Clean your face and go thirsty:
you can tell a tea-drinker by his grime.

Each meal is a bowl of rust-coloured rice:
no salt, no greens, not even a ladle of soup.
Each prisoner must smuggle in food to eat
or else pine for his mother's cooking.

After supper, while the sun sinks,
songs spring out of the silence.
And from the darkness of Jingxi District Prison
appears a little music school.

A prisoner blows on his flute
till it keens and it weeps
and it fills the convicts' ears and hearts,
and it lilts beyond the prison walls,
crossing hills and streams
to where a woman looks out
from the door of her hut
watching the skyline.

Translated from the Vietnamese by Timothy Allen

HÔ CHÍ MINH

Liberation

(from *Prison Diary*)

Everything changes: that's a universal law.
One week of rain, then the sun comes out
and the earth slips off its wet clothes.
And for a thousand miles, the world springs back to life:
warm sun, cool breeze, blooms and blossom,
birdsong in the trees.
Bitter days are followed by sweet.
That's a universal law: everything changes.

The old poets sang of moonlight and rain,
of snowstorms, and mists over hills and streams.
But my poems are made of steel
and each verse is an act of resistance.

Imprisoned: 29 August 1942
Released without charge: 10 September 1943

Translated from the Vietnamese by Timothy Allen

Hô Chí Minh (1890-1969) was President of Vietnam from 1945 to 1969.

Tim Allen writes: 'In August, 1942, a middle-aged Vietnamese gentleman ordered a set of business cards from a Hanoi printer. The cards were to be printed in Chinese. In one corner, they gave his profession as press correspondent'; in another, his nationality as Chinese, resident in Vietnam; and in the centre, his name as Hô Chí Minh. All three pieces of information were false.

He intended the visiting cards as his travelling documents for a short trip into China – he was hoping to meet both with the wartime government of China, led by Lin Seng, and also with its Communist opponents, led by Mao Zedong. With both groups, his intention was to make common cause against the Japanese, carrying with him the fraternal greetings of the Vietminh.

He estimated that the trip would take him four to five weeks. In the event, he never succeeded in meeting any Chinese political leaders, because he was arrested on suspicion of spying shortly after crossing the border. He would spend the next thirteen months being frogmarched between southern Chinese prisons, an experience that forms the subject of his prison diaries.'

AL-SADDIQ AL-RADDI

Nothing

Before you start reading,
put down your pen:
consider the ink,
how it comprehends bleeding

Learn
from the distant horizon
and from narrowing eyes
the expansiveness of vision
and the treachery of hands

Do not blame me – do not blame anyone –
if you die before you read on
before blood is understood

Translated from the Arabic by Sarah Maguire and Atef Alshaer

Al-Saddiq Al-Raddi is one of the leading African poets writing in Arabic today. He has gained a wide audience in his native Sudan for his imaginative approach to poetry and for the delicacy and emotional frankness of his lyrics. Saddiq was born in 1969 and grew up in Omdurman Khartoum where he lived until forced into exile in 2012. From 2006, he was the cultural editor of *Al-Sudani* newspaper until he was sacked from his position for political reasons (along with 22 other colleagues) in July 2012 during the uprising against the dictatorship of Omar Al-Bashir. Saddiq only escaped imprisonment because he was in the UK for the Poetry Parnassus festival at London's Southbank Centre when a series of mass arrests took place. He applied for asylum and now lives in London.

GERÐUR KRISTNÝ

My Brother and Sister

Can't remember myself
without them

didn't really come into being
before they were born
with messages from the Almighty
inlaid in their soles

Haven't been able to decipher them
until now

the reason probably being
that I always walked ahead of them
thus never seeing their footprints

Request to be allowed
to keep the head start
beyond the grave

so that I will never remember myself
without them

Translated from the Icelandic by Sigurður A. Magnússon

MAYA SARISHVILI

To My Father

I know what makes you scream in your sleep –
snakes rising from the candelabras
light up the room with their tongues.
And how frightening is that droning darkness,
poisoned with a treacherous light...
I know how every night you lather your own heart
like soap on your whole body.
How eager to remove the stains
with your own heart's foam.
Perhaps for that very reason
mother rises up from death every night
to plant roses in your slippers,
where you will move your feet in the morning...
Please find the sound of my childhood in our house.
It will probably be somewhere close to a box of sweets.
And if the little marmalade dog barks,
or anything like this,
then the curse has been broken...

Translated from the Georgian by Timothy Kercher and Nene Giorgadze

Maya Sarashvili, born 1968, lives in Tbilisi, works as a primary school teacher and looks after her four children. She won Georgia's top literary prize for her frst collection of poems, *Microscope*. Translator and scholar Ingrid Degraeve writes: 'Female poetry in Georgia has all the characteristics of a diary: it consists of tough statements of what it is like to live as a woman, wife, mother and daughter. The existentialist tone is perhaps reminiscent of the work of Sylvia Plath, who is a considerable model for many female Georgian poets.'

This ice-cutter silence...

This ice-cutter silence
will slice through everything.
Where is the road that is coming for you?
Only the moon will be left like a kite.
I'll follow the line of its string
where there is an easing into losing patience
and an incurable silence
as if the blood lacks a sunset.
Below, a new day will start –
slide into my bed like a black spade into early morning soil –
digging me out from the dreams
that turned me over.

Translated from the Georgian by Timothy Kercher and Nene Giorgadze

FEDERICO GARCÍA LORCA

Romance de la Pena Negra

Sharp as mattocks, rooster beaks pierce the dawn
as Soledad Montoya climbs down the dark mountain.

Yellow copper, her flesh. Scent of horses and shadows.
Her breasts, two smoking anvils, resound with round moans.

Soledad, whom do you ask for, alone and at this hour?
'What does it matter? I ask for the one I ask for.
I seek what I am searching for: my joy and my own self.'

Soledad of my sorrow, hard-mouthed and untameable,
in the end you'll reach the sea, and waves will swallow you.

'Don't remind me of the sea, for if you do the black pain
will unfurl in the land of olives beneath the rumour of leaf-rain.'

Soledad, what hurt you suffer! What great pathetic grief!
Lemon tears bitter with waiting roll into your mouth.

'What enormous pain! I run back and forth like a madwoman,
from hearth to bed-post, my braids dragging on the ground.

What pain! I am turning into jet: black flesh, black clothes.
Ay, my fine linen shifts! Ay, my thighs frail as poppies!'

Soledad, wash your body with the dew of skylarks.
Soledad Montoya, rest your heart in remotest peace.

Far below sings the river, streaming with sky and leaves.
New light crowns itself with yellow squash-flowers.

Oh the pain of the gypsies! Pain so clean and alone.
Pain of hidden river-beds and unapproachable dawns.

Translated from the Spanish by Julith Jedamus

When I Was a Boy

When I was a boy
Grasses and masts stood beside the shore,
And I, lying there,
Couldn't distinguish between them,
For they all rose up to the sky above me.
Only the words of my mother stayed with me
Like a slice of bread wrapped in rustling tissue
And I did not know when my father would return,
For there was another forest beyond the clearing.
Everything held out a hand,
A bull tossed the sun on its horns,
And in the nights the streetlights stroked
My cheeks with the walls,
And the moon, like a great jar, tilted itself
And watered my thirsty sleep.

Translated from the Hebrew by Margalit Benaya

Federico del Sagrado Corazón de Jesús García Lorca (1898–1936) was a Spanish poet, dramatist and theatre director. García Lorca achieved international recognition as an emblematic member of the Generation of '27. He is believed to be one of the thousands who were summarily shot by anti-communist death squads during the Spanish Civil War.

CARLOS DRUMMOND DE ANDRADE

Seven-sided Poem

When I was born, one of those twisted
angels who live in the shadows said:
'Carlos, get ready to be a misfit in life!'

The houses watch the men
who chase after women.
If desire weren't so rampant,
the afternoon might be blue.

The passing streetcar's full of legs:
white and black and yellow legs.
My heart asks why, my God, so many legs?
My eyes, however,
ask no questions.

The man behind the moustache
is serious, simple, and strong.
He hardly ever talks.
Only a very few are friends
with the man behind the glasses and moustache.

My God, why have you forsaken me
if you knew that I wasn't God,
if you knew that I was weak.

World so large, world so wide,
if my name were Clyde,
it would be a rhyme but not an answer.
World so wide, world so large,
my heart's even larger.

I shouldn't tell you,
but this moon
but this brandy
make me sentimental as hell.

Translated from the Brazilian Portuguese by Richard Zenith

MARZANNA BOGUMILA KIELAR

a flock of pigeons blossoms white against the greyish cloth

a flock of pigeons blossoms white against the greyish cloth
of a cloud, over the town, as I'm drawing back the curtains,
and softly flows down:
the day has just breathed in fresh air; naked
– what names does it await now,
in the grey alleyways?

You're asleep, haven't turned your head; your fist clutches
at the sheet, shadow of the night – withdrawing,
it says, composed and assured: 'I will give you back
only for a little while.'

Translated from the Polish by Elzbieta Wójcik-Leese

'Born in 1963, the austerity of Marzanna Bogumila Kielar's mindscape compels
with its monochromy. White, grey, black; chilly, cold, freezing; and occasional
red. This stark concentration is strengthened by the poems' insistent returns to
the same place: northern Poland, where Kielar grew up. "It is the landscape
whose pulse and vibrations I can sense in my blood," she admits. "My first
homeland is a post-German landscape," Kielar explains. She has conducted
field interviews with the inhabitants of the area (which, after the Second
World War, witnessed the deportation of Germans and ethnic Mazurians as
well as the arrival of Ukrainians and Poles) in order to investigate how these
people establish an emotional bond with the space they inhabit, how they
symbolically take it into possession – the questions her poetry asks.' EWL

Carlos Drummond de Andrade (1902–1987) grew up in the Brazilian interior. He
spent most of his life working as a government bureaucrat in Rio de Janeiro, but
his real vocation was writing. Few would dispute his status as Brazil's greatest
poet. Richard Zenith writes: 'His poetry would continually try out new styles –
lyrical, narrative, epic, free verse, blank verse, rhymed and unrhymed sonnets...
And it kept spreading into new territories, including politics, eros, and auto-
biographical memoir. His poetry *ranged* – like the cattle on the sprawling ranch
where he grew up, in the landlocked state of Minas Gerais.

ANNA KÜHN-CICHOCKA

Here the houses...

here the houses
grazed quietly
under the watchful eye
of the church tower
it was high
made of brick
with a six-sided
sharply pointed roof
it seemed to be
a huge pencil
to write down
our misdemeanours
on blue pages of the sky

the organist played beautifully
but his singing was worse
sometimes from a nearby meadow
sheep answered him

at Christmas time
women with their whole heart and throat
tore Christmas carols to shreds
the plaster baby
stopped his ears with his little fists
but God smiled under his moustache
and gave absolution

Translated from the Polish by Sarah Lawson and Malgorzata Koraszweska

On rainy days...

on rainy days
we discovered
a wonderful world of attics
here lived
a clock with a late cuckoo
remembering better times
the old trunk
full of mysteries
wrapped in torn lace
an iron that had run out of steam
and lost its shirt
countless objects
which had already forgotten
who needed them
and for what

we sat in rickety armchairs
the dust danced in the light of a candle
sometimes a floorboard creaked
or a spring moaned
spiders spun
stories about ghosts
and fear
had bigger and bigger eyes

Translated from the Polish by Sarah Lawson and Malgorzata Koraszweska

Anna Kühn-Cichocka (1940–), born in Włocławek, lives in Płock, a town on the Vistula River northwest of Warsaw. Although she had never visited the small town of Dobrzyń nad Wisłą (which lies between Włocławek and Płock), a friend of hers, who had grown up there, told her so much about the place that she decided to write about it herself, imagining herself into the 'feel' of the town and its characters. In 2003 she published a poetry pamphlet called *A Little Town with a View on the River* with her imaginative re-creation of life in Dobrzyń nad Wisłą.

MARIO LUZI

Life True to Life

The city on Sunday
getting late
when there is peace
though a radio moans
out of its stiffened entrails

and if you enter the crevice of a street
clean cut between the banks, you will find
– so sweet it is a pang – what is human
crouched in its cellars and its mezzanines.

a truce, yes, and yet
someone, forehead on the asphalt, is dying
among a few bewildered people
who stop and gather round the accident,

and we are here by fate or chance together
you and I, my partner for an hour or two,
in this maddened circle
beneath the sword with double edge
of judgement or remission,

life true to life
all this that has grown within it
where is it going, I wonder,
slipping or climbing in fits and starts towards its beginning...

although it doesn't matter, although it is our life
and that's that.

Translated from the Italian by Patrick Creagh

SOPHIE DE MELLO BREYNER ANDRESEN

Sibyls

Sibyls of deep caves, of petrification,
Totally loveless and sightless,
Feeding nothingness as if a sacred fire
While shadow unmakes night and day
Into the same light of fleshless horror.

Drive out that foul dew
Of impacted nights, the sweat
Of forces turned against themselves
When words batter the walls
In blind, wild swoops of trapped birds
And the horror of being winged
Shrills like a clock through a vacuum.

Translated from the Portuguese by Ruth Fainlight

Sophie de Mello Breyner Andresen (1919–2004) was born in Porto to a wealthy aristocratic family. She inherited the surname 'Andresen' from her paternal grandfather, a Danish merchant. As a student, she was actively involved in Catholic movements. Politically, she defended constitutional monarchy and openly criticised Salazar's dictatorship. She was a translator of Dante and Shakespeare.

Considered to be one of the major European poets of the 20th century, and the incarnation of the revolutionary 'hermetic' mode of the 50s, Mario Luzi (1914–2005) went on to expand his very personal form of poetic expression towards a more open, narrative lyric style. He also wrote short stories, essays and plays, and was a noted translator of French, English and Spanish poetry. Among his vast body of work there is a fine translation of Shakespeare's *Richard II*.

ANNA ENQUIST

River

So often I have sought in the vicinity of rivers
for proof it was possible; I run into myself
at times mating in tall grass, hear water, wind –
swans flying over measuring unborn time
with wooden wings; the copulation rhythm says
black-white, yes-no, so does your heart and that's
it, a lap is it, is forever

At bad times I sought treacherously halfheartedly
the opposite: how I could let myself slide
breasts cunt and all into that murmuring black mother,
rocked in poisonous embrace done comfortingly away with.

How would I lie then, blue and swollen among
reed stalks, terror of the moorhens? oh no

A strange compromise occurred in
the clear winter night when I, at ten o'clock
or thereabouts, girded myself with skates
and slid forth, forth over black ice with an occasional
silver fish mounted in it, made real haste
for never again, for nowhere

Translated from the Dutch by Lloyd Haft

Anna Enquist (1945–) is the pen name of one of the most popular female
authors in the Netherlands, Christa Widlund-Broer. She is known for both
her poetry and her novels. Born in Amsterdam, Enquist studied piano at the
Music Academy in The Hague and psychology at Leiden University. Her first
poems appeared in the journal *Maatstaaf* in 1988 while her first collection
Soldatenliederen (Soldiers' Songs) was published in 1991 while she was still
working as a psychoanalyst. Thereafter she devoted most of her time to
literature.

EDITH SÖDERGRAN

Violet Dusks

Violet dusks I bear within me from my origins,
naked maidens at play with galloping centaurs...
Yellow sunlit days with gaudy glances,
only sunbeams do true homage to a tender woman's body...
The man has not come, has never been, will never be...
The man in a false mirror the sun's daughter angrily throws against the rock-face,
the man is a lie that white children do not understand,
the man is a rotten fruit that proud lips disdain.

Beautiful sisters, come high up on to the strongest rocks,
we are all warriors, heroines, horsewomen,
eyes of innocence, heavenly foreheads, rose masks,
heavy breakers and birds flown by,
we are the least expected and the deepest red,
stripes of tigers, taut strings, stars without vertigo.

Translated from the Finland Swedish by David McDuff

Edith Södergran (1892–1923) was born in St Petersburg, where her father worked
as an engineer. She grew up knowing Finnish, Swedish and Russian, but
attended a German school and wrote her first literary works in German.
Although in later life she wrote in Swedish, she always considered German
the language she had closest sympathy with. In 1917 the family left Russia and
Edith, who had contracted TB, spent the rest of her life a semi-invalid in a
Karelian village not far from the Russian border called Raivola. She was
intensely excited about the Revolution, believing it would help bring about a
new world order. Far from being isolated from the great events, she witnessed
them as they took place: in Raivola at night she could hear fighting and see
the glow of burning buildings. Edith Södergran's lyrics are generally regarded
as the cornerstone of modernism in Swedish literature. She died, aged only 31,
in 1923.

INGEBORG BACHMANN

Fog Land

In winter my beloved one
is among the beasts of the forest.
The vixen knows that I
must return before morning, and laughs.
How the clouds tremble!
And on my snow-collar falls
a coat of brittle ice.

In winter my beloved one
is a tree among trees and invites
the luck-deserted crows
to her beautiful boughs. She knows
that at dawn the wind will lift
her stiff and frost-trimmed evening-
dress and chase me home.

In winter my beloved one
is among the fish and dumb.
A slave to the waters stirred
by the stroke of her fins within,
I stand on the shore and watch,
till the ice-floes drive me away,
how she plunges, swirls and twists.

And struck again by the hunting-cry
of the bird that stiffens its wings
above me, I fall down flat
on the open field: she plucks
the hens, and the white collar-bone
she throws me I hang round my neck
and go off through the bitter down.

Unfaithful is my beloved one,
I know, she sometimes glides
on high heels to the town,
in the bars with a straw she kisses
the glasses deep in the mouth,
and has words for everyone.
But this language I don't understand.

Fog land have I seen.
Fog heart have I eaten.

Translated from the German by Daniel Huws

INGEBORG BACHMANN

Days in White

These days I get up with the birches
and comb the wheat hair from my forehead
in front of a mirror of ice.

Mixed with my breath
the milk flakes.
So early it frosts up.
And where I breathe on the pane appears
drawn by a childish finger
once more your name, innocence!
After so long.

These days it doesn't pain me
that I'm able to forget
and have to remember.

I'm in love. To white-heat
I love and give thanks with angelic greetings.
I learnt them in flight.

These days I think of the albatross
with whom I soared
up and over
to an undescribed country.

There on the horizon,
brilliant in its destruction,
I'm aware of my fabulous continent
that dismissed me
in a shroud.

I'm alive and from afar I hear its swansong.

Translated from the German by Daniel Huws

The Correspondence of Ingeborg Bachmann and Paul Celan

2008, which saw the publication of the correspondence between perhaps the two most important American poets since the war, Elizabeth Bishop and Robert Lowell, also saw that of the letters between almost certainly the two most important German-language poets of the same period, though neither of them was German. When Paul Celan arrived in Vienna late in 1947 he had come, via Bucharest and Budapest, from Czernowitz, once an outpost of the Austro-Hungarian empire where his parents were part of a German-speaking enclave. Ingeborg Bachmann had then been in Vienna for just over a year, studying philosophy, having come herself from the provincial town of Klagenfurt not far from the Slovenian border. She was six years younger than Celan (Bishop was six years older than Lowell). By May 1948 they had met and were in love, and as this book shows, they remained in close touch until the beginning of the 60s, when, as happened with so many of Celan's friendships, the spurious charges of plagiarism brought against him by Claire Goll and what he saw as the insufficient response by his friends unravelled the ties which should have helped to dismiss the charges as irrelevant fictions. (A last stray note from Celan to Bachmann in 1967 thanks her for recommending him as a potential translator of Akhmatova – Bachmann left her publishers when they instead commissioned a version by someone who had been the author of a Nazi song.) This book makes it easier to understand why Celan was so affected by the charges, but it also gives us an unbearably sad picture of missed opportunities and exhausted hopes. Whereas plenty was known about the relationship between Bishop and Lowell, not much was about Bachmann and Celan's before these letters were released. The facts are startling but far from complete, and the overwhelming feeling the letters leave you with is sadness.

In some ways it was always going to be fraught relationship: Celan's parents had both died in Nazi concentration camps; Bachmann's father had been a member of the NSDAP. A poem Celan gave to Bachmann before leaving Vienna contains the lines 'You shall say to Ruth, to Miriam and to Naomi: | Look, I'm sleeping with her!' 'The surrealist poet Paul Celan whom I met just the other evening together with Weigel at the artist Jené's and who's really fascinating has fallen gloriously in love with me', is how Bachmann announced the beginning in a letter to her parents. 'Unfortunately he's off to Paris in a month's time. My room at the moment is like a poppy-field, that being the kind of flower he likes to shower me with.' If we're interested, and it's hard not to be, we can trace the rest of their relationship through the letters, with the help of the detailed chronology given at the end of the book: Bachmann visited Celan a few times in Paris, they met once at a meeting of the Gruppe 47 in Germany, but in 1952 Celan married. Then in 1957 it all started up again at another literary event, Celan sending her poems and letters and making several trips to her in Munich: 'You were, when I met you, both things for me: the sensuous and the spiritual. That can never come asunder, Ingeborg.' Whether it did or not, this phase of their relationship ended the following year, though the ensuing letters seem to be full of regrets and unresolvedness. After that meetings were few, and usually to do with literary business. Then towards the end the correspondence is invaded by the so-called 'Goll affair'. There are lots of gaps, as is natural, lots of references to telephone calls which seem to have played a bigger role in this distance relationship than the letters. The letters themselves are by turns fascinating and rather humdrum, full of charges and confusions we can't quite understand, tantalisingly incomplete despite the detailed commentary. Bachmann comes out of the correspondence better than Celan. In one long letter that, like several others, was never sent (27 September 1961) she gives an amazingly clear-sighted account of Celan's situation, of why he is ready to 'let himself be buried' by the false criticism levelled against him. And she also says: 'Of all the many injustices and hurtfulnesses I have been exposed to thus far the worst are those that have come from you. Who am I for you after so many years? A phantom, or a reality that no longer corresponds to that phantom? A lot has happened to me and I want to be the person I am, today. Do you even perceive me now? That's what I don't know, and it makes me desperate.' After Celan's death in 1970 Bachmann inserted a dream sequence into her novel *Malina* in which she has a figure learn of the death of her 'lover', who is easily identifiable as a version of Celan. The figure says: 'he was my life. I loved him more than my life.'

VITA ANDERSEN

The Beautiful Room

the room was beautiful
the walls were peach coloured
there were high wood panels
the floor was covered by a thick white shepherd's rug
in the middle of the salmon coloured room
a mattress was lying
covered with a patchwork-quilt
and full of pillows of matching colours
sounds of children's voices came into the room

she was sitting in a corner of the room
completely covered by a blanket
rocking from side to side
whimpering with tiny animal sounds
as if in great distress

she had been there a long time
suddenly she rose
folded the blanket carefully
and placed it neatly on the mattress
let her hands glide over her face and hair
to make it normal
she left the room
closed the door behind her
and said with a normal voice
tidy up now, please
father will be home soon

Translated from the Danish by Jannick Storm and Linda Lappin

Vita Andersen (1944–) was born in Copenhagen and writes poetry and novels for adults and children. In 1977 she spent several months at the International Writing Program at the University of Iowa, where this poem was translated.

NINA CASSIAN

Like Gulliver

My unwieldy lovers – I haul you to shore
like Gulliver dragging a hundred ships,
you colourful scheming bunch
with your teeny swords stiff for battle!

Like Gulliver, I'll give you a break
though you're out to crack my head open
and let you cling to the bloody ropes of my laughter
my heartless, loud-mouthed men.

Translated from the Romanian by Laura Schiff and Virgil Nemoianu

HILDE DOMIN

Catalogue

The heart a snail
with a house
draws in its horns.

The heart a hedgehog.

The heart an owl
in light
fluttering its eyelids.

Bird of passage, climate-changer heart.

The heart a ball
pushed
rolling one centimetre.

Sand-grain heart.

The heart the great
thrower
of every ball.

Translated from the German by Tudor Morris

HALINA POŚWIATOWSKA

These words have existed always...

These words have existed always
in the open smile of a sunflower
in the dark wing of a crow
and even in the frame of a half-opened door

even before there was a door
they existed in the branches of a straight tree

and you want me to have them as mine
to be the wing of the crow
to be the birch and summer
to hum with the sound of beehives open to the sun

Fool. I do not own these words
but borrow them from the wind
from bees and from the sun

Translated from the Polish by Andrzej Busza and Bogdan Czaykowski

Halina Poświatowska (1935–1967) was a lyric poet justly celebrated for her passionate yet unsentimental treatment of love and death. From her childhood under the German occupation she was afflicted with a chronic heart condition. She had treatment for it in the USA in 1958, and then, with scant English, enrolled at Smith College and completed a three-year undergraduate course there. Returning to Poland, she matriculated in Philosophy in Kraków but died before she could finish her doctorate. Her works were collected in four volumes in 1997, of which the first two (several hundred pages) are poems, and the latter two prose and letters. She loved New York, its museums and galleries and, especially, Harlem.

HALINA POŚWIATOWSKA

my face is more and more like the moon...

my face is more and more like the moon
waning
covered with a net of cracks
like a Greek vase
unearthed

full of the memory of touch
of hands of lips
which have long turned into dust

now suitable only
for a museum shelf

it is too brittle
and precious
for everyday use

Translated from the Polish by Andrzej Busza and Bogdan Czaykowski

RUTGER KOPLAND

Three Winter Poems

1

Through godforsaken soaked land
from town to town, hand
in cold hand, I hope I'll never share
that feeling with anyone again. If
I don't have to.

But if I found her now
in the wet grass, or somewhere
in the ploughed earth, what
would I do, what would I?

I know everybody has to die,
still I'd
kiss her cold mouth again,
cover her body, stroke her
hair and again be scared
to wake her up.

2

I wanted to go with you through the meadows
along the canals the brown plumes of the reeds
but a pale sun already came down over the treetops
and farms and I knew I couldn't bear
our shadows getting long and lonely
over the meadows.
I'm scared, you said.

I wanted to go with you through the towns
through the deserted afternoon in the gardens and streets
to a bar where the sun would play for us in
the nylon curtains but I knew I couldn't bear
the silence, long and lonely,
coming between us.
I'm scared, you said.

I wanted to sleep with you, go with
my eyes my hands my mouth like the sun
over the strange landscape of your body
but I knew I couldn't bear
our rising lonely
for a lifetime.
I'm scared, you said.

   3

A still strange sorrow
for which I waited a lifetime
came with you.

It came from your eyes into mine
from your hands under my coat
it came and I let it in.

Finally I saw that everything would
pass like this day
above the country I love.

I'm not saying that it's bad
I'm just saying what I think
I saw.

Translated from the Dutch by Ria Leigh-Loohuizen

Rutger Kopland (1934–2012) made his debut in 1966 and published over 15 volumes of poetry, as well as collections of essays and notes and travel and translation. He was one of the Netherlands' best-loved poets. He spoke to his readers in a quiet, conversational style, using ostensibly simple phrases. His poems seem to evoke a wistful, almost nostalgic atmosphere of a lost paradise, happiness beneath an apple tree or in the grass. But Kopland himself said: 'Everyone finds a lost paradise in my poetry, a longing for it. I don't long for the past, I long for experience, and experience is new, now.'

ANTONÍN BARTUŠEK

Those Few Years

You won't give up.
You still hope.
You keep the fingerprints
of all disasters.
You hope to catch them red-handed.
Snow is falling doubly.
Suddenly we have grey hair,
the two of us.

Translated from the Czech by Ewald Osers

HARUO SHIBUYA

A Young Wife

On a page opened casually
Her eyes are apt to slip away.
While she sings to herself
After her part-time morning job,
She ruminates his smile
Spilt in the small room.

She puts her time in order till he returns
As if cutting paper patterns with a shining blade.
What remains, a bright residue of the order
Lined up by habit, is now
Her somewhat broader day.

She relaxes, leaning at a window.
Then, all at once
The single girl she was,
Opening her eyes wide
On her diffused future,
Returns, and
Sits beside her tenderly.

Translated from the Japanese by James Kirkup

Haruo Shibuya was born in 1924 in Sakhalin. He began writing poems at the age of 17. His first volume of poetry was published in 1962 in Tokyo. He was one of 13 contemporary Japanese poets translated by James Kirkup and published in *Mundus Artium: Japanese, Turkish, Cuban, Arabic Selections* by International Poetry Forum, Pittsburgh in 1976.

JEAN DODO

In My Neighbourhood Market

Seven monkeys dried and smoked
Crouching on a plank
One hundred rusted nails
In a calabash
One thousand cola nuts
Brown or red or white
Powder of gold   powder of nothing   powder of wind
Come on, take a lot, it's cheap

Seven naked kids
In the dust
One hundred merchants sleeping
On their stalls
One hundred piercing voices
Embroider the atmosphere
Powder of gold   powder of nothing   powder of wind
Come on, take a lot, it's cheap

Seven bellying jars
Of good clay
One hundred baby chicks
Without their mothers
One thousand scraps of rags
To clothe queens
Powder of gold   powder of nothing   powder of wind
Come on, take a lot, it's cheap

Seven grave men
Count their coins
One hundred red-headed birds of prey
Glide very high
One thousand grey cockroaches
Play hide-and-seek
Powder of gold   powder of nothing   powder of wind

Seven reed seeds
To paint fingernails
One hundred dried fish
With small black eyes
One thousand copper earrings
Proofs of love
Powder of gold   powder of nothing   powder of wind
Come on, take a lot, it's cheap

Seven days each week
In my neighbourhood
One hundred women buy
Coin by coin
One thousand little things
For their happiness
Powder of gold   powder of nothing   powder of wind
Come on, take a lot, it's cheap

Translated from the French by Elisavietta Ritchie

Jean Dodo, a poet from the Ivory Coast who wrote in French, was awarded the
Prix Nederlands for this poem, which was published in 1979 in *Modern Poetry
in Translation*. He was also awarded a Prix de l'Académie française for his
book *Symphonie en noir et blanc* (Symphony in black and white) in 1976.

RIDHA ZILI

Childhood

The waking of the dawn
the waking of the rooster
the rising bell rings

My two black
eyes
on the nine-times
table

What a school
what a dour list of numbers
sad as a narrow tomb
or cramped parrot's cage.

Translated from the French by Paol Keineg and Candace Slater

VASKO POPA

Bright Lovers

He burns with longing
For her glass breasts
She burns with longing
For his iron shoulders

From the two ends of town
They run all day
Towards each other

The streets rise up
Break his iron shoulders
The streets drop down
Smash her glass breasts

They meet in the middle of town
Radiant and lovely in death
Fall into each other's arms

He turns into
An iron post
She into a glass lamp
Over him

They shine each night
She in him he in her

Translated from the Serbian by Anne Pennington

VASKO POPA

High Lovers

The pavement eats
His sulphur flesh
Drinks mercury from her veins

He takes her in his arms
Lifts her to a cloud
High above the steeples

They love each other there eagerly
Like streaks of young lightning

She bears him
A son a green-eyed sword
And a daughter a red-haired flute

Happy they nurse
Their heavenly children
And go on loving each other

They never come down again
To the gold-eating pavement

Translated from the Serbian by Anne Pennington

ANNA ENQUIST

La Folia

Despair sits straddle-legged at the kitchen table.
If I let that tired cleaning woman have her way,
nothing will come of my day's plans.
She creates a wind of turmoil in the house,
making papers fly up and chill enter the halls.
From closet and drawers she pulls magic
and sticky sorrow from the past, against
my will. 'If you could do just the outside
today,' I say, disguised as a hero. Quickly
I shut the door, which I then lean against dizzy
and panting. How much longer before I
disappear with her, hand in hand, deliriously
dancing above the blazing field?

Translated from the Dutch by Manfred Wolf

Gianni D'Elia (born 1953 in Pesaro) is a poet, novelist and translator of works by, among others, Baudelaire, Gide and Yeats. In October 1997 he attended the Terzo Seminario di Poesia e Traduzione al Palazzo Ducale di Colorno along with Michael Donaghy, Elaine Feinstein and Selima Hill.

GIANNI D'ELIA

Sta(i)rway to Heaven
(in memoriam AM)

A couple of buskers – the girl's face
rosy over the pallor of her youth
numbed by hours on the high street,
the crowd swarming past

freezing them out, indifferent
to the play-list of our hearts,
hearts which long ago filled and shook
to every tremolo, and the song,

Zeppelin or Stones, the song
some old standard of a slacker
generation, you hear it again unchanged
on the greyest of Saturdays.

And the singing girl, the blond guy's electric
guitar, the tiny speaker, the pricey equaliser,
their music stand and the sheets
brown and crumpled at the edges...

we were like them – and not. You recall
long hair blown across a mild and arrogant smile,
the slightly suspicious attitude
of the womb inside the jeans, but also

the indecision, the aimlessness,
played far from the rigged game
where everything was decided.
And if you study her beauty carefully,

her hair falling in curls, the curls
of a frail androgynous Bacchus,
her eyes shut, her throat releasing its
miraculous voice,

you keep within you the sweat of those moments
when your heart ignites and everybody knows
you suffer the ache of living
in a time that prints its history on us

passing in the silence between chords,
in the low frenzy, in the subtle rhythmic shift
when you fret, the feedback shriek,
the fingers sliding wildly up the neck,

which captures that vertigo, the dreadful
orgasmic cadences leading to
the tenderness of the melody releasing
in long waves and surrenders;

to this alien tongue with its joy
in the form of a voice articulating
its only sounds as if it were the meaning
of song itself, without a name.

When she shifts up a key it rhymes –
with her sleeves pulled down on her knuckles
because it's cold playing in the frost,
with her woolly jumper, with the Indian

scarf tied loose about her neck
careless, elegant
with her dancing feet
tiny in their oversize shoes

under oversize trousers, with her throat
making her whole body shake,
with that image of a good girl, with her gifts,
so that you see again in her that vulnerable passionate boredom

and that burning street with no heaven
that took her joy away from the world
and Antonia's smile with all the others.

Translated from the Italian by Michael Donaghy

✦

So much gentleness from unknown men

for no particular reason...

MARINA BORODITSKAYA

So Much Gentleness from Unknown Men...

So much gentleness from unknown men
for no particular reason.
Once in Paris a waiter turned to me: 'Chérie!
Don't forget your cigarettes.'

And in a London market, when
I wanted to buy a Beatles record,
the stall-holder sighed: 'What can I do, love,
if the price goes up again?'

In New York airport, an old black man
took me to the right gate, saying:
'Don't panic, baby, just follow me!'
And I followed in his footsteps.

So much kindness from strange men!
Why the hell should I need more?
Lie peaceful in your oyster, pearl.
Stay calm, Moon, in the heavens.

Translated from the Russian by Ruth Fainlight

Marina Boroditskaya is a Russian poet and translator. She has published
numerous books of children's poetry in Russia, and translated many English-
language children's writers into Russian, including A.A. Milne, Eleanor
Farjeon and Hilaire Belloc. Her most recent translation, the relatively grown-
up *Poets of the Silver Age*, appeared in 2010, and she has also translated John
Donne, Chaucer and Burns, among others. She is the author of five books of
poetry for adults (but dislikes the idea that children's poetry and adult poetry
are somehow different – noting that 'they're made of the same stuff'). Marina
presents the Russian equivalent of *Poetry Please!* on Russian radio – called *The
Literary First Aid Box*, it is inspired by Marina's idea that literature is the best
multivitamin on the market.

ELENI VAKALO

From 'Genealogy'

10

My other grandmother, the older, was from the island and had
five children – boys
Every year when the ships returned, one child

They say that to keep them all alive she had said a charm, that
she should lose whichever was last.
I know the others all reached eighty
And that old grandmother of mine had that baby in her arms when it died

They said she did not weep for it, but never again went down to the ships

Only once, and that was when she said goodbye to one of her sons
And he was my father
The youngest after the dead child

13 A Charm for Women

(You say it to yourself whenever you see something and have a feeling of great love)

> Lighting the lamp on the wall I grew tall
> Planting candles at the grave I grew small

Translated from the Greek by Paul Merchant

Eleni Vakalo (1921–2001) was born in Constantinople, studied archaeology at
the University of Athens and art history at the Sorbonne. She is one of the so-
called 'Poets of Essence', a group of poets who did most of their writing after
the Second World War, the Nazi Occupation and the Greek Civil War, and
had to deal with the ruins (physical and emotional) that were the result of
those historical events and with the accompanying feelings of estrangement
and alienation.

From 'A Conversation on Children's Poetry'

Poetry is about what poetry 'can' do or 'might' do rather than what it will always do. So, it can express 'big ideas in small spaces' and this is convenient and fun. It's very good at not telling the whole story. It doesn't have to conclude and tie things up in the way that plays and novels and films tend to. This means that it can, if it wants to, avoid the falseness of the perfect conclusion. Poems are good at suggesting things which means that the reader or listener can find satisfaction in the open-ended interpretation that is asked for by the poem. Poetry can investigate uses of language. It does this through a very active 'scavenging' process, gobbling up other genres, other uses of language other than its own, other forms and indeed all previous forms of poetry itself. Poetry is good at identifying the culture of the poet. In other words, poets find that they can express something that they feel is a cultural marker. Poetry is good at soap-boxing, saying in effect, 'believe'. This is related to its ability to offer a confession-box to writers, so that they can say, 'this is what I did, what I saw, what I thought'. This enables it to offer poets and readers a kind of running commentary on the self or on the group. Similarly, it's good at witnessing, saying in effect, I am bringing back news of what is 'out there'. Famously, poetry is good at making the familiar unfamiliar and the unfamiliar familiar. Metaphor is one of its most potent ways of doing these two things. Because of the musicality of a good deal of poetry, poetry has the possibility of creating feelings without saying explicitly what those feelings are. This will draw attention to language itself and how we have invented a means of communicating that is not semantic.

If we put all this together, we see that poetry has the potential to offer young people a place that can be an exchange of ideas and feelings, it can offer them a way of being awakened to the potential of language rather than its limits. It can offer them ways of being highly personal and/or highly cultural so that the reader or poet can discover a mixture of 'who I am' and 'who I belong to'. Because it doesn't have to tell the whole story, poetry can offer pupils the idea that there are 'moments' in life as well as 'sequences' and 'consequences'. The lyric tradition, in particular, stands in contrast to the rational-logical process that students are invited to spend a lot of time perfecting elsewhere in the curriculum. This suggests that human experience is more complicated than the rational-logical system offers. It offers a different sense of time. That is, there are 'moments' AND 'continuities' AND 'repetitions', co-existing as we exist.

Michael Rosen (1946–) was brought up in north-west London and is a much loved children's poet and the former Children's Laureate. He has spent a lifetime promoting poetry and reading in schools and is passionate about the children's right to read. His best known children's books such as *We're Going on a Bear Hunt* are classics and learnt by heart by children all over the country. More recently his ardent defence of the Booktrust's free books for children saved the scheme from government cuts.

The Language of Ghosts

Mama, today I discovered the language of ghosts.

What are you talking about, Claudio?

Yes, mama. Seriously, I discovered
the language of ghosts.

To say hello they say: Hoo hoo.
To say yes they say: Hoo.

And how do they say goodbye?

I don't know, they haven't left yet.

translated from the Mexican Spanish by Lawrence Schimel

Gabriela Cantú Westendarp (1972–) is from Monterrey, in the north of Mexico. She has published five collections of poetry, including a book of poems for children, *Los Poemas del Árbol*, in 2009 with the Autonomous University of Nuevo León. She teaches in various schools and colleges.

NGE NGE (KYAUKSE)

A Man Who Is Easily Fooled and a Woman Who Barely Speaks

You may close your eyes and ears but open up your heart
A man and a woman live in a polluted town
The man, who is easily fooled, is quick to believe what he hears
The woman, who barely speaks, thinks things are not for her ears
The man who is easily fooled has infinite trust in her voiceless eyes
The woman who barely speaks is sure that even her heartbeat is mute
The man who is easily fooled survives on what he believes
The woman who barely speaks lives off what she leaves unsaid
The man who is easily fooled is all ears to every speech
The woman who barely speaks makes each action a sign
The man who is easily fooled is eager to sound the alarm
The woman who barely speaks nods approval without a sound
The man who is easily fooled listens to stories
The woman who barely speaks writes poems
The man who is easily fooled hears thunder
The woman who barely speaks conducts lightning
The man who is easily fooled listens out for the deafening crash of falling sky
The woman who barely speaks turns the radio off
The man who is easily fooled waits for the day he'll hear paintings talk
The woman who barely speaks paints on her pulse
The man who is easily fooled keeps an Indian jackdaw
The woman who barely speaks grows a plant

Translated from the Burmese by Pandora and by Olivia McCannon

Nge Nge (Kyaukse) (1984–) lives outside Yangon (Rangoon) and the
metropolis. She writes with great sensitivity to the natural environment but
also with a probing intelligence. In her poems about relationships – such as
the one above – her feminism is amusingly evident. This poem was translated
as part of a *Modern Poetry in Translation* project to link women poets in
Myanmar with women poets in the UK. Burmese poet Pandora provided
literals and helped edit the resulting poems.

Out of Sight

Since you lit the kindling of this brain,
I've learnt to fire-fight by writing poems.
Though I'm a brave coward, my heart
is blistered by the months and years.
I don't want to crack up because of love, darling.
When can we live together?
Since a chance encounter and your reasoning
dowsed the embers of my dignity,
my self-respect quavers, wavers thin as evening smoke.
Our sympathies keep burning out. But I won't give up.
My mind and body still glow with hope.
I hate advice, the cold eye of critique and judgement.
I don't want to display my goods in the window,
or write my price on a yellowing shop tag
hung up by a silk string.
This woman you think of as damaged,
her life almost earthed over,
has been growing away from your philosophies.
You thought me dull, immersed in the classics.
You thought me cool. You thought me frigid.
You struck a spark and set my brain aflame,
and it became a forest fire, rolling forwards.
Where are you hiding, my darling? Where?

Translated from the Burmese by Pandora and by Stephanie Norgate

Ma Ei (1948–) has come through a long history of political turbulence in
Myanmar, and her poems reflect her experiences as a member of the
Communist Party, a rebel, a schoolteacher, widow and divorcee, mother,
editor and writer.

FORUGH FARROKHZAD

In Darkness

I called your name in darkness.
All was silent and the breeze
was ferrying the curtains.
In the tepid sky
a star was on fire,
a star was leaving,
a star was dying.

I called your name.
Your name I called holding
my own being like a bottle
of milk between my hands.
The moon's blue gaze
rapped against the glass.

From the cicada city
a blue song was ascending,
slithering like smoke
against window panes.

All night someone was panting
disappointed inside my chest.
Someone was rising.
Someone was lusting.
Two cold hands were pushing
her away once again.

All through the night
sorrow dripped from black branches.
Someone surprised herself.
Someone voiced your name.
The air, like debris,
collapsed on her head.

My tiny tree was in love with the wind,
the itinerant wind.
Where is the wind's home?
Where is the wind's home?

Translated from the Persian by Sholeh Wolpé

Forugh Farrokhzad (1935–1967) is arguably one of the most significant Iranian
poets of the 20th century. Her poetry was the poetry of protest – protest
through revelation – revelation of the innermost world of women (considered
taboo until then), their intimate secrets and desires, their sorrows, longings,
aspirations and at times even their articulation through silence. She was also
prominent among the group of gifted, bold poets who began the modernist
movement in Iranian poetry, breaking away from the traditional poetic modes,
both in form and subject matter. She died in a car crash at the age of 32.

ARSENY TARKOVSKY

Portrait

There's nobody here at all.
A portrait hangs on the wall.

Over her old, blind eyes
Crawl flies,
      flies,
         flies.

'You in your heaven, under glass –
Are you all right up there?' I ask.

Over her cheek crawls a fly.
I hear the woman reply:

'You down there, in your home –
Are you all right on your own?'

Translated from the Russian by Robert Chandler

Arseny Tarkovsky (1907–1989) was born into a revolutionary family. In 1921, sill a boy, he and his friends published a poem containing an acrostic about Lenin. They were arrested, and sent for execution. Tarkovsky was the only one who escaped. In 1924-25 he worked on a newspaper for railway workers called *Gudok*, writing editorials in verse. In 1925-29 he studied literature in Moscow and began translating poetry from Turkmen, Georgian, Armenian and Arabic. During the Second World War he volunteered as a war-correspondent at the Army Newspaper *Boevaya Trevoga* (War Alarm), and was severely wounded. After the War he prepared his poems for publication but the Party forbade it, so that for a long time he was known only as a translator. He is buried next to Pasternak in Peredelkino. His son Andrei, the filmmaker, predeceased him.

PHILIPPE JACCOTTET

Plus aucun souffle…

Stillness.

As when the morning wind
has had its way
with the last candle.

A silence within us so profound
we would hear a comet
making for the darkness
of our daughters' daughters.

Translated from the French by Ruth Sharman

Born in Switzerland, Philippe Jaccottet (1925–) is one of the most important
and sympathetic figures of the immediate post-war generation of French
poets. He has lived in France, in the Drôme, since 1953, working as a
translator and freelance writer. As well as poetry, he has published notebooks
and critical essays. He is particularly well-known as a translator from German
(Musil, Rilke, Mann, Hölderlin) but has also translated Homer, Plato,
Ungaretti, Montale, Gongora and Mandelstam. Much of his poetry springs
from the locality he inhabits. He is a walker-poet, exceptionally attentive to
the real details of the earth and open also to intimations of its religious sense.

PHILIPPE JACCOTTET

Toi cependant...

But you,

who've either been extinguished,
leaving us fewer ashes
than one evening's fire in the hearth

or live in the invisible, yourself invisible

or lodge, like a seed, deep in our hearts –

whichever is true –

remain as a lesson to us, smiling and patient

like the sun that warms our backs even now
and shines on this table, this page and these grapes.

Translated from the French by Ruth Sharman

Qu'on me le montre...

Show me a man so certain
he shines out in the stillness
like a mountain that catches the last glow
and never trembles beneath the weight of night.

Translated from the French by Ruth Sharman

If You Imagine

If you imagine
if you imagine
little sweetie little sweetie
if you imagine
this will this will this
will last forever
this season of
this season of
season of love
you're fooling yourself
little sweetie little sweetie
you're fooling yourself

If you think little one
if you think ah ah
that that rosy complexion
that waspy waist
those lovely muscles
the enamel nails
nymph thigh
and your light foot
if you think little one
that will that will that
will last forever
you're fooling yourself
little sweetie little sweetie
you're fooling yourself

The lovely days disappear
the lovely holidays
suns and planets
go round in a circle
but you my little one
you go straight

toward you know not what
very slowly draw near
the sudden wrinkle
the weighty fat
the triple chin
the flabby muscle
come gather gather
the roses the roses
roses of life
and may their petals
be a calm sea
of happinesses
come gather gather
if you don't do it
you're fooling yourself
little sweetie little sweetie
you're fooling yourself

Translated from the French by Michael Benedikt

Raymond Queneau (1903–1976) was a novelist, poet and co-founder of the Oulipo movement. As an author, he came to general attention in France with the publication in 1959 of his novel *Zazie dans le métro*. It was adapted for the cinema, directed by Louis Malle, in 1960, and became one of the best known films of the *Nouvelle Vague*. Queneau's poem 'Si tu t'imagines', set by Joseph Kosma, was sung by Juliette Gréco.

TOMAS TRANSTRÖMER

The Couple

They switch off the light and its white shade
glimmers for a moment before dissolving
like a tablet in a glass of darkness. Then up.
The hotel walls shoot up in the black sky.

The movements of love have settled, and they sleep
but their most secret thoughts meet as when
two colours meet and flow into each other
on the wet paper of a schoolboy's painting.

It is dark and silent. But the town has pulled closer
tonight. With quenched windows. The houses have approached.
They stand close up in a throng, waiting,
a crowd whose faces have no expressions.

Translated from the Swedish by Robin Fulton

TAKAGI KYOZO

Lightning Over Beds of Rice Seedlings

Frogs are croaking, and from time to time
there are flashes of lightning over the beds of rice seedlings.

She still hasn't come out.

Rain begins to fall.
I'm getting wet to the skin
but I won't budge from here.

The rain's getting heavier,
and the frogs have already stopped croaking.

It seems very late now.
The lights in her house have all been turned off.

Translated from the Tohoku dialect of Japanese by James Kirkup and Nakano Michio

The Ballad of Widowhood

The two widows sat down and folded their arms
Widowhood between each one:
They'd have chased it out through the window
But the frame is like a cross made of walnut.
They'd have driven it out by the door
But a gale is raging there, and memories.
They'd have wailed it out like a song
But widowhood is deaf.
They'd have flicked it away with their towels,
But widowhood is blind.
They'd have shamed it out with tears
But widowhood is deeper than weeping.
They could only sit with folded arms
Widowhood between them:
One is grey-haired and the other lonely.
And widowhood wears a woman's apron.

Translated from the Ukrainian by Mark Pinchevsky and Alan Sillitoe

Ivan Drach (1936–) is a Ukrainian poet, screenwriter, literary critic and
political activist. He played an important role in the founding of Rukh – the
People's Movement of Ukraine – and led the organisation from 1989 to 1992.

IVAN DRACH

The Ballad of the Bundles

A long time ago there was Grandma Koropchikha –
Whose hands still move and shine for me.
That old grandma couldn't read or write –
But her hands could work, and they still shine for me.
That old grandma baked us cranberry pies
And now she's dead the world has lost its light for me.

If anyone came hungry to her door
She gave each one a bundle.
Those who were cold found warmth at her fire
And left with bundles hugged to their chest.

Those who deceived her stayed that way
But got a bundle nevertheless.

When I have melancholy nightmares
That old woman comes and unties a bundle;
When I have pleasant dreams that smell of cranberries
She comes and ties them all up in a bundle
And now she must be sad inside her grave
With folded arms that cannot tie up bundles...

No magic tablecloth provides all food –
Yet Grannie Koropchickha's bundles did.
I saw them, lifted and undid them all
Then tied them up again, lovingly remembered every knot.
Dear Grandma wore a white headscarf whose ends
Never got the chance to meet beneath her chin:
She was buried in a borrowed one
Since all her own were used in bundles.

Translated from the Ukrainian by Mark Pinchevsky and Alan Sillitoe

Years are passing, and years. And hope

Is like a tin cup toppled in the straw...

JÁNOS PILINSZKY

The Desert of Love

A bridge, and a hot, concrete road–
The day is emptying its pockets,
Lays out, one by one, all its possessions.
You are quite alone in the catatonic twilight.

A landscape like the bed of a wrinkled pit,
With glowing scars, a darkness that dazzles.
Dusk is close. I stand numb with brightness
And blinded by sun. This summer will never leave me for a moment.

Summer. And the flashing heat.
The chickens stand, like burning cherubs,
In the boarded-up, splintered cages.
I know their wings do not even tremble.

Do you still remember? First there was the wind.
And then the earth. Then the cage.
Fire, dung. And every so often
A few wing-flutters, a few empty reflexes.

And thirst. And when I asked for water –
Even today I hear that feverish gulping.
Even now, helplessly, like a stone,
I bear and quench the mirages.

Years are passing, and years. And hope
Is like a tin cup toppled in the straw.

Translated from the Hungarian by Peter Siklós and Ted Hughes

TOON TELLEGEN

Evening

I'm on a train to a summer house in the north
and the scent of wood blows through the open window
of my room on a canal.
Evening.
Beside me sits my grandfather, he is blind and devout,
he's wearing a long black coat,
he sighs.
And that woman over there, with the serious expression,
spilling her tea,
that's my mother: I hadn't expected you,
she says, so far from home.
She pushes my books out of my hands from my knees
onto the ground
and takes me with her in her thoughts:
the sun is shining, it's Sunday, everyone is out for a walk
and greets some unknown person, everyone is reading Gogol in the fresh grass,
everyone is wearing white clothes, everyone
looks into a picnic basket,
and suddenly she's gone, someone
puts on his boots.
My grandfather and I, both sighing,
but only he praying,
we continue our journey northwards. Someone
puts a key in the lock.

Translated from the Dutch by Judith Wilkinson

TOON TELLEGEN

Peace

The peace between you and me
is a dragonfly. Wonderfully beautiful. Sparkling
in the evening sun, skimming
the foolhardy water
between you and me.

Translated from the Dutch by Judith Wilkinson

Toon Tellegen (1941–) was born on one of the islands in the south-west of the
Netherlands. He is one of the best-known Dutch writers, with a long list of
awards to his name. In 2007 he received two major prizes for his entire
oeuvre. He has published more than twenty collections of poetry to date, but
he is also a novelist and a prolific and popular children's author.

Liang Yujing writes: 'Xidu Heshang belongs among the *balinghou* or "post-
1980 poets". The term, now widely used in Chinese poetry criticism, refers to
those born between 1980 and 1989. This group, being the first generation born
after the Cultural Revolution, are less influenced by the past national trauma.
Now in their thirties, they are in the prime of their poetry-writing careers, yet
most of them have not been translated into English. Heshang is a good example
of the vitality of contemporary Chinese poetry in its "new era", which does
not necessarily mean it has totally broken away from its ancient tradition.
People who are familiar with classical Chinese poetry will find a similarity
between the list of repetitions in "Fictionalising Her" and that in many
classical poems.

By the way, Xidu Heshang is a pseudonym that makes me laugh. I dare say
it looks quite weird and unreal even in Chinese. It literally means "west poison
how die" – another instance of his humour.'

XIDU HESHANG

Fictionalising Her

In the third form of primary school,
she pretends her stepfather's hand that stretches over at midnight does not exist.

In the third form of junior school,
she pretends her gym instructor's arm around her waist does not exist.

In the third form of high school,
she pretends the old guy who clings to her hips on the bus does not exist.

In her third year of college,
she pretends the foot of her roommate's boyfriend under the card table does not exist.

On her wedding night,
she pretends the one-month-old foetus in her belly does not exist.

Three years into her marriage,
she pretends the flirting texts on her husband's mobile do not exist.

Seven years into her marriage,
she pretends the plump wife of her boss does not exist.

Eighteen years into her marriage,
she pretends the boy who caresses her son in the room does not exist.

After twenty-eight years of marriage,
she pretends the ever-enlarging tumour in her womb does not exist.

After thirty years of marriage,
she pretends she is fortunate and all the tormenting loneliness in her life does not exist.

Three minutes before death,
she pretends death is painful and her aversion to this world does not exist at all.

Translated from the Chinese by Liang Yujing

CHRISTINE MARENDON

Evening Primrose

In each person there exists a sheer
drop. Darker than campion
which during the day turns inwards
it likes to spread gold
over broad expanses.
So we, animals and humans,
are also vegetation, layers
of the coal age. We are
offshoots, belonging to the species
which pays with pollen and honey
and still awaits the new age.
The flowers, whose language
lacks a word for 'garden',
bend forwards into
the newly flighted scar.
Everything is connected
to not belonging.

Translated from the German by Ken Cockburn

Christine Marendon, born 1964, studied Italian in Erlangen and Siena. She lives in Hamburg where she works with children with special needs. Her poems feature in anthologies including *Jahrbuch der Lyrik 2013*, and she has been widely published in periodicals.

ANGÉLICA FREITAS

I sleep with myself...

I sleep with myself / lying on my stomach I sleep
with myself / turning to the right I sleep with myself / I
sleep with myself hugging myself / there's no night so
long I don't sleep with myself / like a troubadour
inseparable from his lute I sleep with myself / I sleep
with myself beneath the starry sky / I sleep with myself
while other people have birthdays / I sleep
with myself with glasses on sometimes / even in the dark I know
I'm sleeping with myself / and whoever wants to sleep with me
will have to sleep on the side.

Translated from the Brazilian Portuguese by Hilary Kaplan

Angélica Freitas's recent poetry collection, *Um útero é do tamanho de um punho* (The uterus is the size of a fist), was nominated for the Portugal Telecom Prize. Many of the poems in this book consider and critique the notion of 'woman' and some of the poems use Google searches as a compositional technique. Her first book, *Rilke Shake* (Cosac Naify, 2007), has been translated into English and German. She co-edits the poetry journal *Modo de Usar & Co.* from her home in Pelotas, Rio Grande do Sul, Brazil.

ANGÉLICA FREITAS

because a good woman...

because a good woman
is a clean woman
and if she's a clean woman
she's a good woman

millions, millions of years ago
she stood up on two feet
woman was angry and dirty
angry and dirty and barking

because an angry woman
isn't a good woman
and a good woman
is a clean woman

millions, millions of years ago
she stood on her own two feet
she doesn't bark anymore, she's meek
she's meek and good and clean

Translated from the Brazilian Portuguese by Hilary Kaplan

❁

Hurry, take pleasure in the oblique

caress of rain

NATALYA GORBANEVSKAYA

Hurry, take pleasure in the oblique caress of rain...

Hurry, take pleasure in the oblique caress of rain
while the sun shines, while the earth is unparched, the sky not yet dried up,
while Neva and Onega run deep in their banks
and the damp powder has not yet fallen from the musket.

Translated from the Russian by Daniel Weissbort

The MPT Editor

Appendices

ACKNOWLEDGEMENTS

Acknowledgements and thanks are due to the following copyright holders of the works published within this anthology. Royalties from the sale of this book will go to Refugee Council (www.refugeecouncil.org.uk) and we are grateful to all the contributors who have made this possible, including TypeTogether and designer Katy Mawhood. Our thanks also go to King's College Archive, Chrissy Williams and Harriet Downes. All works listed here were first published by *Modern Poetry in Translation*. (For details of individual publication dates, please see the Contents on pp.5–12.)

Author Unknown: 'Dear Fatimeh', translated by Hubert Moore and Nasrin Parvaz. **Author Unknown:** 'The Spirit Lord's Bearkill', translated by Dorothea Grünzweig and Derk Wynand. **Anna Akhmatova:** 'Wild Honey', in a version by Jo Shapcott. **Rafael Alberti:** 'If my voice should die on land...', translated by Robert Hull, from *Pavarotti of the Sidings* (Beafred, 2012), by permission of the publisher. **Samíh al-Qasim:** 'End of Talk with a Jailor', 'Excerpt from an Inquest', translated by Nazih Kassis, by permission of Mohammad Samih al-Qassem. **Al-Saddiq Al-Raddi:** 'Nothing', translated by Sarah Maguire and Atef Alshaer, by permission of the Poetry Translation Centre. **Yehuda Amichai:** 'A Room by the Sea', translated by Dom Moraes; 'When I was a Boy', translated by Margalit Benaya, by permission of Hana Amichai. **Dvora Amir:** 'On the Rim of Abu-Tor', translated by Jennie Feldman. **Vita Andersen:** 'The Beautiful Room', translated by Jannick Storm and Linda Lappin, from *Tryghedsnarkomaner* (Gyldendal, 1977). **Guillaume Apollinaire:** 'My Lou I shall sleep tonight...', translated by Stephen Romer. **Homero Aridjis:** 'In its warmth Summer is a nest...', translated by Michael Schmidt; 'In a valley I saw the dead shades', 'Black Grass', translated by George McWhirter. **Joan Ariete:** 'Why I left', translated by Shon Arieh-Lerer and the author. **Fadhil Assultani:** 'A Tree', translated by Saadi A. Simawe and the author.

Ingeborg Bachmann: 'Fog Land', 'Days in White', translated by Daniel Huws; 'Exile', translated at Spoleto in translation workshops, by permission of Heinz Bachmann, with acknowledgements to Piper and to Jim Kates at Zephyr Press. **Antonín Bartušek:** 'Those Few Years', 'Anniversary in Fribourg', translated by Ewald Osers, by permission of DILIA, the Estate of Antonín Bartušek and the Estate of Ewald Osers. **Giuseppe Belli:** 'La Bbona Famijja'/ 'The Good Life', translated by Dr Paul Howard. **Tahar Ben Jelloun:** From 'The Poet, Neither Guide nor Prophet' translated by Paol Keineg and Candace Slater. **Zsuzsa Beney:** 'The Translator', translated by George Szirtes, by permission of the estate of Zsuzsa Beney. **Yves Berger:** '2nd March: Al Rabweh', translated by John Berger, by permission of John Berger. **Olga Berggolts:** 'Late One Melancholy February Night', translated by Daniel Weissbort. **Tara Bergin:** 'Stag Boy'. **Sujata Bhatt:** 'Another Daphne', from Sujata Bhatt: *Poppies in Translation* (Carcanet Press, 2015), by permission of the publisher. **Marzanna Bogumila Kielar:** 'A flock of pigeons...', translated by Elzbieta Wójcik-Leese. **Yves Bonnefoy:** 'Threats of the Witness', translated by Anthony Rudolf. **Wojciech Bonowicz:** 'Night', translated by Elżbieta Wójcik-Leese. **Marina Boroditskaya:** 'So Much Gentleness from Unknown Men', translated by Ruth

Fainlight. **Bertolt Brecht:** 'When we were first divided into two...' translated by David Constantine from (*Love in a Time of Exile and War* in *Modern Poetry in Translation*, 2014; Norton, 2015), 'The First Sonnet', originally published in German in 1964 as 'Das erste Sonnett', translated by David Constantine, copyright © 1964 by Bertolt-Brecht-Erben / Suhrkamp Verlag, from *Love Poems* by Bertolt Brecht, translated by David Constantine and Tom Kuhn; used by permission of Liveright Publishing Corporation. **Carmen Bugan:** 'Why I Do Not Write in My Native Language'.

Gabriela Cantú Westendarp: 'The Language of Ghosts', translated by Lawrence Schimel. **Nina Cassian:** 'Like Gulliver', 'I wanted to stay', translated by Laura Schiff and Virgil Nemoianu, by permission of Maurice Edwards and Virgil Nemoianu. **Bartolo Cattafi:** 'Winter Figs', translated by Ruth Feldman and Brian Swann, by permission of Ada De Alessandri Cattafi and Brian Swann. **Paul Celan:** 'Tenebrae', 'Psalm', translated by Michael Hamburger, from *Poems of Paul Celan* (Anvil Press Poetry, 1988), by permission of Carcanet Press, with acknowledgements to S. Fischer Verlag, Frankfurt am Main, 1959. **Amarjit Chandan:** 'Punjabi Folksongs from the First World War'. **Hugo Claus:** '1965', translated by David Colmer, from *Even Now* (Archipelago Books, 2013), by permission of the publisher and translator. **Denisa Comănescu:** 'Return from Exile', translated by Adam J. Sorkin. **David and Helen Constantine:** Editorial to 'Getting it Across'.

Gianni D'Elia: 'Sta(i)rway to Heaven', translated by Michael Donaghy. **Mahmoud Darwish:** 'A State of Siege', translated by Sarah Maguire and Sabry Hafez, by permission of the Poetry Translation Centre; from 'Mural', translated by Rema Hammami and John Berger, by permission of the Poetry Translation Centre (*Modern Poetry in Translation*, 2008) and John Berger. **Razmik Davoyan:** 'Somewhere, a birch wood is being stolen...', translated by Armine Tamrazian. **Sophia de Mello Breyner Andresen:** 'Sibyls', translated by Ruth Griffin, by permission of Ella Sher and the Estate of Sophia de Mello Breyner Andresen / SPA, 2016. **Robert Desnos:** 'Tomorrow', 'Springtime', translated by Tim Adès, 'Demain' et 'Printemps' from Robert Desnos: *Destinée arbitraire* (Éditions Gallimard, Paris, 1975). **David Diop:** 'Testimony', From 'Contribution to the Debate on National Poetry', translated by Paol Keineg and Candace Slater. **Jean Dodo:** 'In My Neighbourhood Market', translated by Elisavietta Ritchie. **Hilde Domin:** 'Cologne', 'Catalogue', translated by Tudor Morris. **Alba Donati:** 'Valerio's Story', translated by Stefano de Angelis. **Ivan Drach:** 'The Ballad of Widowhood', 'The Ballad of the Bundles', translated by Alan Sillitoe and Mark Pinchevsky, by permission of Rogers, Coleridge and White. **Mykhailo Draj-Khmara:** 'Swans', translated by Steve Komarnyckyj. **Carlos Drummond de Andrade:** 'Seven-Sided Poem', translated by Richard Zenith. **Sasha Dugdale:** Editorial to 'Scorched Glass'; from 'At the Edge'.

Heinz Ehemann: 'Gerontology or When You Get Old', translated by Shon Arieh-Lerer. **Kristiina Ehin:** 'Cows come from the sea...', translated by Ilmar Lehtpere. **Anna Enquist:** 'River', translated by Lloyd Haft; 'La Folia', translated by Manfred Wolf; by permission of Singel Uitgeverijen and the translators.

Luis Felipe Fabre: 'Doris Najera and Detective Ramirez', 'Infomercial', translated by Cutter Streeby. **Forugh Farrokhzad:** 'In Darkness', translated by Sholeh Wolpé. **Elaine Feinstein:** 'Marina Tsvetaeva'. **Angélika Freitas:** 'I sleep with myself...', 'because a good woman...' translated by Hilary Kaplan. **Du Fu:**

'Ballad of the Military Waggons', translated by Paul Harris.

Federico García Lorca: 'Romance de la Pena Negra', translated by Julith Jedamus. **Eva Gerlach:** 'The Hedgehog', translated by Virginie Kortekaas, by permission of Singel Uitgeverijen and the translator. **Guy Goffette:** 'Elegy for a Friend', translated by Marilyn Hacker, from Marilyn Hacker: *A Stranger's Mirror: New and Selected Poems 1995-2014* (Norton, 2015) by permission of Éditions Gallimard. **Leah Goldberg:** 'The Girl Sings to the River', translated by Robert Friend, by permission of Jean Shapiro Cantu. **George Gömöri:** 'Polishing October', translated by Clive Wilmer and the author. **Natalya Gorbanevskaya:** 'That time I did not save Warsaw, nor Prague later...', 'Hurry, take pleasure in the oblique caress of rain while the sun shines...', 'This from the Diagnosis...', translated by Daniel Weissbort, by permission of Valentina Polukhina. **Georgi Gospodinov:** 'My Mother Reads Poetry', translated by Maria Vassileva and Bilyana Kourtasheva. **Soleïman Adel Guémar:** 'False Departure', translated by Tom Cheesman and John Goodby.

Hai Zi: 'Sonnet: Crown', translated by Chun Ye. **Reesom Haile:** 'African Anthem', translated by Charles Cantelupo. **Choman Hardi:** 'One Moment for Halabja' from Choman Hardi: *Considering the Women* (Bloodaxe Books, 2015), by permission of the publisher. **Ivan Hartel:** 'if I don't recant, someone else will', translated by George Theiner, by permission of Pavel Theiner. **Hô Chí Minh:** 'Entertainment' and 'Liberation' from 'Prison Diary', translated by Timothy Allen. **Miroslav Holub:** 'The fly', 'Wings', 'Five minutes after the air raid', translated by George Theiner, from Miroslav Holub: *Poems Before & After: Collected English Translations* (Bloodaxe Books, 2006), by permission of the publisher. **Peter Huchel:** 'Winter Quarters', translated by Christopher Levenson. **Ted Hughes & Daniel Weissbort:** Editorials to issues 1 and 3 (*Modern Poetry in Translation* 1965, 1967) © Valentina Polukhina and Estate of Ted Hughes and reprinted by permission of Valentina Polukhina and the Estate of Ted Hughes. **Ted Hughes:** 'Introduction' to Poetry International in 1967; 'Introduction' to *Modern Poetry in Translation: An Annual Survey* by Ted Hughes (Persea Books and Modern Poetry in Translation, 1983); 'The *MPT* editor' by Ted Hughes; excerpts from a letter to Daniel Weissbort (unpublished, c. 1982) © Estate of Ted Hughes and reprinted by permission of the Estate of Ted Hughes. **Daniel Huws:** Memories of Ingeborg Bachmann.

Philippe Jaccottet: 'Plus aucun souffle...', 'Toi cependant...', 'Qu'on me le montre√', translated by Ruth Sharman. **Ernst Jandl:** 'oberflaechunguebersetzung', 'die zeit vergeht' © 2005, Deutsche Verlags-Anstalt, München, in der Verlagsgruppe Random House GmbH. **Attila József:** 'What Should a Man Do', translated by John Bátki. **Ferenc Juhász:** 'The Boy Changed into a Stag Cries Out at the Gate of Secrets', translated by Ted Hughes(MPT, 2003) © Estate of Ted Hughes and reprinted by permission of the Estate of Ted Hughes; 'At the Gate of Secrets', translated by Pascale Petit, from *The Huntress* (Seren, 2005), by permission of the publisher.

Zíba Karbassi: 'Writing Cells', translated by Stephen Watts. **Fawzi Karim:** 'The Usual Story', translated by Anthony Howell. **Euphrase Kezilahabi:** 'Thread', 'Sorting the Rice', translated by Annmarie Drury. **Mimi Khalvati:** 'Ghazal: To Hold Me', from Mimi Khalvati: *Child: New and Selected Poems* (Carcanet Press, 2011), by permission of the publisher. **Kim Hyesoon:** 'A Teardrop', translated by Don Mee Choi. **Sarah Kirsch:** 'The Chitchat of Crows', translated by Anne Stokes, *Sämtliche Gedichte* © 2005, Deutsche Verlags-Anstalt, München, in der Verlagsgruppe Random House GmbH, with thanks to the University of Stirling. **Ko Un:** 'Places I want to go', translated by Brother Anthony of Taizé and Lee Sang-Wha, from Ko Un: *First Person Sorrowful*, tr. Brother Anthony of Taizé & Lee Sang-Wha (Bloodaxe Books, 2012). **Edvard Kocbek:** 'Landscape', translated by Michael Scammell and Veno Taufer, by permission of the translators and the Copyright Agency of Slovenia on behalf of the Estate of Edvard Kocbek. **Jiří Kolář:** 'Advice for Sycophants', translated by George Theiner, by permission of Pavel Theiner and the Estate of Jiří Kolář. **Rutger Kopland:** 'Three Winter Poems', translated by Ria Leigh-Loohuizen. **Gerður Kristný:** 'My Brother and Sister', translated by Sigurður A. Magnússon; 'Ægisiða', translated by Victoria Cribb. **Anna Kühn-Cichocka:** 'Here the houses...', 'On rainy days...', translated by Sarah Lawson and Malgorzata Koraszweska. **Shinjiro Kurahara:** 'A Fox', 'A Footprint', translated by William Elliott and Katsumasa Nishihara. **Takagi Kyozo:** 'Poor Harvest', 'Lightning over Beds of Rice Seedlings', translated by James Kirkup and Nakano Michio, by permission of The James Kirkup Collection.

Ivan V. Lalić: 'The Spaces of Hope', translated by Francis R. Jones, by permission of the translator and Carcanet Press Limited. **Paulo Leminski:** 'Things don't start in a story...', 'Poetry is the liberty of language...', translated by Jamie Duncan, by permission of the Leminski Estate. **Primo Levi:** 'The Girl at Pompeii', translated by Martin Bennett; 'Singing', 'The Black Stars', translated by Marco Sonzogni and Harry Thomas. **Gabriel Levin:** 'Self-portrait in Khaki', from Gabriel Levin: *Ostraca* (Anvil Press Poetry, 1999), by permission of Carcanet Press. **Frances Leviston:** 'Reconstruction'. **Anna Lewis:** from 'The Wash House'. **Charlie Louth:** The Correspondence of Ingeborg Bachmann and Paul Celan. **Paula Ludwig:** 'A day and a night it took me...', 'When you return it's always...', translated by Martina Thomson. **Mario Luzi:** 'Life True to Life', translated by Patrick Creagh.

Chris McCabe: 'Ernst Jandl: The Biomechanical Magus'. **Sorley MacLean:** 'Dawn', translated by Cameron Hawke Smith.

Ma Ei: 'Out of Sight', translated by Pandora and Stephanie Norgate. **Nikola Madzirov:** 'Hope Climbed', translated by Graham and Peggy Reid. **Valerio Magrelli:** 'I was lying on an outpatient's bed...', translated by Jamie McKendrick, from Valerio Magrelli: *The Embrace* (Faber & Faber, 2009). **Caroline Maldonado:** On Scotellaro. **Jack Mapanje:** 'Kalikalanje of Ostrich Forest', from Jack Mapanje: *Greetings from Grandpa* (Bloodaxe Books, 2016), by permission of the author and publisher. **Christine Marendon:** 'Evening Primrose', translated by Ken Cockburn. **Harry Martinson:** 'Cable-ship', 'The swamp mosses drink of the stream...', translated by Robin Fulton, from Harry Martinson: *Chickweed Wintergreen: Selected Poems* (Bloodaxe Books, 2010), by permission of the publisher. **Krystyna Miłobędzka:** 'rush upon this house...', 'they are in this photograph!', 'the longer my looking...', 'this will be that sky...', translated by Elżbieta Wójcik-Leese. **Gabriela Mistral:** 'The Foreigner', translated by Arthur McHugh. **Kaneko Misuzu:** 'Stars and Dandelions', translated by Quentin Crisp. **Adriaan Morriën:** 'National Anthem (to be sung standing)', translated by Ria Leigh-Loohuizen.

Vítězslav Nezval: 'Mother Hope', translated by Ewald Osers, by permission of the Estate of Ewald Osers. **Nge Nge (Kyaukse):** 'A Man who is Easily Fooled

and a Woman who Barely Speaks', translated by Pandora and Olivia McCannon.
Liam Ó Muirthíle: 'The Parlour', translated by Bernard O'Donoghue. **Ovid:** from *Tristia*, translated by Paul Batchelor. **Paul van Ostaijen:** 'Dead Sunday', translated by David Colmer. **Jan Boleslaw Ożóg:** 'Ash', translated by Andrzej Busza and Bogdan Czaykowski.

Ūnpoti Pacuṅkuṭaiyār: 'Should clouds refuse to rain because they have in the past...', translated by Vidyan and Thirunavukkarasu Ravinthiran. **Dan Pagis:** 'Roll Call in the Concentration Camp', 'Instructions for Getting Across the Border', 'Scrawled in Pencil in a Sealed Car', translated by Robert Friend, by permission of Jean Shapiro Cantu and ACUM. **Pier Paolo Pasolini:** 'Towards the Baths of Caracalla', translated by N.S. Thompson. **Cesare Pavese:** 'Donne Appassionate', translated by Martin Bennett. **János Pilinszky:** 'The Passion of Ravensbrück' (*MPT*, 1970) 'The Desert of Love' (*MPT*, 1970), translated by Peter Siklós and Ted Hughes © Estate of Ted Hughes and reprinted by permission of the Estate of Ted Hughes; 'Aquarium', 'Knocking', translated by Peter Jay; 'Creative Imagination' in *Our Time*, translated by John Bátki; by permission of Péter Kovács, John Bátki, Peter Jay, Carcanet Press and the Estate of Ted Hughes. **Vasko Popa:** 'How the Mole Came to Be', 'Bright Lovers', 'High Lovers', translated by Anne Pennington; 'The Poplar and the Bystander', 'Cape of Good Hope', 'Swallows' Language', translated by Anne Pennington, from Vasko Popa: *Complete Poems* (Anvil Press Poetry, 2011, revised and expanded by Francis R. Jones), by permission of Carcanet Press; 'Anne Pennington', translated by Anthony Rudolf, Peter Jay and Daniel Weissbort. **Halina Poświatowska:** 'These words have existed always...', 'my face is more and more like the moon...', translated by Andrzej Busza and Bogdan Czaykowski.

Raymond Queneau: 'If You Imagine', translated by Michael Benedikt. **Núria Quevedo:** Cover illustration to 'The Constellation'. **Shazea Quraishi:** 'Carandasi' from Shazea Quraishi: *The Art of Scratching* (Bloodaxe Books, 2015), by permission of the publisher and author.

Miklós Radnóti: 'Letter to My Wife', translated by Stephen Capus. **Jacques Réda:** 'The Fête', translated by Jennie Feldman. **José Rosas Ribeyro:** 'My Grandfather', translated by C.A. de Lomellini and David Tipton. **Raúl Rivero:** 'Stardust', translated by David Shook. **Clemente Rèbora:** 'Voice from a Dead Lookout', translated by Cristina Viti, by permission of Garzanti. **Yannis Ritsos:** 'Return', translated by Robert Hull. **Michael Rosen:** From 'A Conversation on Children's Poetry', (*Modern Poetry in Translation*, 2015). **Tadeusz Różewicz:** 'Chestnut', translated by Geoffrey Thurley, by permission of Wiesława Różewicz. **Valérie Rouzeau:** '01 43 15 50 67', translated by Susan Wicks, from *Talking Vrouz* (Arc Publications, 2013), by permission of the translator.

Ulrike Almut Sandig: 'being inspected', translated by Karen Leeder, by permission of Schöffling & Co. **Maya Sarishvili:** 'To My Father', 'This ice-cutter silence...', translated by Timothy Kercher and Nene Giorgadze. **Rocco Scotellaro:** 'Forlorn Cuckoo, Your Call Keeps Us Awake', 'The Full Moon', translated by Allen Prowle. **Bewketu Seyoum:** 'In Search of Fat', 'Elegy', 'Meditation on the Garden', translated by Chris Beckett and the author, from *In Search of Fat* (Flipped Eye, 2012), by permission of the author. **Haruo Shibuya:** 'A Young Wife', translated by James Kirkup, by permission of The James Kirkup Collection. **Elena Shvarts:** 'Birdsong on the Seabed', translated by Sasha Dugdale, from Elena Shvarts: *Birdsong on the Seabed* (Bloodaxe Books,

2008). **Lal Singh Dil:** 'Nadeen', 'Outcasts', translated by Trilok Chand Ghai. **John E. Smelcer:** 'Spring on the Yukon', 'Owl and Mouse'. **Edith Södergran:** 'Violet Dusks', translated by David McDuff, from Edith Södergran: *Complete Poems*, tr. David McDuff (Bloodaxe Books, 1984), by permission of the translator. **Margarete Steffin:** 'Emboldened, putting off formal address…', translated by David Constantine. **George Szirtes:** 'The Voronezh Variations'. **Wisława Szymborska:** 'Innocence', translated by Jan Darowski; 'Hunger Camp near Jasło', translated by Leonora Mestel © The Wisława Szymborska Foundation.

    Arseny Tarkovsky: 'Portrait', translated by Robert Chandler. **Toon Tellegen:** 'Evening', 'Peace', translated by Judith Wilkinson. **George Theiner:** From 'Helping Those Who Have Been Silenced' by George Theiner, and from a letter to Daniel Weissbort (unpublished, 1968), by permission of Pavel Theiner. **Ned Thomas:** From 'From Minorities to Mosaic' by Ned Thomas. **Tomas Tranströmer:** 'The Couple', 'The Journey's Formulae', translated by Robin Fulton, from *New Collected Poems*, tr. Robin Fulton (Bloodaxe Books, 2011), by permission of the publisher. **Shash Trevett:** 'In Memory', 'Bitter Waters'. **Dimitris Tsaloumas:** 'Rain I', 'Rain II', translated by Helen Constantine and the author. **Marina Tsvetaeva:** 'Poem of the End', translated by Elaine Feinstein (in collaboration with Angela Livingstone), from *Bride of Ice: New Selected Poems* (Carcanet, 2009), by permission of Carcanet Press Limited.

    Liliana Ursu: 'The Tower of Steps', 'Between the Wheat Wells and the Bridal Mirrors', translated by Mihaela Moscaliuc.

    Jón úr Vör: 'Lean Months', translated by Sigurdur A. Magnússon. **Eleni Vakalo:** 'A Charm for Women', translated by Paul Merchant. **Virgil:** 'The Sibyl', from *Aeneid Book VI* by Seamus Heaney (VI, *ll.* 77-97) © Estate of Seamus Heaney and reprinted by permission of Faber and Faber Ltd. **Nikiforos Vrettakos:** 'The Orange Trees of Sparta', translated by Robert Hull.

    Wang Wei: 'Autumnal Dusk in the Mountains', translated by Julian Farmer. **José Watanabe:** 'The Arrangement', translated by C.A. de Lomellini and David Tipton. **Daniel Weissbort:** From 'Ted Hughes and Translation' and 'Hughes Translates Juhász' by Daniel Weissbort), by permission of Valentina Polukhina. **Waldo Williams:** 'The Dead Children', translated by Damian Walford Davies, by permission of Eluned Richards (on behalf of the family).

    Xidu Heshang: 'Fictionalising Her', translated by Liang Yujing.

    Yu Jian: 'Event – Digging', translated by Tao Naikan and Simon Patten. **Yi Lu:** 'Arc', 'Evening Construction Site', translated by Fiona Sze-Lorrain.

    Zahrad: 'The Woman Cleaning Lentils', 'Sentence', translated by Ralph Setian. **Ridha Zili:** 'Childhood', 'Ifrikya the centre of my being', translated by Paol Keineg and Candace Slater.

INDEX OF POETS' AND TRANSLATORS' NAMES

(Notes on the poets appear alongside the first poem listed.)

INDEX OF POEMS AND PROSE PIECES

(Titles or first lines)